Canus Humorous

Lessons on Laughter and Life

from

the Leacock Medal for Humour *Writing*

Dick Bourgeois-Doyle

ISBN: 978-1497587311

DEDICATION

On June 16, 1944, a couple of months after Stephen Leacock's death, Charles Harold (C.H.) Hale, the editor of *the Orillia Packet and Times*, convened a meeting at the local library to identify ways of honouring the humorist and promoting his legacy. The Committee struck that day quickly decided to create an award for books of humour. The award eventually took the form of a silver medal crafted by Emanuel Hahn, the sculptor who also designed the Cariboo quarter, the Bluenose dime, and other Canadian icons.

The Committee later assumed the name "Leacock Associates" to denote individual people working together rather than a featureless institution. The Associates awarded the Stephen Leacock Memorial Medal for Humour for the first time in 1947. This book tries to contribute to their broader mission: "To encourage the growth of Canadian humorous writing."

It is dedicated to Jean Dickson, Pete McGarvey, Judith Rapson, and the other Associates whose volunteer efforts have sustained the medal program and given me something special to read.

CONTENTS

PREFACE

"YOUR BEST …"

There. I did what I was told to do and made my first attempt at humour in this book. In advising me on it, Antanas Sileika, director at Toronto's Humber School for Writers, said "engage your reader immediately" and "make your first line *'your best'...*" - thus my opening above. With this, I also wanted to let you know that I wrote this book with the skills and perspective of a student and to start sharing what I have learned.

The following pages describe my experience studying the books that have won the Stephen Leacock Memorial Medal for Humour, and they do it in the format of lessons on humour writing. Sileika also told me that students in Humber's comedy program seem interested in how Canadian humour has changed over the years, suggesting that my review should cover this issue as well as the personal angle. So, it does.

He offered other advice to get me started, but his greatest help came in connecting me with Dan Needles, a Leacock Medal winner, the mythical Mayor of Mariposa, a playwright, and, for a while, my humour-writing mentor.

"Omit needless words!! ... Just get on with it! ... Toss the adjectives ... Hiding behind passive phrases is for insurance lawyers and bureaucrats," he said, and then "much better ... I think you've got the idea" while stressing that I still had work to do. Encouraging, but always with a prod to do better.

It felt just like winning the Leacock Medal for Humour.

PART I

INTRODUCTION

THE NOT-SO-KIND

CANADIAN SENSE OF HUMOUR

If you want to learn something about yourself and laugh a bit, spend a year studying humour.

If you want to learn more about Canada in the process, read the books recognized by the Stephen Leacock Memorial Medal for Humour, and if you don't have time to experiment with your life in this way, consider this book a passable surrogate.

I've changed the way I look at things since the fall of 2012[1] when I set out to collect and read all of the Leacock Medal books. I wanted to steal techniques, study different writing styles, and laugh. But when you spend hours asking yourself why something strikes you as funny and why something else falls flat, you find the answers not in writing tricks and topics but in the memories, biases, and cares that induce reaction and define who you are.

Robert Thomas Allen, a two-time Leacock medalist who gave this issue a lot of thought,[2] concluded, after watching children, that the humor in a joke doesn't come from the joke itself, but from a lot

---

[1] The centennial of the first publication of Stephen Leacock's *Sunshine Sketches of a Little Town.*

[2] In *A Treasury of Canadian Humour* (Toronto: Canadian Illustrated Library, McClelland and Stewart, 1967), Robert Thomas Allen looks at pioneer days and early 20th century humour in a book that complements the modern era Leacock Medal winners.

of mental pictures, ideas, feelings, and associations that the joke suggests." This explains why we get headaches trying to describe funny – an exercise that triple medal winner Arthur Black compares to "braiding smoke" - and why we usually throw up our hands and brand it a personal thing beyond understanding.[3]

Thinking about these things as I read the Leacock Medal books, I learned that old memories haunt me more than I had realized, and I learned that I have a different home town than I had thought. I now see sad thoughts as the seeds of funny ones, and I get up every morning looking differently at the place where I live.

I also learned that kindness does not always govern my thinking. This rattled me as someone who started the project believing that a unifying theory of Canadian humour might rest in Stephen Leacock's renowned definition: "the kindly contemplation of the incongruities of life and the artistic expression thereof."

We Canadians like to think of ourselves as kind, nice people, and Canadian humour has to function within this perception. But many critics bristle at Leacock's inference that our humour always has to be kind and often call the suggestion "nonsense." In the crusty introduction to *Feast of Stephen*, Robertson Davies said firmly that Leacock "knew better than that."[4] The Leacock Medal books, in fact, reflect both kind and unkind purpose, and I admit that the

[3] Alan Walker, Editor, *The Treasury of Great Canadian Humour (*Toronto: McGraw-Hill Ryerson Ltd 1974) says in his introduction that "humour is either funny or it isn't. No explanations are necessary or even forgivable." (Yet I am sure he would have agreed that things can be made less funny with poor writing.)

[4] Stephen Leacock (author), Robertson Davies (Editor), *Feast of Stephen* (Toronto: McClelland and Stewart, 1970). More recently, historian Don Nerbas said of Leacock's *Arcadian Adventures with the Idle Rich* (Jan.– Feb. 2014 Literary Review of Canada) that "Instead of the kindly --.what we have here is earnest, old-fashioned satire."

ignoble, not nice, and un-Canadian parts made me laugh most.[5] For this reason, I now defend Leacock's statement not as a perfect truth, but as a tool that, like quantum physics and relativity, can provide you with the basis for analysis and new understanding.

With enough education and conceit, you can, of course, pronounce on the "artistic expression thereof" merits of written humour. But even artistry and quality depend on your perspective. The humour writing I admired most last year came as a single made-up word - #Ottawapiskat.[6] The Twitter hashtag unleashed a torrent of jokes about the Canadian government's relationship with aboriginal people. This word draws on another element of the Leacock equation, the relevant "incongruities of life." The Twitter word worked because it touched a raw, moment-in-time Canadian incongruity that overpowered the need for elaborate artistic expression. On the other hand, craftsmen like Davies, Mordecai Richler, and Morley Torgov invoke artistry and lots of words to introduce us to unfamiliar incongruities and make them feel like our own.

Despite my deviation from Canadian niceness, I still see a role for kindly contemplation or, at least, the absence of bile that comes with a separation in distance and time. It beams out of Harry J. Boyle's reminiscing about the Depression years and some of Gregory Clark's war stories.

Leacock's statement thus makes more sense to me when viewed as a three-part formula: Is this written with artistic skill or not? What are the incongruities at work here? And was it motivated by kind or unkind intent? These questions in combination can illuminate that seemingly unknowable - your personal sense of humour – and arm

---

[5] Evidently, I am not alone. Humour researchers have long established that people laugh privately at sexism, sick jokes and other things they deplore in public; see Harvey Mindess, et al., *The Antioch Humor Test,* New York, Avon, 1985.

[6] Attributed to Edmonton First Nations artist and author Aaron Paquette commenting on the Idle No More movement and the northern Ontario reserve Attawapiskat.

you to confront anyone who tries to tell you what is or is not funny. With a collection like the Leacock Medal books, the exercise can also point toward a Canadian sense of humour at the confluence of our incongruities, our varied artistic skills, and our conflictions with kindness.

I commend the Leacock Medal books for this purpose not because others have deemed them humorous or because I happen to find them funny, but because they tell us a lot about Canada.

This includes many things I'm sure you do not know - yet.

So, I invite you to learn more about our country's sense of humour, too much about me, and maybe a bit about yourself.

DBD
May 2014

PART II

THE 1940S

THE FRAMING CONTEXT

Drop by my office in Ottawa, and you will see a blank piece of paper framed and mounted on the wall. I call it my prized work of art, my window on aesthetics, and now my touchstone for the study of Canadian humour. I paid $145 plus shipping charges for the piece of paper about ten years ago. I've never regretted spending the money. The paper holds the original of a cartoon that mocked a book of mine.[7] Newspapers reported my book's release under headlines like 'Canadians suffering from a lack of creativity" which missed the point, but provided the punch line to the empty cartoon.

Because this blank space can still make me laugh, I find it easy to accept writing sage John Gardner's claim that "art has no universal rules"[8] and that every work should be judged by its intent and circumstance. This past year, as I worked my way through the Leacock Medal books, that piece of paper reminded me that even though critics extol what sits on the printed page, we cannot really understand humour without looking at the personal context. (I should ask an art expert to appraise my blank page in the absence of such information.)

Without the circumstance, intent, and personal connection, I would have a different view of the earliest Leacock Medal winners and am not sure how strongly I would have recommended them. Now, I think every Canadian should read these books.

---

[7] The book was *Renaissance II: Canadian Creativity and Innovation in the New Millennium,* edited by Richard I. Doyle (Ottawa: NRC Research Press, 2001). The syndicated cartoon was the work of Edmonton Journal artist Malcom Mayes.

[8] John Gardner, *The Art of Fiction: Notes on Craft for Young Writers,* (New York: Vintage Books, 1985) pp 6-8.

A Drawing of a Drawing of Nothing

1947

OJIBWAY MELODY

BY

HARRY SYMONS

Lesson 1

Be careful how you judge a sixty-eight-year-old book

The two-story, 19th century manor sits in a leafy, established part of Peterborough. I'm glad that I didn't know about the house before I entered it. Learning within its walls convinced me that I was on to something.

"He used to live here; in fact, I bought the house from him," my host said in reference to a famous former inhabitant.

The cordial speaker, Professor Tom Symons, shared this morsel and some funny stories as we discussed my interest in the Leacock Medal books. Symons and his wife Christine had invited me to their home for lemon cake and a cup of tea. My wife and I made the trip from Ottawa in early 2013 not to see the house, not to hear about its past, and not to eat. Michèle came along because she likes road trips, and I came to learn more about Tom's father Harry Lutz Symons, the author of *Ojibway Melody: Stories of Georgian Bay,* the 1947 Leacock Medal book. Little has been published about Harry, and I wanted access to the family archives at Trent University.

All I knew for sure about Harry Symons was that he loved his cottage near Pointe-au-Baril on Georgian Bay and saw it as his sanctuary.[9] With *Ojibway Melody,* he tried to share it, guiding us around the islands, pointing out the good fishing spots, and describing the locals. The book can leave you with the feel of a warm handshake, a pat on the back, and a canoe ride on sparkling waters.

Given Stephen Leacock's association with Ontario cottage country, the 1947 medal judges probably felt that this book made a fitting first winner of the award established in Leacock's honour. Yet it struck me, initially, as a puzzle.

It seems like a stream of consciousness, nothing like the one-liners, jokes, or comic stories that we consume as humour today. *Ojibway Melody*[10] merrily pours out a medley: hunting trips; the legend of Turtle Rock; the whisky-barrel that gave Pointe-au-Baril its name; the crow "Black Lucy"; the rookery of lake birds; and Regatta Day, "with all its fun, and laughter, and excitement, and crowds, and ice cream, and pop, and noise."

At times, the book reads like a transcription of musings over events just as they unfolded, like this unedited bit of narration: "for a while. But hold on a moment. Perhaps that was ... it might just possibly have been ... well YOU know ..."

Harry Symons shifts the verb tense and the perspective of the narrator regularly.[11] The only consistency comes from his affection

---

[9] Harry Symons was a vice-president with Confederation Life in charge of real estate holdings in Toronto and liked to get away from the pressures of the city.

[10] Symons held the full copyright on the book. The first edition of *Ojibway Melody* carried the marks of Copp Clark Co. and Ambassador Books; the former did the printing and the latter was Harry's distributor.

[11] He uses the third person perspective in the first and last chapters ("The Advance Party" and "the Rearguard") and more often the royal first person plural ("we

for "the local focal": Boats and fishing. Canoes, inboards, outboards, and row boats. Pike, lunge and bass. Early in the book, you might think Symons wrote it to celebrate the Ojibway Hotel.[12] But then he talks of the hotel with caution, saying he did not lust for places where "ties and collars" were the norm. Harry says that if such a lifestyle ever takes over Georgian Bay, the area will have "lost its savour and ... the ageless rocks will arise in all their dignity and crumble into dust."

When I read this passage, I started to understand. It sounded like something I had heard others say when I was young and was the kind of thing my own father would have thought. I began to regard Harry Symons as my own dad counselling me raconteur-style to slow down and lighten up a bit.

Harry praised simple pleasures: "First we swing our feet out of bed, and dangle them over the side, and keep our toes off the floor just in case it is cold. Then we yawn a good deal and grumble, and flex our arms, and wish we were back in bed ... And quite often we just do give up and crawl back in again ..."

This kind of talk humoured my father's generation because it was struggling with the strains of careers, family, and a changing society. In the 1940s, Canadians also wanted to think about things other than war. *Ojibway Melody,* though written in 1944 and 1945, met that need. It only mentions the World War II context in a vague reference to "the labour shortage in wartime." The incongruity of this book exists, not in the text alone, but between its dark background and cheery content.

---

rocked on our toes") after initiating his story with "I."

12 The landmark Ojibway Hotel endures to this day in the form of a clubhouse and community centre.

Harry Symons [13] had special reason to block out the violence and seek refuge in the boats and fishing around Georgian Bay.

Born in Toronto in 1893, Harry loved physical exertion and the outdoors. He even quarterbacked for the Toronto Argonauts, served as captain of the University of Toronto varsity football team, and sailed competitively. He spent summers on a survey crew, camping and hiking through the wilderness around Georgian Bay. The beauty of the forests and the waters fixed in his head and would turn out to be important to his psyche and survival.

When World War I broke out in 1914, Harry Symons left university and joined the army to serve on the frontlines in Europe, where his mind clenched onto images of the islands around the Bay. In August 1916, he transferred to the Royal Flying Corps and the cockpit of a Sopwith Camel. Harry survived, scoring enough kills to place him in the "Ace" category. Yet he never talked much about the war, and after his death in 1961, aviation historians described his exploits as "unknown to all but the most diligent researchers."[14]

The future Leacock medalist did not consider the war-time heroics nearly as important as his post-plane-crash stay in an English hospital. That's where he met a nurse named Dorothy.[15] After he returned to Canada with Dorothy at his side, he bought the Georgian Bay cottage "Yoctangee," put the war behind him, pursued a career in real estate and insurance, and started a family that would eventually include Tom and seven other children.

---

[13] Personal papers that include the original typed manuscript of Ojibway Melody can be accessed with prior permission at Trent University Archives, Trent University, Peterborough, Ontario, Thomas H. B. Symons Fonds, 1929-99 Accession number 01-003 (box 4 folder 6)

[14] H. *Creagen, "H.L. Symons - Ace & Author,"* Canadian Aviation Historical Society Journal, Vol. 2, No. 4 (Winter 1964) 113.

[15] The convalescent hospital was established by Harry's future father-in-law, the wealthy Canadian lawyer and businessman William Perkins Bull. Other patients at the centre during this period included decorated pilot Billy Bishop and future governor general Georges Vanier.

Tom Symons[16] had talked to me on the phone and had sent me some records as well as having invited me to his Peterborough home, which I learned, only after taking off my boots and sitting down, carries formal designation as Marchbanks House, a historic site and former home of novelist Robertson Davies. Davies wrote his Leacock Medal winning novel in this house. W.O. Mitchell and others also honoured by the Leacock prize regularly visited the place and sat in the chair that held my butt that early 2013 afternoon. Tom, who also showed me the artist's cast for the first Leacock Medal,[17] told me all this to encourage me in my project. He wanted, in particular, to share the story of his dad's book *Ojibway Melody* and the impact it has had on the academic study of Canada.

"The book ... means a great deal to me. I often think of it because it gives me answers when I am considering things - it helps as a compass when I have difficult chores from time to time," said Tom Symons. "First of all, it reads the way my father talked and I enjoy that. I can hear his voice, but I also hear his respect and his concern for others. The book is all about it – between the lines sometimes."

He was touched, in particular, by his father's empathy for the Ojibway people.

"That chapter is superb," said the author's son, now well into his eighties. "I was raised with that concern, and I am sure that that is one of the reasons Trent was the first university in Canada to have a department of native studies."

Tom Symons, the first president of that university and a founder of the field of Canadian Studies, served as Chair of the 1970s national

---

16 For more on Harry's son, see Ralph Heintzman, ed., *Tom Symons: A Canadian Life* (Ottawa: University of Ottawa Press, 2011), which featured contributions from many Canadian politicians, writers, and scholars.

17 Harry Symons' family has possession of sculptor Emanuel Hahn's original cast of Stephen Leacock's face in profile and the Sunshine and Mosquito back used to mint the Leacock medals.

Commission on the subject of Canada.[18] The Commission's 1976 report *To Know Ourselves*[19] set out the roadmap for the subsequent study of Canada and the promotion of Canadians as a people that mix sensitivity with conviction, qualities that Symons saw in his dad's book *Ojibway Melody*.

"My interest in the rapport between French and English people is drawn from the book," said Tom. "You sometimes don't recognize the deeper values of the author because it is written so amiably, but the book is a touchstone for me and the things I value."

This conversation convinced me that every Canadian could benefit from a trip to the cottage described in the first Leacock Medal winning book and, again, made me think that I might be on to something with this project.

It also gave me hope that a person who, like *Ojibway Melody*, is over sixty years old and a little tattered on the edges might still have something worthwhile to say about Canadian humour.

Writing Exercise

In the voice of a former fishing guide from Georgian Bay, describe your first day at work as a stockbroker on Bay Street in 1987.

[18] Tom Symons, born May 30, 1929 also served as Chair of the Ontario Heritage Trust, the Ontario Human Rights Commission, and the Historic Sites and Monuments Board.

[19] The history of Canadian Studies and the Commission are outlined in the Canadian Encyclopedia (online) - Canadian Studies - author S. McMullin http://www.thecanadianencyclopedia.com/articles/canadian-studies accessed September 28, 2013

1948

SARAH BINKS

BY PAUL HIEBERT

Lesson 2

Sometimes the packaging is everything

The book shelf at home holds a first edition, first-printing copy of the 1948 Leacock Medal winner, *Sarah Binks,* that I bought last year from a used book store in Winnipeg. The store considered it a treasured "old friend"[20] and sent it to me inside two layers of packaging.

The book bears the signature of the author, Paul Hiebert,[21] but I "treasure" it because of another scribble on the front page: the names of the original owners, Don and Helen Penner, a Manitoba couple who changed laws and affected the practice of medicine in Canada. In their seventies, the Penners packed up their books and other possessions to pass a decade of

---

[20] Burton Lysecki Books, Osborne Street, email to DBD October 18, 2012.

[21] One of the best resources on what is termed "Binksiana" is the University of Saskatchewan Paul Hiebert Digital Fonds - http://library2.usask.ca/hiebert/node/7 An example of the resources here include Hiebert's modest letter committing his personal material to the University in the imagined native province of his heroine.

retirement helping hospitals in Africa.[22]

This story wrapped around my book gives it value.

In the same way, *Sarah Binks,* a poetry collection packaged in a biography-style narrative, has value because of the premise wrapped around it.

It always surprises me a little when I meet people who have never heard of *Sarah Binks.* Canadian humour circles celebrate her as "iconic," in a way that doesn't abuse the word too much. *Canada Reads* short-listed *Sarah* in 2003 with Will Ferguson as her advocate,[23] and humorist Charles Gordon says the book comes as close as anything to being the "quintessentially Canadian" work, stressing that it's also "damned funny."[24]

The humour flows from knowing that we come close to being as unsophisticated as the book suggests, but not quite. Some non-Canadian readers miss the joke and regard *Sarah* as a serious study, and that's pretty funny too.

Like all great satire, *Sarah Binks* invites interpretation. You could even say the book, a pretend life history that mocks literary

---

[22] Dr. Donald W. Penner was a colleague professor of Paul Hiebert at the University of Manitoba when *Sarah Binks* was published. Penner became one of "Canada's foremost pathologists and a pioneer in blood alcohol research, whose work would eventually lead to stricter national laws." His wife Helen helped design quality assurance and control programs for the College of American Pathologists. In 1988, in their seventies, Don and Helen moved to Africa where Dr. Penner worked as a hospital pathologist, and the couple helped with medical training and recruitment programs in Kenya. They did not return to Winnipeg for ten years, both past the age of eighty. Helen died in January 2004. Don passed away a few months later. My information on the Penners is from public sources and the University of Manitoba.

[23] CBC, "Book Profile: *Sarah Binks,*" http://www.cbc.ca/books/booksandauthors/2010/08/sarah-binks.html accessed September 29, 2013.

[24] Charles Gordon, afterword to *Sarah Binks*, by Paul Hiebert (New Canadian Library edition, 2010).

awards, won the Leacock Medal for Humour for making fun of the Leacock Medal for Humour.

The imaginary Sarah writes bad poetry, lots of it, and this ability to produce quantity over quality brings her the peculiar Wheat Pool Medal and fictional fame in her native province. Among "the highest awards … ever … bestowed upon one of Saskatchewan's Daughters" and the "highest award in the bestowal of Saskatchewan people,"[25] the Wheat Pool Medal recognizes increased production in unspecified fields and, like crop planting, does so through a rotational system.

You might laugh at some of Sarah's award-winning bad poetry in isolation, but that over-the-top, gushing account of her modest life experience amplifies the humour. As the biographer, Hiebert tells us earnestly that Sarah's literary influences include the hired man and a neighbor, Mathilda, the least cross-eyed of the Schwantzhacker sisters. He reports with admiration that the *Horse-Breeders Gazette* and other farm publications profiled her poems and that an agricultural fair honoured her work with the presentation of a horse thermometer. Sarah would die tragically trying to take her own temperature with the poetry prize.

So, at least a few people noticed the irony when *Sarah*, the book, won the new and not-yet-acclaimed literary award, the Leacock Medal, in 1948.

Hiebert was the kind of person who would have recognized and appreciated it too.

---

25 The version used for most of these references is Paul Hiebert, *Sarah Binks* (London: Geoffrey Cumberlege / Oxford University Press, 1947).

He understood convolution. An academic and chemistry researcher, Hiebert won the Governor General's Medal in 1924 for his science.[26] This might lead you to think that his spoof on poetry and the arts was the condescension of a hard scientist. But, before his shift to chemistry, Hiebert studied literature and ultimately earned an M.A. in the arcane field of Gothic and Teutonic philology. He knew the subject of his satire well, and I believe the book had an edge because Hiebert had a specific target in mind even though he did not want to overtly ridicule any individual.[27]

Although *Sarah* directs its lampoon more broadly on the field of literary criticism, it covers other terrain from prairie politics and the cultural charms of early 20th century Canada to the drama of adolescent introspection. Hiebert also calls on many writing tricks including slapstick notions like geology-based poetry and names like Chief Buffalo Chip, Colonel MacSqueamish, Rosalind Drool, Professor Marrowfat, and Windheaver, the politician.

---

26 He got his B.A. at the University of Manitoba (1916) and the M.A. at Toronto (1917). I was inspired to learn that he did his Governor General's Award work as a Fellow of the National Research Council of Canada, my employer. We are imaginary colleagues (as per the National Research Council Report on Scholarships and Fellowships 1932: Hiebert, Paul. G., M.Sc. McGill 1922, Ph.D., 1924. NRC Bursary 1922-23, Fellowship 1923-24, under Otto Maas, Properties of Pure Hydrogen peroxide, accessed NRC Archives, Ottawa, November 2012).

27 Although I have nothing more than coincidence to support the view, I am convinced that Hiebert modeled Sarah in part on E. Pauline Johnson, the late 19th and early 20th century Canadian poetess of mixed aboriginal–European ancestry. Each woman gained great fame through means not directly tied to the quality of her poetry: Pauline through public readings and performances, Sarah through the sale of magazine subscriptions, the collection of product labels, and quantity. The list of similarities between Pauline and Sarah runs from their associations with the Liberal Party, the titles and subjects of their sentimental "Song" poetry, and their relationships with their grandfathers to their deaths, memorials, and aftermath. Even Sarah's geology-based poems, such as the last one, "Up from the Magma," echo Pauline Johnson's final works and her legend for the magma-formed Siwash Rock in Vancouver's Stanley Park. Johnson's celebrity and the resentment of her work in the stuffier Canadian literary circles were in ascendency during Hiebert's literature studies. Hiebert is quoted, however, as saying that Sarah was not a reflection of any single person.

Sarah's odes to pigs, skunks, and farm-based love jerk around, change voice, and ooze conceited sounds from every pore. But they usually rhyme, and follow a metrical structure much of the time, and short of reprinting whole poems along with Hiebert's laudatory packaging, I would struggle to describe precisely how and why Sarah's poems are so "damned funny."

So, maybe, I should be charitable to those who read the book as the story of a real poetess. But one reason I treasure the copy on my shelf comes from thinking that Don and Helen Penner got the joke and, like the early Leacock Medal judges and other Canadians, might have been laughing at themselves too.

Writing Exercise

Write the worst four-line poem you possibly can and then explain why it is the best bit of verse ever written.

1949

TRUTHFULLY YOURS

BY ANGÉLINE HANGO

Lesson 3

They may think you're funny for the Wrong Reasons

"When drunk, papa often struck maman ... And he would swear and push furniture around, and want to fight everybody," Angéline Hango tells us in the opening pages of her Leacock Medal winner *Truthfully Yours.*

In this book, a memoir, Hango describes the childhood embarrassments, hurts, and instability flowing from her father's alcoholism and her mother's struggle to cope in small town Quebec.

I wasn't shocked to learn that the author first submitted the book under a pseudonym and that she didn't consider it to be particularly funny when she wrote it in 1948. She penned it as catharsis, and the award for humour that came a year later surprised her. Hango was forty-four at that time. Last year, I contacted her son

Roy in Vermont, and he told me that his mother appreciated the Leacock honour, but did not regard herself as a humorist or a professional writer of any kind. Though she lived to the age of ninety,[28] Hango never wrote anything for publication after the Leacock Medal.[29] In fact, two decades passed before she would even look at her medal-winning book again, re-read it, and, for the first time, laugh.[30]

The "Truthfully" in the book's title refers to Hango's pledge to break from her life-long habit of "fibbing" about her family, a practice she refines in school, social settings, and eventually the workplace.

Although a capable chef and salesman when sober, her father keeps his income on soft footing and destabilizes the family with his drinking. Hango and her younger sister go off to a convent school for protection from the disturbances at home. Maman works tirelessly and thanklessly as a seamstress to finance their education and board.

At the nunnery school, the two girls learn English, music, and more, but feel out of place among the better-dressed, upper class students. They lie in order to fit in. Later, the book tells of unwanted advances from older men and more "fibs."

"So, where was the humour?" you ask.

Some commentators suggest that 1940s readers found their amusement in material that is "a touch politically incorrect by today's standards:"[31] this being the 1940s stereotype of alcoholic, illiterate,

---

28 Roy A. Hango, email to DBD April 17, 2013.

29 She was, however, working on a manuscript about travel in Morocco at the time of her death from a stroke in 1995.

30 Sheila McCook, "Optimism helps writers," Ottawa Citizen, Jan. 21, 1970, p.45

31 AbeBooks, book description written by bookseller (Finefinds Collection Management, Kaslo, BC, Canada), http://www.abebooks.com (accessed October 15, 2012).

and superstitious backwoods French Canadians and, more generally, the seemingly comic presentation of an abusive circumstance.

For this distortion, the publisher, Oxford University Press, bears some responsibility. It sprinkled cheery cartoons throughout the book and branded the story as a "riotous" and "revealing" picture of "life in rural French Canada" with characters of unsurpassed ignorance in "the business world." As for the bumpy parts of Hango's early life, the original book jacket makes only light and vague mention of the author's "odd" and embarrassing relatives.

Oxford took other liberties, saying, without any stipulation, that *Truthfully Yours* described "many, many love affairs involving every man she (Hango) met from the doorman at the department store to each and every one of her sister's beaux" [32] when those "love affairs" are, in the actual text, clearly awkward encounters or imagined events presented by Hango to show her susceptibility to infatuation.

Hango may have unintentionally contributed to this portrayal of French Canadian life by intertwining the edgier elements of her story with reminiscences on her ancestry, her religion, and traditions such as Christmas Eve réveillon. She also slips into caricature when talking of life as an unmarried "old maid" at the age of twenty-one and in describing her very Quebeçois mother.

"Whenever we made her try to pronounce words in English, she would twist her face all up, as if a person had to wear a different face

---

[32] Angéline Hango, *Truthfully Yours* (Toronto: Oxford University Press, 1948) - from the book jacket cover.

to speak a different tongue," the author says. "The sounds that came out did not resemble any language."

Okay. That and some other parts might be funny.

Hango tells us that her convent cohorts "had a vague notion that anybody that lived in the States was fabulously rich or immensely interesting." With this presumption, she cites "the States" as her home to ensure that her school-yard tormentors are "simply awed into silence." Pondering the art of fibbing, Hango says when a man catches you in a lie, he "would just take it for granted that he misunderstood ... or that he remembered incorrectly" but "not a female, she will pin you down."

If the task of the humorist is to tell the truth with affection, Hango makes a creditable addition to the list of Leacock medalists because of her sense of irony, forgiving take on her family, and decision to speak truthfully. I liked *Truthfully Yours*, but I'm amused most because the book was mistakenly celebrated as a comic take on French Canadian life when first published and now it can be regarded as politically incorrect by those who wrongly assume that intention. [33]

---

[33] The 1949 Leacock medalist went by several different names during her life. She was born on February 2, 1905, and baptized Marie Rose Angéline Roy in the Saguenay-Lac-Saint-Jean region of Quebec. She first distributed the manuscript for *Truthfully Yours* under the pseudonym Angéline Bleuets (meaning Angéline Blueberries — a reference to the pejorative nickname for the people of Lac-Saint-Jean). The text of her book never reveals any of the main characters' names. The pseudonym was the name under which she won the $500 Oxford–Crowell Award for her manuscript, setting the stage for her book's later publication in 1948 by Oxford University Press. By the time the book's jacket was being typeset, she went public under her married name, Hango. Marie Rose Angéline Roy had married John Raymond Hango in 1932 in Arvida. (The groom picked up his unusual last name from inventive immigration officials in the United States, where he landed from Finland with the family name Heino.) She had lived in Montreal for many years and was once cited as Rose Hango. Angéline Hango later remarried, initially assuming the surname Hango-Burke. After she died on November 9, 1995, in Montreal, she was remembered by some as Angéline Burke.

It illustrates the limitations of literary criticism,[34] and that makes me laugh.

Writing Exercise

In five hundred words, explain why children must always tell the truth and adults must lie.

[34] For a thoughtful and interesting examination of the book in isolation of those perceptions, read Bina Freiwald, "The Interpellated Subject Lies Back: Angeline Hango's *Truthfully Yours*," *Essays on Canadian Writing* 58 (1996): 36–59. In an e-mail to DBD, October 10, 2012, Bina Freiwald stated, " my essay ... was part of my research on Canadian women's autobiographical writing, with the emphasis on the text."

PART III

THE 1950'S

THE EVOLUTION OF CANADIAN HUMOUR

"First you have to take all of his skin off, right from his head down to his toes. That's so you can get at his muscles and organs easier."

I was talking to a researcher[35] in the Department of Ecology and Evolutionary Biology at the University of Toronto to see if scientific models could be applied to the evolution of Canadian humour. Interestingly, she showed me how to dismember a frog while talking about the subject.

American writer and wit E.B. White likened the study of humour to dissecting a frog and is often quoted, in a simplified version, as explaining "Few people are interested and the frog dies of it." This remark has killed many attempts to study humour.

"He was wrong," I was told by the white-coated ecologist. "Lots of people care about what frog bodies can tell us."

She was surprisingly enthused about the evolution of humour and had lots of ideas, even offering to generate a phylogenetic tree to show inferred relationships between the various species of humour. I passed. But her definition of evolution swayed my thinking.

In *Humour: Its Theory and Technique, The Greatest Pages of American*

---

[35] Rebecca Batstone (marine biologist, beloved daughter, and U of T Ph.D. student), in discussion with DBD, December 2012.

Humour, and other writings, Stephen Leacock described the evolution of humour as a climb up a ladder to higher forms, away from ridicule toward the sublime.

But science experts view evolution, instead, as a continual process of adaptation to change and adjustment to environmental conditions. I think Canadian humour as expressed in the Leacock Medal books maps more easily against this scientific definition.

These books reflect not only that "Framing Context" of personal experience, but also the cultural and social environment surrounding the author.

One book begs dissection from this evolutionary perspective because its publisher issued it twice, in different versions, over a quarter of a century apart: the fourth medal winner and the first of the 1950s, *Turvey*.

1950

TURVEY

BY EARLE BIRNEY

Lesson 4

How one word can change a book

In my dentist's office one morning in the fall of 2012, while I fumbled with my earphones, the female computer voice on my e-reader blurted out a loud stream of F-word[36] swearing. It made a lasting impression on those around me, and the hygienists and office staff still talk about it over a year later. My audio version of the picaresque novel *Turvey*, like my 1976 hardcover copy, bears the word "unexpurgated" in the title. This means that, unlike the version that won the Leacock Medal in 1950, it has lots of "F words."

When the publisher, McClelland and Stewart (M&S), reviewed Earle Birney's original manuscript, it feared negative reviews and reader reaction to the "army talk," references to "bodily functions," and words that the late 1940s editors picked out as "vulgar."[37] The

[36] The word ends in u-c-k.

boss, Jack McClelland, pushed for milder language, believing that the prevailing Canadian sensibilities would not tolerate F-word swearing.

Birney fought back saying he would rather produce a dirty-talking piece of reality than an expurgated best-seller. There was a standoff. The B.C. writer and World War II veteran, still burning over military bureaucracy, wanted to satirize this aspect of war while that memory was hot, and he knew that the book would have to sound authentic to resonate with soldiers.

As evidenced by the different versions of *Turvey,* Birney lost the standoff with McClelland. He knew that he wouldn't get the swear words by the church-based Ryerson Press, his usual publisher and the one that handled his poetry, and had been worn down by rejections from foreign publishers who thought his book was too Canadian or conversely that it didn't have enough "Mounties, trappers, and pious habitants,"[38] Birney acquiesced and accepted the F-word deletions. M&S produced its sanitized *Turvey* in 1949, and this clean version won the Leacock Medal a year later.

Even with the swearing lifted out, *Turvey* probably had a ring of authenticity. Before the end of the book, the fighting leaves some characters with horrible wounds while others suffer disease and a few die. It is, after all, a war story.

Yet it's also seriously funny.

The reason the humour survives the story's frame lies in the

---

37 My main resource for stories around the publication of *Turvey* is the comprehensive *Earle Birney: A Life*, by Elspeth Cameron (Toronto: Viking, 1994); see p. 320 in particular.

38 Cameron, *Earle Birney: A Life*, p. 329.

personality of protagonist Private Thomas Leadbeater Turvey. Turvey embodies all the Canadian soldiers who signed up with naive intentions and little idea of what they had ahead of them.

His story borders on farce. But the detail and characters make it all seem just plausible. Turvey comes from a small town, Skookam Falls, in the Interior of British Columbia. Like his creator Birney, he identifies with B.C. totally, and aside from a general desire to defeat fascism, Turvey wants nothing more than to serve with his best friend Mac Macgillicuddy in a B.C. regiment, the Kootenay Highlanders. Turvey's quest to get transferred and to get to the "sharp end" of military service provides the drama and drive to the story.

The humour breaks out of Turvey's misfortunes along the way. Sometimes he suffers bad luck, but more often he creates his own problems through gullibility and his interest in the opposite sex. Accident-prone, simple-minded, and light on education and commitment, Turvey does not excel at military life.

By the end of the book, the army has tried him out as a driver, a batman, a guard, a courier, and in many other jobs. Although he finally makes it across the English Channel, he arrives in Europe well after D-Day and on the heels of the fighting. Turvey never sees what most in the World War II military called "real action."

Being one step removed from the horror, Turvey's enthusiasm seems almost reasonable, and this makes it possible to laugh at individual incidents. His path takes him into a minefield after a night at an English pub, into a confrontation with his own jacket which he mistakes for a German paratrooper, and into prison for making too much noise with female companions while AWOL.

Despite the misadventure, Turvey seems heroic in facing the real object of the satire, the institutions and the administration that surround him. The book takes aim, in particular, at the army's human resource systems and IQ-style evaluations which initially rank Turvey as sub-par and almost sub-human. The book concludes with him scoring extremely high after years of repeated test-taking practice.

It takes skill to find humour in grim situations, and even greater skill to make it genuine when editors pluck real-world vocabulary out of the mouths of your characters. Birney achieves his desired effect in the expurgated *Turvey* without the swearing by filling the army-talk conversations with subjects like alcohol, venereal disease, and the brass. He also made sure that war still bled into the story through a smattering of second-hand accounts.

This helped to make *Turvey* a window on a soldier's life in one post-war era. In another one, the book was also bolstered by Birney's original wording.

Canadian society changed over the next quarter-century, and in the post-Vietnam, post-Woodstock, post-Lenny Bruce, George Carlin, National Lampoon, M.A.S.H. world, M&S decided the time was right to dust off the original manuscript and send the swearing out into the world in the "unexpurgated" version of *Turvey* that I bought and read. My hardcover book sits in a slick Robert-Crumb-Keep-on-Truckin-type jacket that reminds me of seventies-style subversion.

In this unexpurgated text, Birney, the poet, made creative use of the four-letter words. They rarely appear in the same combinations. By my count, he uses F*** in five different ways: "What the F***,""Flying F***," "F*** you," "I'm F***-ed," and "F***-ing". A harsh C word appears twice in novel combinations: "those ****s back in Ottawa," and "that ****-faced sergeant." And Birney injects the bodily function-related S*** as follows: "Holy S***," "Sunday S***," "The S*** of the Commandant," "S***-faced turkies," "Up S*** creek," "that recruitin' S***," "Horse S***," "Have to sweat S***," "Pinch of coon- S***,"and "S***-brown battle dress."[39] In 1949, Jack McClelland blocked the publication of these phrases and

[39] One word, however, popular in many military circumstances, did not survive even into the liberated 1976 version of *Turvey*, and according to Birney was there in the first manuscript submitted to McClelland and Stewart in the 1940s (Earl Birney Collection, Thomas Fisher Rare Book Library, University of Toronto). That word was "C***-sucker."

stopped a book that could have pushed the Canadian humour envelope. But, from the perspective of a bookselling businessman, he may have been right about his market.

The expurgated *Turvey,* even with the swear words lifted out, still ran into trouble and drew criticism for its language. In this environment, the Leacock Medal judges might have easily passed over my seemingly crude, but more authentic 1976 swearing-filled version of *Turvey* if it had been available for the medal competition in 1950. Over six decades later, publications like the *New York Times* still fuss over the word in print and people like me still resort to prissy asterisks and the term "F-word" to represent it.

But I know that *Turvey* would have been a better book and could have had more impact if left "unexpurgated," and I am glad that the publisher eventually issued it in this format. I am also glad that this was the version I read - except for that one day in my dentist's office.

Writing Exercise

Describe a group of soldiers raging about the brass in the aftermath of a firefight without using swear words or mentioning foul language.

1951

THE ROVING I

BY ERIC NICOL

Lesson 5

Finding your own "moveable feast"

As a teen in 1960s Ontario, I fantasized that some heavenly intervention might allow me to pass high school French so I could go off to Paris and hang out with someone who might be named Collette, Michèle, or something like that. Ernest Hemingway's death, image, and aftermath loomed large in pop culture and in young male minds at that time.

He told us, "If you're lucky enough to have lived in Paris as a young man, then wherever you go for the rest of your life, it stays with you," adding that celebrated comment "for Paris is a moveable feast."[40]

---

40 The quote, attributed to Hemingway by his biographer, A.E. Hotchner, and slapped on the cover of a post-suicide collection, now strikes me as too cute or rehearsed to be authentic conversation, but the connotation make sense.

Paris was not in the cards for me. Instead, I moved to Vancouver where I had relatives, a place at Simon Fraser University, and my own experiences. They eventually led me to meet writer Eric Nicol and to spend an afternoon at his Point Grey home.[41] For these and other reasons, Nicol's book *The Roving I*, the first of three to win the Leacock Medal for him, mixed Paris and Vancouver together in my mind.

In this 1951 medal winner, Nicol tells of ordinary things: a visit to the library, a ride on a train, and a walk through city streets. There's not much interaction with other people. Yet the book holds your interest because those streets run through Paris, and the train takes you across the French countryside. Nicol wrote the book during his time as a graduate student at the Sorbonne in the late 1940s. He assembled *The Roving I* as a travel narrative aimed at a Canadian audience drawing it from the columns that helped pay his expenses in the City of Light. Eric Nicol's later books also repackaged newspaper columns, but those collections often lacked any unifying theme. *The Roving I* had the story-like framework of his year in Paris, and this makes it an easier read.

Thousands of Canadians around Nicol's age had seen Europe the hard way a few years earlier; Nicol, however, passed his military service in Ottawa offices, and having been "spared the hostilities," he could ride on the post-war wave that regarded Paris with a smile. Nicol, with his master's degree in French literature from UBC, had genuine affection for Parisian life, and this shows too.

The tone of the book and many of its observations may seem

---

41 I interviewed him for Vancouver radio station CJVB in 1978. Nicol (1919-2011) lived in that same house from 1957 to the end of his life.

quaint in an Internet world. Yet some passages could have been written yesterday, and pretty much all of it remains funny. This is because Nicol describes the walks through the streets of the everyday with weird words and silly detail - as he did on his day at the bibliothèque: "A little man saved from midgetdom only by his bowler. With hands resting on his behind, he fluffs out the wings of his swallowtail coat (circa 1885), like a nervous blowfly."[42]

Nicol's inclination to elaborate the ordinary while skating over the elaborate sparkles in his description of a side trip to Florence. In it, he devotes two and a half pages to the process of eating spaghetti and only a paragraph to the Uffizi. He not only elevates mundane events with his descriptions, but manages to generate stories of things that never happened - like an imagined date with a woman who might have been named "Collette" had she shown up. Nicol never fully explains the decision to leave the Sorbonne before completing his doctorate, but he felt lonely. He laments not having someone with whom to share his Paris experience.

What Hemingway meant by "moveable feast," of course, was that the 1920s Paris of artists, writers, and poets was his personal foundation: the learning, the relationships, and the experiences that he would feed upon for the rest of his life. Nicol, at the age of thirty, had passed out of the young man stage (his Collette imaginings notwithstanding) when he attended university in Paris. As a published author and veteran journalist, he had already found his comic voice and decided that British Columbia would be his touchstone.

This meant that Nicol brought his own moveable feast[43] to Paris and to the book that allowed him to share those Sorbonne days with thousands of Canadians including one living in Ottawa, who still feasts on young man thoughts of Vancouver from time to time.

---

[42] This excerpt was also highlighted by Michael Nolan in "Eric Nicol," in *Dictionary of Literary Biography*, vol. 362, *Canadian Literary Humorists*, ed. Paul Matthew St. Pierre (Detroit: Gale, 2011). Anyone interested in substantive bios of humour writers should access the St. Pierre collection.

[43] On the subject of moveable feasts, the ever modest Nicol said, "In the feast of life, I have been a digestive biscuit." Allen Twigg, "Tribute to Eric Nicol," *BC Bookworld*, Spring 2011, pp.17–18.

Writing Exercise

In a paragraph, explain why Sudbury, Ontario is your "moveable feast."

1952

THE SALT-BOX

BY JAN HILLIARD

Lesson 6

How to embrace uncertainty

I used to think that age and experience would bring more certainty to my life. But aside from some aspects of politics and the importance of comfortable pants, fewer things seem definite with the passing of time. The 1952 winner of the Leacock Medal, *The Salt-Box* by Jan Hilliard, reminded me that this is not such a bad thing.

Artist Kay Grant[44] used the pseudonym Jan Hilliard when she decided, in her early forties, to shift gears, pick up a pen, and write the story of her unsettled childhood in small town Nova Scotia. The false name sheltered her family and friends and allowed her to sprinkle a little fiction on the largely factual.

---

[44] Grant was her married surname. Hilda Kay was her full maiden name. She told friends she did not like Hilda as a name, and she adopted her maiden surname as her first name and possibly converted Hilda into Hilliard for the pseudonym. (David Skene-Melvin, "Hilda Kay Grant," *Globe and Mail*, sec. A16, June 25, 1996). She was born November 29, 1910.

A salt-box house with its two-story main building and sloping extension looks like the wooden box used to store salt in colonial-era kitchens. Old salt-box buildings are common sights down east, and all of them have a ramshackle feel. But Grant's family home enjoys a particular unstable quality - inside and out. Her mother dies when she is young, and afterward, her father, an Englishman who never appreciated the charm of Nova Scotia's wind and sea, hits the road for long periods searching for gold mines in British Columbia while leaving his five kids in the care of their Aunt Belle. He supports Belle and the children with an allowance from relations in Britain.

With each departure, Grant's father pledges to strike it rich, get established, and relocate everyone to the west coast. The family never makes the move but lives in a permanent state of uncertainty, always thinking it was about to leave for B.C.

The old house and light income keep their lives rustic and minimal. In fact, upon reading the horses, buggies, and wilderness-filled manuscript, Grant's U.S. publisher decided that the primitive Nova Scotian home sounded implausible when set in the 1920s. For the benefit of urban American readers, it edited the story to place it decades earlier than the reality.

Yet Belle, the children, and the others who share the home love the old salt-box and, as it turns out, even the instability. They not only accept the hovering possibility of a big move as their norm, but draw a kind of energy from it: uncertainty gave the family a common concern and a feeling of continuous excitement. Near the end of the book, the family finally sells the salt-box and then promptly turns around to rent it back from the new owner.

Like her predecessor Angéline Hango and other Leacock medalists to follow, Grant had, in mid-life, come to terms with the tense part of her childhood and felt obliged to share it in a written recollection. But unlike Hango, Grant deliberately crafted *The Salt-Box* with the goal of making readers laugh. She consciously exploited the humour inherent in a situation constantly on the edge of change.

A graduate of the Grand Central School of Art in New York,

Grant had already dedicated her life to artistic expression and had more than a passing interest in writing before producing this, her first book. Her *Salt-Box* story recalls her wandering father's writing aspirations and describes her childhood exposure to books and authors like "Stevenson, Barrie, George Eliot, Charlotte Brontë, Sir Walter Scott ... *Lorna Doone* ... *The Water Babies* and *Jane Eyre* ... *Alice in Wonderland* ... (and the) *Pickwick Papers*" as well as poetry from Omar Khayyám to Robert Service.

Before returning to the visual arts full time in her late fifties, Grant wrote a total of nine published books. They included several novels with the pseudonym Jan Hilliard as well as two biographies and a book on gardening under her own Kay Grant name.[45] Although she sought to be humorous only in that first book,[46] Grant showed some talent in setting up funny scenes, playing up irony, and even modelling Stephen Leacock in the attempt.

She echoes Leacock's *Sunshine Sketches* in episodes like Uncle Harry's foray into the cranberry business; he decided it "would not demand too much muscular energy. God grew the berries, and all you had to do was pick them." Harry makes a deal to lease land from a semi-shrewd local with a promise to share the profits. After learning all that cranberry cultivation entails, Harry decides to invest nothing, do nothing, collect nothing, and thus share nothing for the summer spent as a leasing landholder.

45 Some other books by Kay Grant: *Robert Stevenson, Engineer and Sea-builder* (New York: Meredith Press, 1969); *Samuel Cunard, Pioneer of the Atlantic Steamship* (London: Abelard-Schuman, 1967); and *Small City Gardens* (Toronto: Abelard-Schuman, 1967), coauthored with William S. Brett.

46 McCook, "Optimism helps writers" (see n. 30).

In *the Salt-Box,* Grant clearly wants to focus on the positive and the affection she feels for idiosyncratic personalities such as her "fun" New York-based, English-born Aunt Emily and her teacher, Miss Higby, "a spare, big-boned spinster of indeterminate age, with thin gray hair strained back over red ears, who always looked as though she had dressed in a hurry ... (but boy) ...she could teach!"

The Salt-Box not only accepts an imperfect childhood, it celebrates instability and the possibility of change, and, again, prods people like me with a reminder that we should reconsider any yearning for death-and-taxes-style certainty in life.

I found it sad to read that no one staged a memorial or funeral service in Toronto for Grant when she died there in 1996 at the age of eighty-five.[47] A recognized water colorist and writer, she deserved commemoration. But Grant, knowing from childhood how to laugh at life's ephemeral nature, might have seen a bit of humour in her quiet passing.

One thing, besides politics and pants, now strikes me as certain: if you want to pursue a career as an artist of any kind, you should get used to the certainty of uncertainty and try to see the funny side.

Writing Exercise

Write a memoir-style short story about your childhood in Tornado Alley.

[47] When she died in Toronto on May 11, 1996, no services were held. Her ashes were later interred in her husband's family plot (the Grant family) back in Nova Scotia (New Glasgow). Obituary of Kay Grant, *Globe and Mail,* May 13, 1996.

1953

THE BATTLE OF BALTINGLASS

BY LAWRENCE EARL

Lesson 7

How the basics of politics never change

The drama, the character, and the humour make *The Battle of Baltinglass* an entertaining story. But I keep my copy of the book handy, not as a compelling narrative, but as a manual and technical reference on the people part of politics.

Set in rural Ireland in the early 1950s, the story might not, at first, appear relevant to 21st century Realpolitik powered by Twitter, tipping-points, robocalls, and the viral Internet. Yet it covers all the bases in the true story of a local campaign that eventually toppled a national government.

A mountain village in County Wiklow, Baltinglass remains bucolic and quiet as a community where people tend to mind their own business until 1950. The appointment of a new sub-postmaster that year shakes things up and launches the story told by the seventh winner of the Leacock Medal.

The government grants the post office position to Mick Farrell, a young local with political connections but no post office experience. Villagers might have turned a blind eye to Mick's failings had they not seen his appointment as an injustice to two innocent others: Helen Cooke and her elderly Aunt Katie. The job had been in the Cooke family for eighty years. Katie had held it officially, but Helen had done the work on her behalf. The people of Baltinglass see Helen, a "tiny, shy-seeming" and unmarried woman of fifty-five, as dependent and vulnerable and as someone who had done the job to perfection.

Sympathy for Helen induces a movement to get her reinstated. The crusade runs well over a year before culminating in Mick's resignation and Helen's return to the post office. Meanwhile, a broader debate over political favoritism takes hold around the Baltinglass hubbub. It ultimately forces out the responsible politician (the Labour Party Minister of Posts and Telegraphs James Everett) and then the whole government (the Inter-Party Coalition).

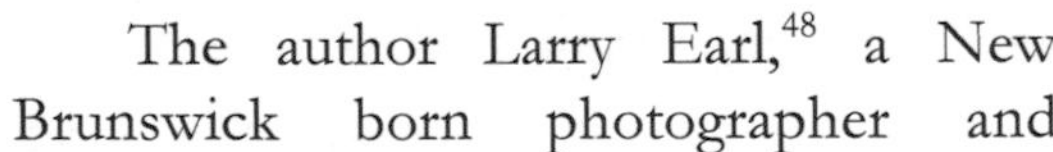

The author Larry Earl,[48] a New Brunswick born photographer and

---

48 Lawrence Earl was born Lawrence Wiezel in Saint John, New Brunswick. He died in 2005 at the age of ninety, back in Canada, after spending most of his life in London, England. He covered the invasion of Normandy first-hand. His photos were used on the cover of *Time* magazine and in *National Geographic*, *Maclean's*, and the *Saturday Evening Post.* In 1943, he married Jane Armstrong, a woman recognized as one of only two female foreign correspondents during WWII. *New Brunswick Literary Encyclopedia*, s.v. "Lawrence Earl" (by Matt Belyea), http://w3.stu.ca/stu/sites/nble/e/earl_lawrence.html (accessed October 15, 2013); Obituary of Lawrence Earl, *Saint John High School Alumni News*, vol. 21, May 2006; *Canadian Books and Authors*, s.v. "Lawrence Earl," see http://www.canadianauthors.net/e/earl_lawrence; and University of New Brunswick, ""UNB to Confer Three Honorary Degrees at Convocation." news release cited on UNB website, September 21, 2005.

reporter, was working in Britain at the time. Baltinglass appealed to his sense of humour as well as his journalist side. Against the Tolstoy standard for dispassionate narrators, Earl's style sounds a little shaky and over the top at times, but his words always seem aimed at reporting the facts of the story. He had lots of material to draw on. Newspapers filled their pages with the battle of Baltinglass and its aftermath; the controversy generated letters to the editor, fiery hearings, debates in Parliament, and even a popular song about the battle. Earl not only choreographs all these facts into a story, but also provides a snapshot of the Irish politics of Catholics and Protestants, the village poor and city rich, and the Republicans and those who would deign to associate with the British Royal family. The combination makes for a lively read, and like an earlier book written by Larry Earl, it would, in the right hands, make for a good movie.[49]

But for a one-time political hack like me, the book serves as something else. It acts like a happy souvenir of the politics of Legion halls, door knocking, letters, and draught beer. It records, as a readable reference, all the elements of an election campaign: (1) a core team as well as committees for collective decisions; (2) rapid-response media relations; (3) a demand for justice; (4) titillating David-and-Goliath narratives; and (5) a determination to focus, focus, focus. All will sound familiar to anyone at a party headquarters or in a well-run local campaign. The book embraces principles that seem as valid now as they were in that Irish mountain town.

Today political events move so fast, they're hard to understand. But *Baltinglass* provides me with a reference and a way to study the chain reaction in slow motion when real people interacted in what was once real time.

---

49 Earl's book *Yangtse Incident* (1950) tells another true story, that of the HMS *Amethyst* and its attack and escape during the revolution in China in 1949. The movie based on it was a British box office success in 1957 and starred Richard Todd and Donald Houston. Earl wrote five other books: *Crocodile Fever* (1954), *The Frozen Jungle* (1955), *She Loved a Wicked City* (1962), *The Riddle of a Haunted River* (1962), and *Risk* (1969). *New Brunswick Literary Encyclopedia*, s.v. "Lawrence Earl," http://w3.stu.ca/stu/sites/nble/e/earl_lawrence.html (accessed Oct. 15, 2013).

Writing Exercise

Write a short story that tells how a pothole brought down the government of New Brunswick.

1954

PARDON MY PARKA

BY JOAN WALKER

Lesson 8

The limits of self-deprecating humour

I laugh when I look at my copy of the 1954 Leacock Medal winner, *Pardon My Parka,* by Joan Walker,[50] because of the irony. I didn't find the book particularly funny and probably liked it the least of the award-winning bunch. Yet I paid more for it than any other book.

I had a hard time finding a copy, eventually ordered one from a rare book dealer, and paid around 200 times its original 35-cent sticker price. Some people might see the book's rarity as a good thing.

---

50 Joan Suter Walker, born in London on November 21, 1908, worked in advertising and as a feature writer, editor, and journalist in Britain before marrying Canadian major James Rankin Walker. She wrote other books and contributed regularly to the *Globe and Mail,* specializing in reviews of humour. She reviewed many books that would eventually win the Leacock Medal.

Walker wrote it to be a fun account of her experience as a British war bride, struggling to get established in Val D'Or, Quebec just ten years after the town's gold mine opened. Most of the book tells her story in a cheerful and positive way.

"Anyone can be a pioneer," she says. "All you have to do is fall in love with a Canadian Major during a London blackout."

But more than a few times, Walker resorts to racial and cultural stereotypes that go beyond what you can excuse as just a feature of another era or as awkward attempts at humour. [51] These comments stick in my mind and taint the whole book despite her breezy, self-deprecating style.

Walker admits upfront to being a privileged Brit "who can barely tell a cow from a sheep, and couldn't care less." Back in London, her family paid others to do the housekeeping, and Walker says that even when she worked as a Fleet Street journalist, she put a high priority on socializing and sleeping in. Parties, cigarettes, and alcohol fill her stories, and she shops and soaks in the tub whenever possible. These pursuits, of course, collide with northern life, particularly when she treks off on camping trips to battle black flies and moose.

Reflecting her interest in comforts, she always brings her story back to the multi-year quest to build, furnish, and occupy her bungalow. Walker wrangles with contractors, fights to get municipal services hooked up, and slogs through the mud. She and her husband rely on an outhouse in winter, tote water up-hill, and readjust financing every step of the way.

The book often reads like a yarn written to impress the writer's friends back in Blighty, and its greatest sales success came initially in Britain. But Walker generally treats the physical environment kindly,

---

[51] Robert Thomas Allen tells of even greater transgressions in the search for humour in Canada during the Victorian era, when people with disabilities and anyone struggling to speak English warranted ridicule. Allen, *A Treasury of Canadian Humour*, pp. 18–19 (see n. 2).

rarely commenting on the snow and cold, and she never directs her aggravation at the Canadian soldier who brought her to the wilds of northern Quebec. Even when relating extreme disappointment and a desire to strangle someone, she won't label the villain as anything more than a "dirty so and so," "such and such," or "son of a gun."

For this reason, her cultural shots and race references seem to leap off the page.

Walker belittles the "notoriously prolific" French Canadians and summons her Swiss finishing school background to condemn the locals for their "hideous" language skills and flawed manners. In one early passage, she mourns the treatment Chopin's Prelude in C received from a pianist passing through Val D'Or. She did not know him at the time and describes him only as "a coloured" man, adding that his name was Oscar Peterson. At other points, she complains of being treated like a "Chinese Coolie."

Whether you could excuse those remarks as a symptom of another age or not, it's hard to skip over Joan's portrait of Indian children in the closing chapters.

"They are dirty and smelly, and their noses always run. They are naturally cruel to animals," she says.[52]

Mercifully, Walker doesn't slip all the way back to the Victorian era when Canadians evidently found their laughs not only in the

---

[52] Joan Walker, *Pardon my Parka* (London: Morrison and Gibb, 1954), p. 181. Citations are to the Morrison and Gibb edition.

plight of convicts and the underprivileged, but also "anyone with a physical disability." [53]

Still, her comments definitely give off a whiff of the "dirty and smelly" side of Victorian "gentility," and they reminded me of the limits of self-deprecating humour as a mollifying context. My humour guru (commenting on my writing) noted that "it gets tiresome quickly, draws attention to the author, and interferes with the story."[54] Walker's book shows that self-deprecation also grates and seems insincere when juxtaposed with slights at others.

Despite all of this, I think that you might want to read the book for a snapshot of the life of a war bride. Close to fifty thousand of them came to Canada after World War II. They undoubtedly had a bit of a shock, felt the separation from familiar surroundings, and missed family and friends, but did it for love. Joan Walker's book captures that part of the Canadian experience, and I believe she tries to be honest and open about her personal take as someone of privilege.[55] I just wish she had had an underprivileged editor.

Writing Exercise

After exaggerated self-deprecation, set out your solution to the tensions in the Middle East based on stereotypes.

---

[53] Judging by our 19th century humour magazines (*The Moon*, *The Grumbler*, and even *Grip* and *Punch in Canada*), early Canadians did, unfortunately, see funniness in the "Chinese, Catholics, Jews, Germans, Dutch ... French Canadians" and others who seemed different and struggled to speak English. See Allen, *A Treasury of Canadian Humour*, pp. 18–19 (see n. 2).

[54] Rajee Tupak Needles (email message to DBD, September 2013).

[55] Joan and her husband, the former major J.R. Walker, finished their bungalow in Val D'Or, but soon moved to northern Ontario, and later settled just outside of Oshawa. Despite her early cigarettes-and-parties lifestyle, Joan Walker lived well into her eighties. The couple spent over a decade of their retirement in a comfortable bungalow overlooking the ocean in a privileged part of the Britain-like Oak Bay area of Victoria, B.C.

1955

LEAVEN OF MALICE

BY ROBERTSON DAVIES

Lesson 9

When more words are better

My friends and relatives in Kawartha Lakes farm country might beat me with a pitch fork if I tried to talk to them the way Robertson Davies liked to write. His prose has an intelligence and wit that critics often classed as urbane, but, as shown in the 1955 Leacock Medal winner *Leaven of Malice,* it also fumes with condescension and pretentions that make for a funny book, but might not go over well as spoken words.

Davies starts one chapter thus: "It was not for Gloster Ridley only that November 1st was embittered by the incident of the fraudulent engagement notice." Another begins: "In the music room of the Waverly University Library, Pearl Vambrace had abandoned herself to a deplorable form of self-indulgence."

The author also decorates his descriptions with odd adjectives in long streams like the one that tells us "Matthew Snelgrove read his evening copy of *The Bellman* with a special gloomy relish, for it never failed to yield several instances in which rampant democracy had been guilty of some foolishness which could never, he was convinced, have happened under the old squirearchy - particularly if a sufficient number of squires happened also to be lawyers." Try reading that out loud.

Unlike most of us, Davies seemed attracted to sentences with an air of affectation. They worked for him in this book and others because he was trying to satirize pomposity, and his prose makes you feel the stuffiness.

In a sentence introducing the lawyer Snelgrove, for example, Davies, as narrator, repeats and repeats a phrase in a way that breaks lots of writing-course rules:

> "a lawyer in reality but also a lawyer in a score of stagey mannerisms ... a lawyer who joined the tips of his fingers while listening to a client; a lawyer who closed his eyes and smacked his lips disconcertingly while others talked; a lawyer who tugged and polished his long nose with a very large handkerchief; a lawyer who coughed dryly before speaking; a lawyer who used his eyeglasses not so much as aids to vision as for peeping over, snatching from the nose, rubbing on the lapel, and wagging in his listener's face."

I admire writers who do things I would never think to do and make them work. Having been told by wise teachers to economize with language and only put down on paper what readers need to know, I strive to omit needless words and might have cut out the repetition about the lawyer. Yet the echoing creates a mood and seems to beat a logical path to the legal battles that ensue, and I wouldn't delete the adjectives from clusters like "gloomy relish" and "rampant democracy," as the nouns would not convey the same incongruity if left unadorned. The definition of needless seems to change with the circumstance and intent.

The format of a satirical novel gave these words their circumstance. As for intent, *Leaven of Malice* wants you to see the humour imbedded in snooty society. It even opens with a practical joke packaged in formality – that phony engagement announcement in the *Evening Bellman:* "Professor and Mrs. Walter Vambrace are pleased to announce the engagement of their daughter, Pearl Veronica, to Solomon Bridgetower, Esq." The Vambrace and Bridgetower families were feuding and thus the joke, the embarrassment, and the quest to find the culprit.[56]

The pretentions make great prose for the purpose served. But, as my country cousins would attest, it doesn't do well as oral interaction, and perhaps, this hints at why Davies failed miserably in efforts to convert *Leaven of Malice* into plays both on Broadway (as Tyronne Guthrie's adaptation *Love and Libel*) and later in Canada.[57]

Professional snot and *New York Times* critic Clive Barnes trashed the play, saying that hotels should give "hardship discounts ... to people who have just seen *Leaven of Malice*" and that the play did not merely fall "beneath international standards, but fail(s) at even a provincial level."[58] I wish I had been around to console Davies.

By his own admission, Barnes, who dismissed Davies as "an academic," never read the novel, knew the author only as a failed playwright, and predictably bristled at the play's jokes about conventional theatre. The critic also saw the story as focused on

---

[56] Davies attended Queen's University in Kingston and Balliol College at Oxford. The college's graduates include three British prime ministers, and many other figures from politics and the arts, such as philosopher Adam Smith.

[57] Davies, who acted at the Old Vic in London after his days at Oxford and who helped establish the Stratford Theatre Festival, loved the theatre and was frustrated by his limited success as a playwright.

[58] Clive Barnes, "Leaven of Malice badly acted nonsense," Globe and Mail, June 10, 1975.

Vambrace, the professor who bumbles within it.

But in the novel version which I liked, Davies followed Ridley, the editor of the *Bellman,* as the protagonist who observes, learns, and brings the story full circle.

In the first pages, Ridley fusses in anticipation of an honourary degree from the university. At the end of the book, he decides, after the parade of pretension and pomposity, that he doesn't want validation from the academic community, after all.

It's too bad Davies,[59] who wrote the novel with confidence and authority while editor of the *Peterborough Examiner* and living the role of Ridley,[60] wasn't satisfied with his success in printed words and instead sought validation in the spoken-word world of the theatre. It could have been worse though; he could have tried out his text in lectures to my friends and relatives in the Kawartha country around Peterborough.[61]

---

[59] William Robertson Davies, born in 1913 in Thamesville, Ontario, is among the most celebrated figures in Canadian literature, but even his publisher (Penguin) did not always identify him as a writer, regularly listing his professions as actor, publisher, and professor. When Davies died in 1995, the CBC broadcasted his funeral live.

[60] *Leaven of Malice* features a newspaper editor pestered by a would-be freelance writer who ends up being the hapless scoundrel of the story. During this period, the author's older brother, Fred Davies, had pestered Robertson, the editor of the *Peterborough Examiner*, for freelance work including funding for a trip to Nassau in the Bahamas, where Fred died in a car accident just months before *Leaven of Malice* was published. Val Ross, *Robertson Davies: A Portrait in Mosaic* (Toronto: McClelland and Stewart, 2008), p. 138.

[61] Davies was thinking about Kingston, Ontario, when he painted the town of Salterton in this book and its trilogical companions *Tempest-Tost* (1951) and *A Mixture of Frailties* (1958). When it was first released, *Leaven of Malice*, as a novel, suffered one noteworthy critical review. It came from a columnist who could have stood in for many characters in the book: Arnold Edinborough, a university lecturer, lay preacher in the Anglican Church, and editor of the *Whig-Standard*, the newspaper located in Kingston. (Val Ross, *Robertson Davies: A Portrait in Mosaic*, p. 142). With all due respect to the late Mr. Edinborough, that makes me laugh.

Writing Exercise

Imitate the long, one-sentence description of a lawyer above to introduce a plumber.

1956

SHALL WE JOIN THE LADIES

BY ERIC NICOL

Lesson 10

Why travel writers need a place to call home

I often liken Eric Nicol's newspaper columns to a bunch of chocolates.

When I lived in Lotus Land and read the Vancouver Province,[62] his sense of humour always broke up the day and brightened it like a treat. But like chocolates, a bunch of them can be a bit much if devoured without pause.

This applies to a lot of humour

62 Before his 1986 retirement, Nicol wrote more than six thousand humour columns for the *Vancouver Province*. He also produced thirty-nine books as well as plays and magazine articles. He kept writing past the age of ninety, being funny and intrigued by the opposite sex, even after a diagnosis of Alzheimer's. As I finished this book, I was laughing at his last (*Script Tease*) and wishing that my book could just touch its hem. I was stunned to read Nicol's memorial service in February 2011 described as "embarrassingly small" and that "precious little" reference was made to his career and "stature as a writer" at it. (Twigg, "Tribute to Eric Nicol," p. 17; see n. 43.) I think I will adjust my aspiration for enduring literary fame.

writing. *A Book of Canadian Humour,* an anthology published in the 1950s, even defines "comic relief" as "the interspersion of tragic scenes which will enable the audience to endure the comedy."[63] That book cautions readers against the rapid consumption of humour. The same warning could be applied to the 1956 Leacock Medal winner by Eric Nicol.

I usually try to read Nicol's books in a number of short sessions when they are collections of columns. But because my goal was to finish sixty-six books in one year, I broke my rule with this one and pushed through it.

Of the three Leacock Medal winning books written by Nicol, two wrap themselves around international travel. The first tells of his time as a student in Paris, and the third book presents tips for globe trotters. But this winner in the middle, *Shall We Join the Ladies,* strings disconnected stories together in a compilation that seems at times, like the overwhelming bunch of sweets. His subjects run from the sex changes behind the title of the book to how to stay warm: "women are wonderful, money is more so, but there is really nothing like central heating" and "I put on so many socks people thought I had elephantiasis".

The humour helped me along, and I'm glad I read the book in one burst because at the end, I recognized a unifying theme after all - travel - again.

I might not have seen this travel angle without consuming the collection in a rush for two reasons. First, many of the stories are detached from any real sense of place. They celebrate routine tasks like buying a shoe or minor adventures like riding a bike. The other reason that this probably would not strike you as "travel writing" at first comes from its homage to staying home. As evident in all his Leacock Medal books, home for Nicol was and always would be

63 John Daniel Robins and Margaret V. Ray, eds., *A Book of Canadian Humour* (Toronto: Ryerson Press, 1951). Writer and academic John Daniel Robins died the year after the book's publication, at the age of sixty-eight.

Vancouver,[64] and you realize this is where he likes to be as you work through his stories: "I think I'll spend most of my holiday at a quiet little place I know, near the beach, tennis courts, golf course, yet handy to the city and serving first-rate victuals. You guessed it."

It all culminates in the final chapter which sets out his reasons for staying in British Columbia when so many suggest that professional success can only be achieved abroad or at the very least in the east. "For a writer, such a plan (staying in B.C.) indicates a sorry lack of ambition." But he argues that his home town is destined to be great, and he wants to be part of it. I understand that for sure.

At the same time, he wants to see other countries even though his trips "can never be more than that of the yo-yo that flies forth from the hand for the joy of whizzing straight back" home. He hoped "to see the world in a series of zips out and zips back, so that the graph of (his) voyages will look like a lie detector - with the hiccups." I understand that too.

So, like Nicol's two other medal winners, *Shall We Join the Ladies* really tells us about travel. In order to travel, you have to be leaving someplace behind, someplace that gives you a basis to evaluate the new places, and someplace to address your observations. You can't say you are travelling unless you have someplace else to call home.

Nicol seemed to know that better than most people and even many travel writers. This idea made the box that holds his bunch of treats together. But I only saw it after all the chocolates were finished.

Writing Exercise

Explain why you refused a free trip around the world to stay at home in Hamilton.

---

64 When he won his first Leacock Medal in 1951, Nichol, who was born in Kingston, Ontario, told reporters that he considered himself a "Vancouver native." (the *Globe and Mail,* "The Winners," May 5, 1951) p. 8.

1957

THE GRASS IS NEVER GREENER

BY ROBERT THOMAS ALLEN

Lesson 11

When "home" is not a place

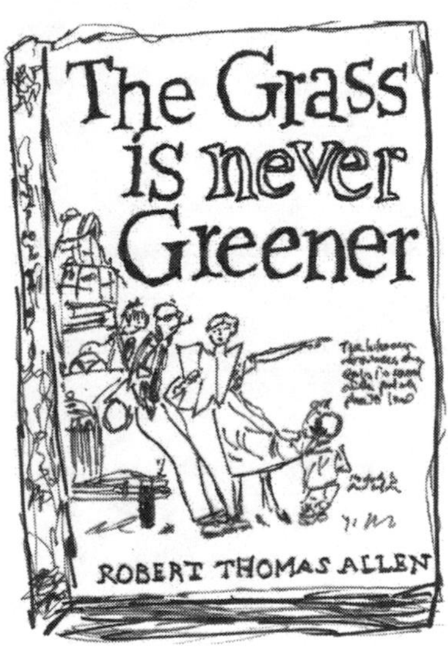

In 1976, my cousin Rod, then in his early thirties, was working in an odious cardboard box factory near Oshawa, Ontario. One night, he came home to his bare apartment to find a brown envelope wrapped around a tax refund of $500. Rod had never held so much unencumbered money in his hands before, and it changed his life. He quit his job, stuffed his possessions into a trunk, and jumped on a train to B.C. where he lived with me before moving to California, the sunny setting for the rest of his life.

Rod's $500 life-changing story has always made me smile, and it makes it easier for me than perhaps many other early 21st century readers to accept the pack-up-and-move premise of the eleventh Leacock Medal book, *The Grass is Never Greener,* Robert Thomas Allen's search for "the Perfect Place to Live."

By the mid-1950s, Allen, born in 1911, had had enough success as a freelance "magazine writer" to cause him to dream about breaking away from his Toronto advertising job. His fantasy congeals around the possibility of selling his home for a $2000 to $3,000 profit and using those proceeds to live in a warmer spot. He was equipped with a Chev that he bought for $400 in 1934, the year of his wedding.

When I first read the jacket notes, I wondered whether the book would really mark a vigorous contribution to Canadian culture. Published in the U.S., it purportedly told of life in the U.S., and Allen's publisher promoted it primarily in the U.S. market as the work of a "fresh humorist" for "American readers."

But the book follows the adventures of a very Canadian family. In fact, a lot of the story takes place in Canada: first during the set up to Allen's plunge into itinerant, freelance employment; [65] then a transition time in an Ontario cottage; then back in Toronto and a spell on a small farm outside the city. In between, he hauls his wife and two young daughters around on a long road trip, settling for a while in a beach house in Florida, then a town in Arizona near the Mexican border, and finally in Pasadena before heading back to Canada, temporarily.

One Canadian concern that frames the travels comes in references to climate and in comparisons to winters in Toronto. Allen judges most places in this way and uses the weather to structure

65 Although he spent much of his adult life in the U.S., Allen became a Canadian symbol. The bespectacled figure used for decades by the *Toronto Star's* Duncan Macpherson to represent "the Canadian everyman" in editorial cartoons was widely known to have been based upon Robert Thomas Allen, or at least was inspired by his writings. Macpherson said that "if (Stephen) Leacock were alive, he would be lucky to win the Robert Thomas Allen Medal for Humour."

many of his choices.

Much of the humor, however, comes from concerns that are neither Canadian nor American, neither warm nor cold. They surround children and schools, husbands and wives, making money and spending it. These issues preoccupied 1950s, post-war readers of the book, and Robert Thomas Allen tried to make them seem a little less serious.

Allen wrote in "a gentle, self-mocking, quietly insightful and sneakily profound manner" that tried to ensnare readers with charm to teach a life lesson.

Some of the humour about pipe-smoking men and hairdo-loving women seems more than a little quaint ("there are no schools that teach men how to teach women how to drive"), and corporal punishment for children, domestic turmoil, and archaic terms like "retarded" stand out as reminders that the book was of a different time, particularly when they sit in a work by a man whom other writers remember as enlightened and kind.

"He was a sweet, sweet man … as polite as any human ever was, soft spoken, but had a wry smile and a twinkle," says author and columnist Roy MacGregor, who knew Allen in the 1970s. "He was so Canadian that the word 'sorry' was minted for him … never a sour word, never … a flash of anger."[66]

Although Allen's style eventually fell out of fashion, *The Grass is Never Greener* startled me as a 21st century reader with the extent to which some themes still resonate. His musings on celebrity Self-Help books (Gene Autry was one fifties personality who indulged in the field) are not much different than satire of today's psychology for sale, and, of course, that issue of where and how to live our lives endures.

At times, the search for "the Perfect Place to Live" premise

---

[66] Roy MacGregor (Globe and Mail Columnist and author) email to DBD, February 28, 2014. Also the source of the "sneakily profound" comment.

seems faint, and Allen twists some stories to fit the theme in a way that may be a little contrived. But it worked for me, in part because of my late cousin Rod, but also because I knew that Allen's struggle over where to live was authentic and lasted most of his life.

He and his wife liked California, and the book ends with them back on the U.S. west coast where he feels "good to know ... (they)... don't have to move around anymore ... (and) can dig in, for good." One page later, the editor added this note "When this manuscript went to press, the author and his family had started back to Toronto."

Even that did not end the real life story. Allen would return to Florida repeatedly, his daughters lived much of their lives as Americans, and in 1983 Allen and his wife finally settled around San Diego where the writer spent his final years.[67] The "Perfect Place to Live" for U.S.-loving, ultra-typical Canadian Robert Thomas Allen was evidently many places, and he came to recognize "the only way to get the best out of anything is to make the best of the good things you've got" wherever you are.

This left me thinking that my California cousin, whose lifestyle cut short his years, might still be around if he had looked at the world like Robert Thomas Allen did.

Writing Exercise

Write a short story about a family that leaves the heat of Arizona for the cooler climate of Fort Vermilion, Alberta.

---

67 Allen, who died in 1990, felt comfortable living in many different places, but he was very proud of Toronto where he was born in 1911. He celebrated his native city in books, like *When Toronto Was for Kids* (McClelland and Stewart, 1961), which were tagged by reviewers as unique descriptions of both Toronto and a Canadian childhood in the 1920s. Allen wrote fourteen books in all. Two won the Stephen Leacock Medal. He was also one of the first winners of the Ruth Schwartz Children's Book Award for *The Violin* (1977).

1958

GIRDLE ME A GLOBE

BY ERIC NICOL

Lesson 12

Why the best story is not always the dramatic one

Eric Nicol must have regarded 1958 as a good year. By then, he had established himself as a regular newspaper columnist, he had the means to travel for a year at a time, and his book, *Girdle Me a Globe,* brought him his third Leacock Medal.[68]

Nicol had even more reasons to be happy. But anyone who skimmed his new book or read sections out of context might have thought he was a hopeless grumbler.

In the book, Nicol's report on a year-long, round-the-world trip, he complains a lot, details the aggravation of packing clothes, and fusses over dinner jackets and satin pants. Nicol describes foreign laundries in epic terms, shudders over the ordeal of standing on marble floors,

---

[68] Nicol remained the only triple Leacock Medal winner until 1980 when Donald Jack matched his record.

and talks of the multi-gauge Australian railway with terror.

He was joking, as usual, and cloaked those every day events in drama to poke at people who see the foreign world as alluring, yet unjustifiably inconvenient. He suggests that their ideal would be an old inn where "the food is dreadful and the beds have lumps" as the "solid foundation of real suffering" for future travel war stories.

Drama around the mundane can often make a story more readable than drama around drama. Other writers achieve similar effect by presenting dramatic events in matter-of-fact, low-key ways.[69]

Through this, Nicol's book also jabs at travel writing and swaggering travel writers who use their trade for personal puffery. He rebuffs the practice by filling his own book with minor experiences and suggests we adopt "a certain manner, a superiority that has no need to assert itself, like that of the veteran of many battles" rather than bragging about foreign adventures. If you only want to impress people, Nicol says it should be enough to assume a mysterious "far-away look" when any dark corner of the world is mentioned in social settings.

Even with these bits, the book could seem, on the surface, to be just a catalogue of funny fussiness or at best a collection of witty essays. Yet the stories in sum create satire in the Swift tradition. Because Nicol avoided personal attacks and meanness in his writing, few readers and reviewers regarded him as a satirist. But as a journalist who attracted a contempt of court citation for his views on capital punishment, he had a point of view on many issues and often slipped it into your brain while you were laughing. Labelling *Girdle Me*

69 2012 Leacock Medal winner *The Sisters Brothers* by Patrick deWitt is a good example.

a Globe as a compilation of light stories about laundry, trains, and foreign food would miss the point and would be a bit like branding *Gulliver's Travels* as a children's book about horses and giants.

Instead of trying to amaze us with cocktail-party place dropping, Eric Nicol wanted to share international travel by showing it as something all can appreciate and understand. To this end, he typically dwells on the everyday problems with which many Canadians can identify while only briefly mentioning his time in countries like Ceylon and Syria and cities like Baghdad and Karachi. He talks about bathrooms and showers, eating and sleeping, and other necessities common everywhere, shows that many inconveniences can be wiped away with a laugh, and reminds me that a travel experience often depends more on your sense of humour and what is in your mind than your surroundings.

Eric Nicol makes you smile because he is smiling a lot himself, and, again, he had reason to do so in 1958. His trip around the world and his book brought him back to the kind of life and theme he celebrated in his first Leacock Medal winner, *The Roving I*: the experience of a Canadian abroad. He says in that earlier book that he "would like to thank (his) wife for her unfailing help and encouragement during the preparation of this book," adding "but, I'm not married."

Eight years later with *Girdle Me a Globe*, Nicol describes a world tour that was also his honeymoon and dedicates the story to his new wife, "who held my hand all the way."[70] It was a good year for him, and his book made me think of my own good ones, travelling with the one who holds my hand, keeps travel drama in check, and makes me laugh.

Writing Exercise

Tell, in dramatic terms, about getting a bad haircut in a foreign country.

70 Nicol's first wife was Myrl Heselton. He had three children. He remarried in 1986. His second wife was writer Mary Razzell.

PART IV

THE 1960'S

NOSTALGIAS AND NASTINESS

I think that I should've received the 1959 Leacock Medal for Humour - even though I was only six years old at the time. The Leacock Associates didn't make an award that year,[71] reportedly because of a lack of qualifying entries, [72] and many people close to me believe that I was responsible for the best work of printed Canadian humour in the year previous - my kindergarten report card. Unfortunately, no one thought to enter it.

Although the report rated me as acceptable in "Punctuality" and "Personal Cleanliness," it ran out a long column of F's for areas like "Co-operates with his teacher" and "Muscular Co-ordination." My teacher, the prescient Miss Joblin, added: "Richard's lack in co-operation is due mainly to lack in attention. His little mind seems completely occupied with his own ideas." My parents may not have considered these elements humorous, but they and many others found great amusement in my direct contribution.

This came when the then five-year-old me added a careful,

---

[71] The Leacock Medal website merely states - 1959 *** No Award Made *** - some reports suggest that a change in judging procedures prevented an award decision that year; others say simply that 1959 was not a humorous year in Canada.

[72] The Associates could have honoured Robertson Davies for *A Mixture of Frailties*, the follow-up to *Leaven of Malice*, or *Maclean's* Editor Ralph Allen's *Peace River Country*, both published in 1958, but they were evidently not submitted for consideration.

cursive forgery on the line for "Parent's signature."

"Who did you think you were going to fool?" my parents asked that day and others as the story of the counterfeiter kid was told and retold. Four decades later, the local paper cited the forming incident in an article about me.[73]

I think this story attests not only to the personal nature of funny, but also to the varied forms that written Canadian humour can take. A few critics toss all of the Leacock Medal books, all Canadian humour, and even all Canadians into a single, dull, hoser, "combine-harvester"[74] bin that does not have much of a sense of humour and does not produce much that is funny.

Even those who feel Canadians lack sophistication can have opinions, of course, and can rightfully say whether they personally find something funny or not. But I really believe they sit on cracking ice when they suggest that Canadian humour is homogeneous or even homogenized. The subset represented by the Leacock Medal books contains its fair share of those parochial pleasantries. But the books, as a collection, also satirize and parody with an urbane appreciation for social context.

Consistent with the adapting-to-change definition of evolution, the Leacock Medal winners fluctuate. This may be most evident in the 1960s when books like W.O. Mitchell's *Jake and the Kid* and Harry J. Boyle's *Homebrew and Patches* actually do talk of combines and harvests in homespun nostalgias while other books take hard shots at war and mock modern society with biting wit and a degree of nastiness. The book that won the first medal of the 1960s, in fact, uses different formats in a blend of comedy and pathos. It's kinda like that report card.

---

73 *Port Perry Star,* "Area Native wins national award," March 27, 2000.

74 For a good example, see John Allemang, review of *The Penguin Anthology of Canadian Humour*, ed. Will Ferguson, *Globe and Mail,* March 15, 2006.

1960

JUST ADD WATER AND STIR

BY PIERRE BERTON

Lesson 13

Why someone would abandon humour writing

Like that of many Canadians, my last memory of Pierre Berton[75] comes from his appearance on the CBC's Rick Mercer Report in 2004. Eighty-four years old at the time and fated to die later that year, Berton took part in the TV program to demonstrate how to roll a joint.

The image made people laugh because most Canadians knew Berton as a literary icon and as part of a generation not tied to notorious marijuana use. I'm grateful for the scene because it will remind me forever of just how funny Pierre Berton could be.

Despite all the achievements that marked Berton's life, the television vignette purposely celebrated his funny side and stressed it by highlighting Berton's Leacock Medal for Humour. However, setting aside the joint-rolling lesson, he had, arguably, reached his peak as a humorist in *Just Add Water and Stir*, the book that earned

[75] Pierre Francis de Marigny Berton was born on July 12, 1920 in Whitehorse, Yukon. A comprehensive resource on Berton is the 2008 biography by historian A.B. McKillop, (*Pierre Berton: A Biography*).

him that 1960 Leacock Medal.[76]

Berton devoted his subsequent writing to history and other serious subjects, where he achieved most of his literary success. In 1960, his career was taking him away from magazines and newspapers into television and radio. This gave him different opportunities to indulge his personality and to poke at politics and culture, and he decided to direct his writing to ambitions that required research and respect.

As someone who aspired to make Canada's history accessible, Berton had a challenge. He needed to link the fact-laden, pursed-lipped world of academia to the language and the imagery that make books interesting. Perhaps, he didn't want to risk eroding his reputation with the brand of humorist, which some writers think marks you for a spot at the children's table and the basement of the CanLit outhouse.

Too bad. I think *Just Add Water and Stir* pulls it off, fluctuating between humour and the deadly serious in a way that makes a coherent sounding whole. It leaves you smiling, but it also includes pieces that are grim. Berton struggled to describe the book calling it "a random collection of satirical essays, rude remarks, used anecdotes, thumbnail sketches, ancient wheezes, old nostalgias, wry comments, limp doggerel, intemperate recipes, vagrant opinions, and crude drawings ..." (they were crude – I may be Berton's peer as an illustrator).

Although officially an editor and journalist, Berton admired parody and satire and imbeds his editorial comments on education in episodes entitled "Fun with Dick and Jane" and "Little Red Riding Hood." His observations on the changing Canadian society include

---

[76] Although Berton had started to dabble in other media by that time, he was still known primarily as a newspaper columnist, and the book draws heavily from his pieces in the *Toronto Star*. He rarely drifted into humour writing again. One exception came, however, not long after he won the Leacock Medal. This was *The Secret World of Og*, which he wrote for his own children.

essays on the size-of-your-office corporate culture and his "Modest Proposal for a Divorce Ceremony."[77] In critiques of popular periodicals, he attacks *Time, Vogue,* and *Mayfair*, but lauds *Mad Magazine.*[78]

The outrage in Berton's humorous pieces is recognizable because it echoes the opinions in the accompanying somber pieces on social reform, racial profiling, capital punishment, wiretapping, and torture in Canadian prisons. He also rants about commercialization, politics, and mass media. But, surprisingly at first reading, his harshest words fall on food recipes, the issue behind the title of the book.

Berton calls "just add water and stir" the "most hideous phrase to enter the language," (adding that) "the greatest and most monstrous villainy foisted on the consuming public has been instant coffee." In the middle of the book, via a pink paper insert, he tries to counter the 1950s version of fast food with his own semi-serious recipes. They're different. Rather than setting out an ordered combination of ingredients and steps for preparation, they tell stories of making a soup, some baked beans, and a plate of corned beef hash.

Anticipation and the joy of food fill these recipe-yarns.

The phrase "just add water and stir" makes an ideal title for this

---

77 More Swiftian humour complete with a "Worst Man" and the father taking back the Bride.

78 In *Just Add Water and Stir*, Berton also lampoons 1950s society in "modern fables" that mock commercial enterprise ("The Great Detergent Premium Race," "Goliath Tobacco's Big Comeback," and "The Legend of (a Las Vegas-like) Healing Mountain," and in verse like "A Toast to (the) Woodbine (Racetrack in Toronto)" and "The Sixty-Five Days of Christmas" as well as parodies of 1950s television shows like *Perry Mason* and *Gunsmoke.*

book because it evokes a bouillabaisse blend of different kinds of spices with meaty chunks, but it also speaks directly to Berton's overriding message and the notion that pulls the mix together: that people should care about things.

"We live in a dehydrated age and we are in mortal danger of having our souls dehydrated as well," he says explaining that "in the kitchen ... we will cheerfully eat sawdust, as long as it can be poured straight from the package to the plate."

For him, instant coffee reflects a society increasingly coloured by "not caring" - in this case, not caring about the effort taken to cultivate the coffee beans and not caring enough to honour your guests with a decent beverage. We would classify the recipes and food rants as humour, but many words - about people not caring - could have been easily injected into his pieces on legalized torture and capital punishment.

The book closes with some of those "old nostalgias," around his father, his childhood during the Depression, and his early days in journalism.[79] Berton was still in his thirties when this book was produced, and I am not sure he really had the credentials for quality nostalgia, but his words stimulated my own. I miss the funny Pierre Berton, Ben Wicks, Barbara Frum, W.O. Mitchell, Peter Gzowski, Eric Nicol, Mordecai Richler, Gary Lautens, Bob Johnstone, Max Ferguson, and all the others who, through a mix of humour and caring, gave meaning to the word "Canadian" for most of my life.

Berton's book amplifies this impulse for nostalgia with profiles of Glenn Gould, Charles Templeton, Russ Baker, and others. But *Just Add Water* also admonishes people like me who become wistful over a past that doesn't seem to exist any longer. Berton says it "still exists ... as (it) always did...You (just) do not see it any more, my friend." Perhaps this jab is a better reason to be grateful for my last, joint-rolling memory of Berton. It ties the history of Canadian humour to

---

[79] In this book, he also celebrated the UBC student paper (*The Ubyssey* - a training ground for a number of Leacock Medalists like Eric Nicol, Earle Birney, and Mark Leiren-Young) and his work at the defunct *Vancouver News-Herald*.

Mercer and his generation of extant Canadian personalities who care, help define our country today, and persist in doing it proudly branded as humorists.

Writing Exercise

Write a funny short story that shows the inanity of capital punishment.

1961

MICE IN THE BEER

BY NORMAN WARD

Lesson 14

The power of simple sentences and plain talk

If my Mariposa-Mayor[80] mentor had one wish for me, it would be a better appreciation of short sentences, active verbs, and simple prose. He would give me boot in the butt for the pretentious alliteration that starts this paragraph.

I still struggle to recognize that simple is not merely clearer, but also livelier and blame my failings on being a bureaucrat and scholar want to-be, over-exposed to same influences that plagued the 1961 Leacock Medal winner, Professor Norman Ward.

Historian Jack Granatstein once said that Ward's writing was "as dry as the Prairie soil of the dust bowl years" and that his prose "sits on the page like so many cow flaps in a farmer's field."[81] He was,

[80] The Mayor of Mariposa is an honorary title, currently held by Dan Needles. Past mayors include Harry J. Boyle and other Leacock medalists as well as distinguished and entertaining supporters of the Leacock Associates.

[81] In 1969 Ward was designated the official biographer of James G. Gardiner, a former premier of Saskatchewan. Granatstein made these "cow flap" comments in a newspaper review of the Gardiner biography.

however, directing those comments at the wordiness of Ward's scholarly work, not at his humour writing.

Ward spent over four decades as a professor at the University of Saskatchewan[82] where he sharpened his opinions but evidently felt restrained.[83] The serious political scientist[84] saw humour writing as a sand box - a place to play, to be creative, and to express thoughts without worrying about the facts or the professional implications. Ward, whose book *Mice in the Beer* won the medal in 1961, could make reviewers laugh until they cried[85] with his humourous work and his mastery of what was labelled the "Gentle Art of Satire."[86] His writing seems mild on the surface, but it hides prickliness below the veneer.

Early in *Mice in the Beer,* he covers himself by stating for the record that this book is "fiction, in the sense that the events and conversations chronicled here did not happen as recorded." Maybe Ward felt it was necessary to make that clear because much of his

---

82 Norman Ward not only spent most of his career at the University of Saskatchewan, he spent most of his life there. He died on February 4, 1990 at the age of seventy-one. He had retired in 1985 after forty years at UofS. His funeral was held in the university's Convocation Hall.

83 Ward was a busy humour writer during the 1960s and 1970s, writing articles as well as *Mice* and two follow-up books, *The Fully Processed Cheese,* published in 1964, and *Her Majesty's Mice* in 1977. But his greatest national recognitions, including election to the Royal Society of Canada, came for his work as a political science and economics researcher. Ward's Order of Canada citation, in fact, only cites his services as an economist and political scientist, not as a creative writer.

84 One of Norman Ward's books, the fourth edition of *The Government of Canada* (University of Toronto Press) was the first Canadian book to be translated into and published in Punjabi.

85 "Laughed until I cried" is how the *Globe and Mail* reviewer Joan Walker described the book.

86 The Gentle Art of Satire is an expression you don't hear too often. Google produced just 204 immediate web references for the phrase. We usually describe "satire" as "biting" or "bitter," and the Net coughs up over a million hits for those expressions.

book mocks the university world. In his opening piece, "A Meeting of Minds," Ward explains to a passing workman that musing over an academic article with eyes closed, sitting under a tree is considered work for a university professor.

"When I write articles, my wife calls it loafing," says the man.

But he commends Ward as well: "For a fellow who never does anything but read books ... you seem to know a lot."

Gentle, but making a point. This style of humour flows out of the low-key prairie voice[87] that Ward says adorns "conversation with homely asides and earthy aphorisms," is expressed in simple declarative sentences, and enlivened only by references to farm concerns like "bloat, heaves, and various other murrains that disturb our animal friends from time to time."

The prairie perspective is not easily impressed and looks at "the banking belts of Toronto and Montreal" and my own town of Ottawa with skepticism. Ward proposes, for example, that the winners of federal elections should stay home in Saskatchewan because the "losers, being demonstrably less smart than their victorious opponents, could probably be allowed to take their places in Ottawa without damage to the public weal." Ward says the national capital is overrun by Ottawa terriers, a reference not to a "special breed of dog, but a cynical frame of mind" linked to alcohol.

"Half the business and political history of this country could be told in terms of its alcoholic content," says a politician in the book.

---

[87] Norman Ward, known as a voice of the Prairies and solidly associated with Saskatchewan throughout his career, was, in fact, born and raised in Hamilton, Ontario, where he attended university before earning his doctoral degree at the University of Toronto. The only institutions to recognize him with honourary degrees were the Ontario universities McMaster (1974) and Queens (1977).

With this, I squirmed and assumed Ward would suggest that the "mice" here in Ottawa were the culprits drinking up the nation's beer. But again, he avoids naming a specific target when telling the story behind the book's title.

A bottle-collector explains that mice crawl into empties, "attracted by the malty smell." They lick up the drops, spin around, and expire. Ward loves the intoxicated mouse story because anything that can discredit animals "should be widely publicized, so as to make man seem a little better by comparison."

He thinks humans need all the help they can get - not only politicians, Ottawa bureaucrats, and eastern bankers, but also bird watchers and teachers, pig farmers and cowboys, students and cemetery salesmen, and, persistently, academics and people like Ward himself.

By the end, you realize that we are all like the "mice in the beer." Canadians - we scurry around, lap up a few drops of delight, act silly, and die.

Not a particularly cheery thought, but if we can find enough drops in life, we can, like the mouse in the bottle, leave this world with a "face ... wreathed in smiles (with) ... ears ... at a rakish angle (and) ... happy." Norman Ward, the sober academic, evidently found his droplets in simple language, plain talk, and the art of writing gentle satire.

So, I will think of him and drunken mice the next time I try to edit my own writing.

Writing Exercise

In plain language and simple declarative sentences, write a paragraph describing a university professor's research on ways to insert dead mice into beer bottles.

1962

JAKE AND THE KID

BY W.O. MITCHELL

Lesson 15

Why we like idealized images

The shiny shoes, pressed pants, and neatness pictured on my copy of W.O. Mitchell's[88] *Jake and the Kid* would amuse anyone who has ever lived on a farm. The Rockwell-like artwork features a spotless barn interior that looks out into bright daylight where a young boy sits on a horse. An older man in clean shoes and straight coveralls holds a strap coming from the bridle.

At times, reading *Jake and the Kid* feels like a stroll through a Norman Rockwell painting. It's a saving-kittens-at-Christmas version of the Canadian Prairies that makes you nod and smile. This is not a bad experience, but the book's real value comes in its relevance to the real world where you

---

88 William Ormond (W.O.) Mitchell (1914–98) influenced a generation of authors as a teacher: he was a writer in residence at Trent University, the University of Calgary, the University of Alberta, the University of Toronto's Massey College, the University of Windsor, and the Banff Centre. He also studied at the U of A and the University of Manitoba and mentored others outside of formal settings, encouraging many in his time as literary editor for *Maclean's* magazine. Mitchell has been credited with "discovering" writers like Ray Bradbury and fellow Leacock Medal winners Farley Mowat and Ernest Buckler. David O'Rourke, *Essays on Canadian Writing* 20 (Winter 1980): 149–59.

have to watch your step and what you step into.

The book, which won the Leacock Medal in 1962,[89] features the relationship between Jake, the hired hand, and "The Kid," an unnamed boy who tells the story and who helps his mother farm while his father is overseas during World War II. The Kid's life revolves around the farm, school, and the mythical town of Crocus, Saskatchewan.[90]

Starving to make sense of the world, the boy soaks up Jake's every word with wide-eyes and the certainty that his hero "always knows what he is talking about."

Too old for World War II, Jake often talks about days at Vimy Ridge in the Great War and his battles with Boers before that. In fact, the farm hand never passes over a chance to reference anything he can relate to the Kid's problems. Jake's recollections of "Looie" Riel and "Wilf" Laurier seem dubious and conflict with historical facts. But he seems to believe this stuff himself and always has a goal beyond self-aggrandizement. In everything he says, he's just trying to assure the Kid and make life a little easier.

Jake explains to the Kid that the difference between women and other humans is their preoccupation with having things "just so," and it rings true. Miss Henchbaw, the teacher, is always insisting on

---

89 W.O. Mitchell was not an unqualified admirer of Stephen Leacock, once calling him "a little slapstick." Mitchell said Virginia Woolf was his greatest influence.

90 Mitchell started writing Jake stories in the early 1940s and then polished them into a popular CBC radio series in the 1950s.

decimal points being in just the right place, and the Kid's Ma takes great care every Sunday to saliva down each and every hair on her son's head before church.

The stories are comforting and easy to absorb.[91] Jake's explanations are simultaneously innocent and shrewd, nonsensical and common-sense, and we smile because it all has an undertone of caring and a desire to lessen the hardship. Jake is not alone. Crocus has other yarn spinners who have all seen "the deepest snow, the worst dust storms, the biggest hailstones ... Rust and dust and hail and sawfly and cutworm and drought." "Terrible things," but Jake and his cohorts make their fears seem silly with tall tales.

Half-way through the book, in "The Liar Hunter" episode, one character explains, "These men lie about the things that hurt them most ... If a man can laugh at them he's won half the battle ... When he exaggerates things he isn't lying really; it's a defense, ... He can either do that or squeal."

In the same way, it doesn't matter much that W.O. Mitchell's paradise in the prairie never really existed. Like the Rockwell-ish painting on my book, the thought of someone like Jake watching over you makes a good reference when wrestling with reality in any era.

The popularity of *Jake and the Kid* in books, radio, and TV over many decades suggests lots of Canadians are like me: inclined to the idea of a boy trying to make sense of the world and a regular guy trying to make life a little softer with his stories.[92]

---

[91] Mitchell was, during his time, the recognized author of the bestselling book in Canada, *Who Has Seen the Wind.* Its sales were approaching the million mark before his passing. It had displaced *Maria Chapdelaine*, a novel set in French Canada around the time of Mitchell's birth.

[92] Mitchell's son Ormond and Ormond's wife Barbara are both literary scholars. They produced a well-reviewed and uniquely intimate biography of W.O. in two volumes: *The Life of W.O. Mitchell, Beginnings to Who has seen the Wind, 1914 to 1947*, and *The Life of W.O. Mitchell, The years of Fame, 1948-1998.*

Writing Exercise

Identify the thought that frightens you most. Then describe it in exaggerated, silly terms.

1963

THREE CHEERS FOR ME

BY DONALD JACK

Lesson 16

When it's time to see the humour

As a World War II ambulance driver at Camp Borden, my mother attended an average of six to eight fatal air crashes per month. She learned what a body looks like after it passes through a propeller and what it smells like while still smoldering.[93] Dramatic stuff. But whenever asked about her role in the War, she talked about her time as chauffeur to a famous pilot.

"I drove Billy Bishop to drink" was her one-line response.[94]

By the time Donald Jack wrote his war story, *Three Cheers for Me,*

---

[93] You could stop a thousand people on any street in this country today and not find one person who was aware that over 2,000 military men died on Canadian soil during World War II. These were the pilots, crew, and others killed in air crashes and ground accidents around training bases. (These events are described in "The Great Canadian Air Battle", Dr. Jean Martin, Canadian Military Journal, Spring 2002).

[94] Bishop, a flying ace in WWI, was a senior air force officer who promoted recruitment during WWII.

the 1963 Leacock Medal winner, other concerns were starting to displace the pain of World War II, and veterans like Mom were more and more prone to focus on funny memories.

The British-born Jack had served in the Royal Air Force, moved to Canada, and established himself in a less demanding situation as a playwright and author.[95] He too could laugh about war more often, but, as a writer, he also knew that a good story is more than a one-line joke like my mom's; so *Three Cheers for Me* surrounds the humour with description and drama, never shying away from the trenches, muddy battles, and hairy dog fights.

Yet it is very funny.

The Bandy books, three of which would win the Leacock Medal, are first-person accounts of the life of Bartholomew Wolfe Bandy, a sometimes smart, but luckless, Canadian medical school dropout who heads to the frontlines in 1916 and later fights from the cockpit of a Sopwith Camel. The realism of the stories convinced some early readers and reviewers that they were nonfiction memoirs.

I found myself laughing at the battle scenes not because of what happens in them, but because of Donald Jack's set up beforehand. When Bandy was preparing to leave for Europe, his father, a self-righteous minister in the Ottawa Valley still shaken by the fifty-year-old *Origin of Species,* described the Great War as a battle "not just against the barbaric legions of the heathen Hun, but against all revolutionaries, theorists, anarchists, and Charles Darwin !" He and others saw the greatest dangers in the temptations of alcohol and scoffed at bleak stories of battle wounds and trench foot.

---

[95] Jack was not yet a Canadian citizen when he wrote this book. He only came to Canada in 1951 and worked on survey crews in Alberta and as a bank teller in Toronto before turning to theatre and writing, which led to a job with Academy Award-winning Crawley Films in Ottawa. Two years later Crawley fired him. In 1957 Donald Jack's *Breakthrough* was the first Canadian TV play to be simultaneously telecast to the United States. His third play, *The Canvas Barricade*, produced in 1961, was the first original Canadian play performed on the main stage of the Stratford Festival.

"Plain carelessness," one church elder tells Bandy. "No excuse at all. It may be a little damp at the front, but to let your feet get that way is inexcusable ... (I hear) the generals are thinking of punishing anyone who so abuses his extremities."

As he watches the passing bodies, sits in the mud, and listens to the shells fall, Bandy reads letters from his mother who hopes that he's keeping up his piano lessons while abroad, adding that her son must be having "an interesting time over there, seeing Westminster Abbey and the Tower of London." The correspondence from Canada crescendos when Bandy starts receiving letters of condolence ("My Dear Bartholomew ... we sympathize with you in your misfortune ... despite everything we are still your friends") with no explanation. Eventually, an aunt tells Bandy that his father had been caught in an indiscretion in the cornfield.

Another force that keeps the book light is the love story based on narrowed eyes. Bandy falls for the young English woman Katherine Lewis, whose face was characterized by a squint. At first, Bandy says simply that "she had a slight squint" and later a squint to be "self-conscious about." Then, he notices that "Her squint ... suits her" and eventually confesses that "That faint squint of hers affected me strongly." Bandy later thinks there is "something almost erotic about (her squint)."[96]

Jack manages the mix of humour and horror pretty well, but it probably wasn't easy. Even though *Three Cheers for Me* ends with a cliff-hanger inference of more to come[97] and even though Jack would

---

[96] Jack's relationship with his own wife likely affected his stories. In 1986, when she fell ill, Jack returned to his native England with her. He stopped writing for many years after her death in 1991. But when Jack, born on December 6, 1924, died in 2003, he had started to write again, working on another volume of *The Bandy Papers*. Obituaries of Donald Jack (*National Post* and *Globe and Mail* June 2003).

[97] The book ended suggesting that the future was to bring an "awful new significance ... to the expression *War is Hell*."

eventually write many more Bandy books,[98] a second one did not appear for over a decade.

Despite those 1960's inclinations to think of chauffeuring celebrities instead of corpses, it still took a bit of work to find humour in war.

Writing Exercise

Recount a conversation between two wartime cabinet ministers talking about the importance of table manners and dry cleaning services on the frontlines

98 Jack wrote with military discipline, saying his dedication came from "reminding myself of how lucky I am to be able to be the only thing I ever really wanted to be — a writer." Jack wrote forty TV plays, several radio plays, four stage plays, and thirty-five film scripts. Leacock medals came for three of the nine volumes of *The Bandy Papers*: *Three Cheers for Me* in 1963, *That's Me in the Middle* in 1974, and *Me Bandy, You Cissie* in 1980. One of his two nonfiction books, *Rogues, Rebels and Geniuses*, was about the history of medicine. The other, *Sinc, Betty and the Morning Man*, was the history of the Toronto radio station CFRB.

1964

HOMEBREW AND PATCHES

BY HARRY J. BOYLE

Lesson 17

How to laugh in hard economic times

The smell of manure never faded, chores filled their days, and, except for an orange "all the way from Florida" one Christmas, few luxuries visited their home. Yet my maternal grandparents and their seven kids managed to pass through the Great Depression with their sense of humour intact. They even laughed about those years and felt privileged to have spent them on that central Ontario farm.

At a parallel place, over two hundred miles to the west near Goderich, Harry J. Boyle[99] was absorbing the stories and meeting the characters that he would, decades later, package in the 1964 Leacock Medal winner *Homebrew and Patches.*[100] Having grown up with similar people around me, I was ready to accept Boyle's stories as true.

---

[99] Harry J. Boyle was born at the village of St. Augustine, near Goderich in 1915; he died in Toronto on 22 January 2005.

[100] His second Leacock Medal came in 1975 for a novel, *The Luck of the Irish.*

This might have been a little naive, but I am not alone. Others thought they were true too.

Harry Boyle would go on to author many other books, win many awards, and become one of Canada's top broadcasting personalities. But when *Homebrew and Patches* was published, he was still a relatively new writer and the dates and details of his own life were not widely known. His one previous book, *Mostly in Clover*, described the life of a young boy in 1920's rural Ontario. Its popularity demanded a sequel, and *Patches* met that need by following the same boy, regularly presumed to be the young Boyle himself, into adolescence and the Great Depression.

Boyle used the boy as a way of telling a bigger story. He wanted readers to know that the bleak image of the "Dirty Thirties" was only part of the experience. He said the time was a mix of good and bad, sad and amusing.

Many of his stories celebrated neighbourliness and efforts to "make do" by putting "patches on patches." But more often this book finds humour by focusing on features of life that unfold independently of the economic circumstance - the rites of passage for a teenager with one foot on his path to the future and one on the family farm. The book tells of experimentation with shaving, tobacco, alcohol-laced medications, school dances, and the opposite sex. Most farm boys learned "a little by observation, gleaned some more information from older boys who were probably as ignorant as ourselves and listened carefully to the talk of the threshing gang." Boyle adds, however, that all of this was at least better than a dreaded "man-to-man" talk with your dad.

When a local teen pregnancy and hurried marriage forces the issue, the narrator's father sits down next to his son and says "Been meaning to have a talk with you ...urr ... Anything you want to—is there—well—I mean—do you have anything on your mind? ...(you will be) going to town next year and you'll be- be — Meeting girls ... there's a few things ya got to remember ... (silence) ...That was too bad about Bert and Janey ... Those things happen and they don't do anybody any good ... course they got married ... Now you got to watch out for that sort of thing."

Then the older participant in the conversation stands up in relief and says, in words that could have fallen from any farm father's mouth, "Well, I'm going back to see if the cattle have enough salt. I'm might' glad we had this talk."

And the painful event is over for both son and father.

When *Homebrew and Patches* first appeared, reviewers praised Boyle's ability to recall conversations like that and to describe people and events from many years before in detail. This is why most readers assumed the stories to be true. But I think Boyle made a lot of it up. One reason, ironically, lies in the detail of the recollections. I'm sure, even under deep hypnosis, I couldn't recall the specifics of conversations of two weeks ago like Boyle did with respect to events three decades earlier.

Another reason for doubt is the timeframe itself. Although told in the first person with persistent references to "my mother," "my father," and "me" throughout, the book doesn't match the exact chronology of the author's own life. Boyle was born in 1915 and would have been well into his late teens by the time the fingers of the economic collapse reached into rural Southwestern Ontario. The real life Boyle, who got his first radio job at the age of sixteen, was off to college[101] and the working world not on the farm.[102]

---

[101] Boyle finished high school in 1931 and went to college in Waterloo. While still in his teens, he published his own magazine and worked as a newspaper stringer for papers that included the *London Free Press* and the *Toronto Globe and Mail.*

[102] His first assignment with the CBC, after joining it in 1942, was as a farm commentator. Later he was promoted to programme director of the Trans-Canada

He could make his stories detailed and authentic sounding not because he lived all of them, but because he focused on those things that never change, are as vivid as yesterday, and are humorous no matter when they take place.

Measured against Boyle's primary goals - disrupting our view of the Depression and making us smile - it matters little whether it was all fact or not. *Homebrew and Patches* is probably best considered a mix of bright reminiscences and a bit of fiction - like an orange all the way from Florida with just a whiff of manure.

Writing Exercise

Write the text message exchange between a 21st century farm father and his son talking about the facts of life for the first time.

Network and executive producer for television. In 1968, he joined the Canadian Radio-Television and Telecommunications Commission (CRTC) and was later appointed CRTC Chair.

1965

WAR STORIES

BY GREGORY CLARK

Lesson 18

How to keep sane in the insane

Gregory Clark's 1965 Leacock Medal book describes bloody, plodding conflict in the two world wars. Its title, *War Stories*, is not misleading. But collectively, these stories also describe a different battle: the one to stay sane amid the insane and to maintain a sense of humour.

I hope to never have the face-to-face familiarity with war that Gregory Clark had. But like all of humanity and its peculiar subset of aspiring writers, I have my own interest in Clark's experience and example.

Books about war often take one of two approaches: the soldier's close-up experience of death and ruin or the military strategist's sanitized view from afar.

But Clark, a decorated Vimy Ridge officer in the First World War and an embedded correspondent throughout the Second, speaks as a veteran soldier who also has the journalist's capacity to analyze and observe.[103] The combination of detachment and personal

103 Born in Toronto on September 25, 1892, Clark died in the city on February 3,

experience gave him the inclination to look at the absurdities of war with sensitivity.

The book draws its material from Clark's feature articles in *Weekend Magazine*.[104] In *War Stories*, the difficult subject matter and the magazine format were merged into a refined technique. Almost all are either heart-wrenching stories with a lighter twist at the end - or humorous episodes punctuated by a reminder of war.

Clark tells of a mob attack on a French woman who had been involved with a German soldier. Then the story jumps ahead to the day years later when "The German boy came back and married her." The sad tale of an old Italian woman transforms when she's revealed to be the protector of escaping Allied POW's.

In a lighter story, Clark describes a day spent fly fishing in southern England. He realizes that he is standing in streams celebrated by the iconic book *Where the Bright Waters Meet.* The day ends with a supper of fresh fish and talk of the book.

But that's not the end of this story. One last sentence adds a typical Clark twist: "The order presently came; and the young men piled into their lorries; and we went on down to the sea." It was 1944. The men were off to Normandy.

Gregory Clark was in his fifties during the Second World War, and he could have easily avoided the grimness that time around. He had done his part in 1916 at Sanctuary Wood. In that battle, his battalion dropped from 22 officers and 680 men to 3 officers and 78

1977. He worked for the *Toronto Star* from 1911 to 1947. His father was the editor-in-chief of the *Star*. His great-nephew is broadcaster Tom Clark.

104 For many years, Clark's columns featured art work by his fishing buddy, cartoonist Jimmie Frise. In 1947 Clark and Frise joined the *Montreal Standard* (it became *Weekend Magazine*) as a team, but Frise died the next year at the age of fifty-seven. Afterward, Clark's stories were illustrated by Duncan Macpherson.

men in just two days of fighting. Four months later, after reinforcements, the same battalion lost another thousand men at the Somme. But Clark returned to the battles a few decades later and worked the World War II frontlines only coming home after the death of James Murray Clark of the Regina Rifle Regiment in 1944.

Somehow Clark emerged from the wars, the loss of his son, and later personal tragedies with the ability to hold onto those thoughts of fly-fishing, to care for others, and to celebrate the softer side up to the end of his own life. Again, the answer may lie in the combined journalist-soldier capacity to stand back and observe even though you still relate and feel.

This may be, more than any technical writing tricks, the greatest lesson Greg Clark's *War Stories* offers to those of us who hope to write, persevere, and keep a sense of humour in the wake of our own inevitable heartbreaks and setbacks.[105]

Writing Exercise

As a first-wave soldier, realistically describe D-Day ending your story with a humorous twist.

105 For a thorough biography, check out - *The Life & Times of Greg Clark: Canada's Favorite Story Teller* by Jock Carroll (1981).

1966

NURSERY RHYMES TO BE READ ALOUD BY YOUNG PARENTS WITH OLD CHILDREN

BY GEORGE BAIN

Lesson 19

Mixing formats for more than a sum of the parts

If you ripped every second page out of George Bain's *Nursery Rhymes to be read aloud by young parents with old children,* you'd have a book that could sit on the shelf between Dr. Seuss and Winnie-the-Pooh. Every second page of the 1966 Leacock Medal winner speaks in a fun, three-to-eight-year-old-kid kind of way.

Yet whole and intact, Bain's book belongs on the hard to reach shelves alongside works of literature. Colourful illustrations and verse laid out in the abecedarium (A is for ape, B is for beaver) style for kids fill half the book. But each of these pages sits opposite one of prose, biological information, and facts about the animal.

Bain, a respected journalist,[106] proposed the two-pronged format

106 George Bain (1920 - 2006), was celebrated for using the F... word in print. In 1968 when Prime Minister Pierre Trudeau swore in the House of Commons, most media only reported that Trudeau used an obscenity or quoted him as saying the words "fuddle duddle." Bain set the record straight, using the four letters for the first time in a major Canadian publication (the *Globe and Mail*).

under the premise that young parents needed ammunition to beat back inquisitive children. Children who, upon hearing funny verses, react with "persistent whys, whens, and hows."

You can learn a lot - from the scientific names of fish to whether a zebra is white with black stripes or a marked black animal. On the letter-G animal, the Gnu, we learn of the "Brindled Gnu" and that there never was a "zoologist named Watt" and no sub-species "known as Watt's Gnu." Useful stuff when dealing with kids.

The two sides of the book feed off each other, making the whole more than the sum of a kid's book and a bunch of facts and a reminder of the power that lies in mixing formats. Like other Leacock Medal books, a mix elevates simple content with an incongruous context. But unlike the others, *Nursery Rhymes* wouldn't have succeeded with words alone. The drawings and ornate lettering made the parody work. The Leacock Medal awarders could have justly split the prize between the illustrator, Nova Scotian artist Colette MacNeil, and Bain. Nevertheless, Bain[107] deserves full credit for a concept that spoke to the times. His book reflects the backend of the baby boom when babies were becoming children, homes were being built, and family concerns were ascending. Many parents needed a laugh. I wish I'd had the book when my kids were little.

Although my copy is fragile and the dust jacket is tattered, I may lend it to some parents to see if the same mental gymnastics remain part of raising kids in the Internet age. In any case, I'm pretty sure that young parents can still use a laugh.

---

107 A political journalist, George Bain injected humour into his regular columns and wrote mock newspaper reports, like his pretend Letters from Lilac, Saskatchewan . Bain authored other humorous books. They included *I've Been Around and Around and Around*, *Letters from Lilac*, *Champagne is for Breakfast*, and *Gotcha.*

Writing Exercise

Write ten lines of verse for adult readers followed by prose that explains it to an eight-year-old.

1967

NEEDHAM'S INFERNO

BY RICHARD J. NEEDHAM

Lesson 20

Breaking all the rules

When I was a teenager, we all knew about the *Globe and Mail* columnist Richard J. Needham because he had caused a disturbance down the road at Whitby's Henry Street High School.[108] In early 1967, the year Needham won the Leacock Medal for Humour, he caught our attention not because of his award or his writing, but because of his address to the Henry Street "School Spirit Week" assembly. He told three hundred fresh faces that he was in favour of "freedom of drink, freedom of sex, voluntary education and the abolishment of all laws except those restraining murder and property damage."[109] Needham said that "Sex, liquor and gambling laws are not worth observing" adding that "The only way to change them is to refuse to obey them." The next day students staged a protest, and we read newspapers for the first time.[110]

In life and in his writing, Needham seems unrestrained by rules.

---

108 *Globe and Mail*, "Principal feels strike sparked by Needham," April 28, 1967, p. 51.

109 Walter T. Crandall, "Trends," *The Youth's Instructor*, September 1967, p. 5.

110 I attended high school in Port Perry, about 30 km away.

Whereas other humorists take a breather once in a while, Needham jumps from one sentence to the next without letting up. He could serve up one joke, one bit of nonsense, one sardonic shot after another after another after another for pages and pages as he did throughout most of his medal-winning book *Needham's Inferno.*

In a single paragraph, he lists a dozen methods used to deliver columns and irritate his editor: "carved on tree in High Park, engraved on the head of a pin, signalled with flags from a flotilla in the lake ... spelled out by a circus elephant ... rhythmic clanking .. through the radiators in Morse code ... 200-foot totem pole... (squirrels) each with a fortune cookie between its teeth ... in Sanskrit or maybe Australian." He peppers stories with gibberish and nonsense names like "Fifi Farenheit," "Claude Hopper," "Earnest Consideration," "Alice Aforethought," and his own alter ego, the booze-loving "Rudolph J. Needleberry."

In his *Globe and Mail* columns and this collection, he keeps readers on edge with an energetic and sometimes nasty silliness. For no reason beyond irreverence, he maligns his paper with epithets like "The Mop and Pail" and "The Goat and Snail," names that struck a chord and persist to today. In reference to his managing editor,[111] Needham throws out adjectives like "solitary, nasty, brutish, and short" adding that "when he pollutes the waters of Lake Simcoe with his presence, he is often mistaken for a snapping turtle."

Needham was not just flame-thrower ruthless, but sometimes crude and often lecherous. Many ruminations poke across the boundaries of what is politically correct. His columns, as captured in *Inferno*, were a reflection of those other times. They echo the *Mad Men* sexism and deride the presumed female obsession with finding a "first-class man." Needham describes the desperations of a woman who lowered her standards by telling us with sarcasm that she even "went out with men who wore hats, men who wore rimless spectacles, and ... who wore sharply pointed shoes with paper-thin soles ... who read Zane Grey ... who carefully studied and added up the restaurant bill ... who took her to Fort York (and) the Royal

---

[111] A future Senator (Richard J. Doyle)

Ontario Museum ... who sucked Clorets just before they kissed ... who put their correct names and addresses on LCBO purchase slips" and other flawed beings.

Needham was not using humour in frustration as a struggling single person. With a long marriage, grown children, and grandchildren, he was looking at the sixties singles scene with the same detached amusement he applied to politics, business, and even his own profession. In a Faustian tale, he makes a pact with the devil and then reveals that "Daily newspaper columnists don't have any souls." He makes you feel sorry for poor naive Satan.

If *Needham's Inferno* ended around the hundred-page mark, it could be filed away as a string of comical, but random thoughts and quotable, but disconnected comments. But the book shifts into essays that hint at libertarian themes, comment on issues like education, wax on morality and ethics, and satirize government rules. He predicts an institution to fight obesity called the Food Control Board of Ontario.

Needham was from the generation of newspaper reporters who entered the field with little formal education and came up in an apprenticeship. For many, reading was limited to the materials of their trade. But Needham seems comfortable referencing Dante, Plato, Cervantes, Melville, Faulkner, Balzac, Flaubert, Goethe, and particularly Albert Camus as well as characters and concepts from opera and theatre. There is a depth to his madness that's easier to feel than to explain. It stings, cries political reform, and philosophizes. And it's silly. It pushes the definition of Canadian humour well beyond kindly contemplation.

It would be hard to officially place Richard J. Needham on a platform above Leacock medalists like W.O. Mitchell, Mordecai Richler, and Robertson Davies or to hold him up as exemplary of Canadian sensibilities. But when I'm all alone and thinking of nothing in particular, it's Needham, Needhamisms and "School Spirit Week" at Henry Street High School that pop into my mind most often, cause my head to shake, and make me laugh.

Writing Exercise

List twelve ways you could deliver an assignment to your creative writing professor without using the mail, the Internet, or recording devices.

1968

"AND NOW … HERE'S MAX"

BY MAX FERGUSON

Lesson 21

How to stay creative within a bureaucracy

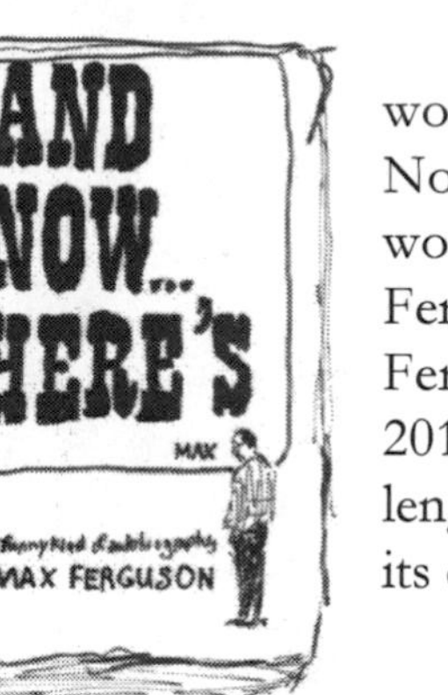

CBC Radio fired me after just one day of work. It was Friday September 18, 1981.[112] Not a good day. But at least I can say I worked at CBC at the same time as Max Ferguson, and I can appreciate why, when Ferguson passed away at eighty-nine in March 2013, he was eulogized as much for the length of his half century radio career as for its content.

It's not easy to keep up the creativity for that long, particularly amid all the constraint and bureaucracy of an institution like the CBC. Part of the answer for Ferguson was, ironically, to get fired. He shared the story of his firing, re-hiring under contract, and resulting pay increase along with other anecdotes in his 1968 Leacock Medal memoir *"And Now ... Here's Max,"*[113] a book written at about the half way mark in his long career and life.

---

112 By union rules, the corporation had to pay me a salary when trying me out as a researcher for the CBC Vancouver noon hour show. I know the date because of clippings on the labour news story I screwed up.

113 The title of the book was the standard introduction to his radio shows as delivered by the then well-known CBC announcer Allan McFee.

Ferguson called it "a funny kind of autobiography," and it's a bit different. He shares very little of his personal life in it. But because of his popularity, CBC fans were willing to shell out for his radio war stories alone. In each, Ferguson describes characters, practical jokes, and mishap induced by administration. His friendly style makes the stories easy to read. Some are pretty funny. Others are not so effective because cited personalities are no longer known and the premise of CBC domination of electronic media is dated.

The book starts in 1946 with Ferguson's first radio job (at the private station CFPL in his hometown of London, Ontario). He earns $25 per week, $5 over the norm in recognition of his unusual qualification of a university education. CBC recruits him for its Halifax, Nova Scotia operations in December of that year. In Halifax, he falls into the role of performer rather than announcer when the station management directs him to host a "cowboy" music show called *After Breakfast Breakdown.*

In a story now well known as Canadian broadcasting lore, Ferguson tells us that he doesn't like the music, is embarrassed, and decides to cloak himself on air in the persona of "Old Rawhide," an elderly cowboy who ridiculed the music he was playing. To Ferguson's surprise, the character becomes a hit. At one point, some nine thousand listeners in Atlantic Canada write in requesting photos of Old Rawhide. Ferguson amuses himself by adding other characters to the show, which eventually moves to the CBC flagship operations in Toronto where it accesses a national audience.

Through the late 1940s and early 1950s, Ferguson, as Rawhide, anchors one of CBC Radio's most popular programs. Yet, as his book reveals, he was not paid a cent for his Rawhide work during those glory days. Formally, Ferguson was a regular CBC staff announcer paid only for routine on-air duties. In a circumstance many in government bureaucracies would recognize, CBC management says his job classification does not allow for a raise or any incremental pay for his optional work on what was one of the network's most popular programs. Ferguson decides to test the "optional" nature of the arrangement by staying home.

With Ferguson's termination in the works, a CBC executive[114] suggests that he leave, become a private sector producer, and provide the Rawhide show to the network as a contractor and non-CBC employee. Ferguson takes the advice - and immediately receives a fee that is four times his former CBC-employee salary. The best part of the deal for Ferguson is the freedom to mock his meal ticket and to move his family back to Nova Scotia.[115] By the end of the book, Ferguson's stature as a performer reaches the point where he can drop the Rawhide character altogether and pursue a more flexible style in *The Max Ferguson Show.* In the following years, Ferguson produces daily skits, parodies of literary classics, and satires of current events. He uses his show to promote alternative music, folk music, and what is now known as world music. Very few cowboys.

He is creative and often off the wall. In one skit, he performs as two talking heads that had been grafted onto one body to allow CBC to pay a single performing fee for two voices. This tells me he and his colleagues could laugh about the bureaucracy around them. And this might be the main reason why he managed to do so well and to stick it out for a lot longer than just one day.

Writing Exercise

Explain how you could get a raise by being fired from your current job.

[114] The CBC executive was Harry J. Boyle, a Leacock Medal winner himself.

[115] Overall, I would class this book as a Nova Scotian story.

1969

YOU'RE ONLY AS OLD AS YOU ACT

BY STUART TRUEMAN

Lesson 22

A formula for generic Canadian humour

No covered bridges, no swirling tidal waters, and no lobster-eating Acadians in the 1969 Leacock Medal winner - this disappoints me and my Bourgeois side because the author Stuart Trueman was normally an energetic promoter of New Brunswick.[116] Trueman worked his entire career and lived his eighty-four years around his native Saint John.[117]

Yet, when reading his Leacock Medal book, you might not recognize any stories as being associated with the place he cared about and called home.

---

116 One of the men credited with the "discovery" of Magnetic Hill, Trueman served in many official tourism roles including, for close to thirty years, as an alternate member of the commission overseeing the Roosevelt Campobello International Park.

117 Stuart Trueman worked (for two papers in Saint John, New Brunswick, the *Telegraph Journal* and the *Evening Times Globe)* as a journalist for over sixty years in total if you count his post-retirement freelance work. He died in 1995. Initially a cartoonist, Trueman began work at the age of eighteen right out of high school. He illustrated his 1969 Leacock Medal winning book, and others. As a twenty-one-year-old reporter, on May 19, 1932, he interviewed Amelia Earhart as she was preparing for her flight across the Atlantic.

The book, *You're Only as Old as You Act,* bundles up a collection of stories about family, friendships, and other absorptions not tied to geography or local culture. Trueman had published most of them earlier in magazines that served national audiences and may have written them purposely to suit a generic Canadian sense of humour.

He had it mastered even though he didn't consider himself a humorist at all or even a particularly funny writer. Trueman called himself a reporter who could write in a light-style when required, and, in this book, his technical reporter skill stands out. His writing is crisp and efficient. But these pieces also follow a humour recipe of sorts. They often tell of a well-meaning hoser whose plans go wrong and have the opposite effect of what might have been expected.

In "The Considerate Shopper," Trueman advises readers to speak pleasantly to "sales girls" so that they know you appreciate the "tiring hours they put in" and because the act will encourage "faster service." He then counts out the dominoes that tumble after his compliment is taken as an accusation, his attempts to explain are seen as an awkward joke, and his apology is viewed as an inappropriate advance. Similar luck befalls the salesman who thinks success in fishing will make him popular at the White Birches Lake Fishing Club.

One Christmas season, Trueman's friend Roly Haskins has his head turned by exposure to four speeches on keeping up "the goodwill of Yuletide ... all the year." When Roly decides to leave his Christmas tree and decorations up, neighbours brand him a tightwad "trying to make one tree last two Christmases." His persistent good will wishing causes friends to assume he has something to sell and then "the rumour flew around that Roly was going into politics and shouldn't be trusted."

Although Trueman follows a pattern, it's not enough by itself. His quirky yet authentic-sounding descriptions make it all work. My no-New Brunswick misgivings aside, it's all pretty funny, and that mix of a well-meaning hoser, unintentional consequences, and writing skill probably still makes a valid formula for generic Canadian humour.[118]

Writing Exercise

Tell the story of a forty-year-old former boy scout who ends up in jail for helping elderly people cross streets in heavy traffic.

118 Trueman wrote thirteen other books and had hundreds of articles in publications like *Weekend Magazine*, *Maclean's*, and the *Saturday Evening Post.* He wrote two books after the age of seventy. They were cookbooks with New Brunswick heritage recipes co-written with his wife, Mildred. *New Brunswick Literary Encyclopedia*, s.v. "Stuart Trueman" (by Amanda Palmer), http://w3.stu.ca/stu/sites/nble/t/trueman_stuart.html (accessed Nov. 2, 2013).

PART V

THE 1970'S REGIONS AND RELIGIONS

My wife was born overseas, spent her early life in another country, and has immediate family in Europe. She went through childhood in Quebec and lived in Iqaluit for most of her twenties, but identifies with her Acadian roots in New Brunswick. My daughter spent most of her adult life in Nova Scotia and Newfoundland and married into Atlantic Canada but now lives with her husband in an apartment near Yonge and Bloor in downtown Toronto. My son has lived and worked for years in Alberta and Saskatchewan. I have divided my own life between Southern Ontario and British Columbia. If we start reaching out to in-laws and other family, we pull in Montreal, PEI, Manitoba, and other corners of the country. We do our best at representing all parts of Canada. Yet if my family were a literary award, some critic would surely point out that we are not perfect.

One of the peculiar lenses used to examine national honours in Canada and other countries comes from the notion that all cultures, regions, and interests should be represented equitably, and by this measure, the Leacock Medal will always fall short in a big way because it honours works in English only. This by necessity snubs over a quarter of the country.

Knowing this and the Ontario origins of the medal, I entered this project presuming an Anglo/central Canadian bias to the selections, perhaps twisted by Toronto-centric publishing - and I could suggest one if pressed. But looking over the books and thinking about the authors, I'm generally impressed by the assortment of regions and cultures represented.

From the early days with books like Saskatchewan's *Sarah Binks* and the Nova Scotian *Salt-Box,* the Leacock Medal has attracted and recognized entries from across the country with subjects that reflected regions other than those within stone-throwing distance of Toronto. Even rural Quebec was featured in those first winners in the books by the English-educated francophone Angéline Hango and the Englishwoman in Val D'Or Joan Walker. Decades later, Quebec's Roch Carrier squeaks in as well. While some books pass through more than one region, and others seem to exist in the clouds over the whole country, a rough count suggests a fairly even distribution on a provincial basis - for what that's worth.

But a head count is a poor measure of a region's profile. The two New Brunswick authors, Trueman and Earl, don't talk about their home province whereas the books by writers like Mitchell, Ward, and Braithewaite are painfully prairie. Books by B.C. authors split between those like *Writing in the Rain* and *Bachelor Brothers' Bed and Breakfast* which vigorously promote west coast life and those that chose another setting.

You might be surprised to learn that ten books tell stories set on foreign soil. *War Stories,* two of the Bandy books, and parts of *Turvey* focus on World War II Europe; *The Battle of Baltinglass* and *Beyond Belfast* are very Irish, whereas *Luck of the Irish* is not; and you could see *The Sisters Brothers*, *Generica*, *The Grass is Never Greener*, and *Me Bandy, You Cissie* as American.

A number of Ontario books focus on rural life, and while Stuart McLean, Arthur Black, and Pierre Berton wrote Leacock Medal books as Torontonians, the Toronto references are often light, and I only really thought of the Big Smoke while reading *Winter Tulips* by Joe Kertes and those books drawn from Toronto newspaper columns like those of Richard J. Needham, Joey Slinger, and Gary Lautens. This is significant, I suppose. Still, Hogtown venues, it seems, have not inspired creative humour disproportionately. Even Paul Quarrington's *King Leary,* which recounts a road trip to Toronto, reminds me first of another city, the national capital, which provides the setting for the political story *The Best Laid Plans.*

I also see Kertes as representative of something more interesting than the venue for his love story: this is the impact of Jewish Canadian writers on the Leacock Medal list. Montrealers like Mordecai Richler, Donald Bell, Ted Allan, and Josh Freed do a compelling job of sharing that side of their city, and this might be expected. In the 1970s, two Leacock Medal books told the lesser known stories of Jewish life in other centres: North Winnipeg and Northern Ontario. Regions and religion also rear their heads in Harry J. Boyle's 1976 winner.

Yet this decade, the 1970s, makes a particularly good point to consider regional and cultural voices in the Leacock Medal books because of the two that explore Newfoundland.

Ray Guy, a proud native Newfoundlander, wrote one. An outsider wrote the other book.

This other Newfoundland book begins in a Toronto bar and ends up back in Ontario with the author having added a new member to his family and new references to his own clan's list of Canadian regional interests.

1970

THE BOAT WHO WOULDN'T FLOAT

BY FARLEY MOWAT

Lesson 23

How to echo character in the setting

"You know that he disgraced himself," he said. "It was reported in the papers."

"He what??"

"He drank heavily, was rude in his speech ... and he dropped his pants and mooned the audience – well, actually, he lifted his kilt," the distinguished Leacock Associate explained in recalling the 1970 Leacock Medal banquet that honoured Farley Mowat. I read the newspaper report later. It stressed that the abused audience members had forked out $8.00 each for the meal and entertainment.

"Oh ... I see," I said, remembering 1970 as my first year of university and relieved that the reporters were watching Farley and not me.

In the book that induced that evening of ignominy, Farley Mowat doesn't hide his fondness for alcohol and adventuresome behaviour. He tells of a night riding dark waves and confesses to being "fog-chilled, unutterably lonely, and scared to death," and then says that "Since rum is a known and accepted antidote for all three conditions," he turned to it in quantity. Booze, whether in the form of rum, brandy, or screech, flows freely. I counted almost one hundred references to alcohol over the book's 260 pages. Mowat seems to be trying to float himself.

Although these words come as close as he ever gets to an admission, Mowat was, when he lived the experience of his 1970 Leacock Medal book, going through a rough patch, chugging along aimlessly with holes on all sides. His boat wasn't doing so well either.

The Boat Who Wouldn't Float recounts a genuine adventure.[119] It's also a porthole into Farley Mowat's life. If the story as told is sound, he and the publisher Jack McClelland reached their alcohol-soaked agreement to buy a boat late one night in a Toronto bar. That summer, in the mid-1960s, Mowat goes out to Newfoundland, buys a two-masted schooner, the *Happy Adventurer*,[120] and plots a summer away from personal stresses.

It seems like a plan. Mowat has been a sailor since his youth, and

---

119 Farley Mowat produced dozens of books, numerous magazine articles, and short stories in his sixty-plus-year career as a writer.

120 The boat had many names from *the Black Joke* to "*Itchy-Ass-Sally*," which was an easier to pronounce alteration of *Itchatchozale Aid,* the name proposed by the Basque descendants on Saint-Pierre and Miquelon. The name that stuck, *the Happy Adventurer,* was taken from the flagship of the 17th century pirate Peter Easton, who made Newfoundland his base.

McClelland served as the skipper on torpedo boats during World War II. But the two men are not prepared for what lays ahead in the fog around Newfoundland. Engine problems, leaks, and a malfunctioning compass plague the boat. Bad decisions, booze smugglers, and a magnetic attraction to poor weather add to the trials.

Though Mowat doesn't expose his dissolving first marriage in the book, he merges his other relationships with the leaky *Boat* story. One is his great friendship with McClelland. The publisher was only on the vessel for a small part of the time, but he floats around in the background, always making sure that Farley has supplies and a crew.

Mowat recruits one crew member himself: a "golden-haired young fugitive from Toronto by the name of Claire (Wheeler)," who was on the French island of Saint-Pierre to study languages and who would eventually become the second and final Mrs. Farley Mowat. Claire wins his heart when she falls overboard using the boat's over-the-railing head and comes up from a slimy harbour laughing.

The other relationships are those between boat and man, man and sea, and Farley and Newfoundland.[121] Some critics accused Mowat of painting Newfoundland people as cartoonish, with characters like Enos, the man charged with boat repair. Enos eats bacon by removing "his badly fitting dentures," holding them between his thumb and forefinger, and making them open, shut, and chew "with a dexterity that argued long practice." But I think that, even in these passages, Mowat's words convey a genuine love for the place and an admiration for the people whom he once described as epitomizing "all the qualities that make the human species viable ... worthwhile ... durable."

The leaky boat and floundering Farley, mixed with humour, heart-pumping adventure, and a sense of place, stick in my mind most because of a passage featuring the short sentence "We pumped." Mowat uses it seven times in just two pages. The first time, he repeats it with just a few words in between, then slowly fades

---

[121] Mowat knew the island well and had written about life there in an earlier book, *This Rock within the Sea (1968).*

into long intervals of thundering engines, jammed equipment, and flotsam-filled bilge, and finally paragraphs of dimming anxiety until - suddenly - the "We pumped" spurts out a reminder of the circumstance. Just as I wondered if the shtick would be carried too far, it came to an end. That I might sense when to stop gave me hope that I can develop that kind of rhythm and the skill to merge character with circumstance if I work at my writing and if I can find the time.

Maybe I do have enough time. This past year, Mowat and his wife Claire sent me a post card that they both signed.[122] Their note began: "Many thanks for ... the good things you said about *The Boat Who Wouldn't Float* ..." That was nice. But the real gift came at the end when they made me think I could be at this for another thirty years. Octogenarian Claire and ninety-two-year-old Farley said "We are still writing."[123] They didn't say whether he was still drinking.

Writing Exercise

In three paragraphs, tell the story of a voyageur riding over rapids in a leaky canoe using the phrase "I scratched" seven times.

---

122 The postcard itself could be many decades old. It had a caption quoting from *Never Cry Wolf* and a trademark reference citing a group named "Canadian and American Wolf Defenders" in Carmel Valley, California. The *California Archives Online*, in fact, records the group's existence as being limited to one year: 1972.

123 Mowat, born May 12, 1921, produced forty-three books over his career; some were children's novels, some were autobiographical, and others were essay collections. At the age of eighty-seven, he published *Otherwise*, about his early life and his years on the front lines of WWII. It was presumed by many reviewers to be his last book. Two years later he wrote and published *Eastern Passage*, continuing the story of his life where *Otherwise* had left off. He passed away just shy of ninety-three on May 6, 2014.

1971

CHILDREN, WIVES, AND OTHER WILDLIFE

BY ROBERT THOMAS ALLEN

Lesson 24

Why writing means thinking

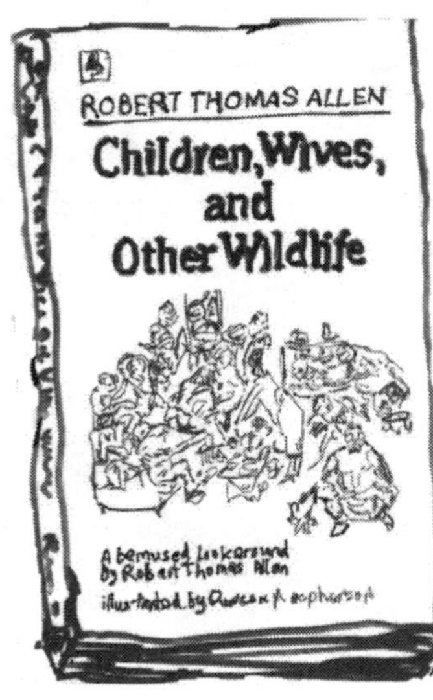

"Sorry, we don't hire women here." I cringe remembering how many times that phrase slid across my lips. In the 1970s, I helped manage a forestry company that worked out of remote camps with crews sharing tents for weeks on end. We didn't think, and we used working conditions to justify our discrimination.

The same cringing sensation gripped my neck this year when I pulled the 1971 Leacock Medal book down from the shelf and looked at the cover. *Children, Wives, and Other Wildlife* by Robert Thomas Allen seemingly bundles adult women with things childlike and untamed. Allen produced the book in an era when the law still permitted gender discrimination in the workplace.[124] People like me merrily abided by it.

124 The book was published in the same year (1970) as the *Report of the Royal Commission on the Status of Women in Canada* which initiated changes in these laws.

But the book title was misleading. Allen, in reality, sat on the other side of the fence, and his book may actually have been mocking sexism with its title. While capable of playing with gender stereotypes, Allen had no patience with male chauvinism.

"The next time I see a guy sitting behind a wheel honking at a woman driver, then shaking his head slowly and looking over at me with a long-suffering smile as if we belong to some secret club, I'm going to go over and start letting the air out of his tires," he says. "Just so that he won't get the idea that I agree with him."

His essays on "wives" are satirical and sometimes silly, but also a tribute to women who support, care, and struggle without abundant appreciation.

Like most essay collections, *Children* tries to categorize the pieces but it is really a mixture. Allen's subjects include schools and learning, the treatment of animals, the natural environment, encroachments on cottage country, and a curmudgeon grab bag of "All Kinds of Complaints." Still, the essays share a common voice because all share a foundation of progressive thinking. [125]

Allen was my age and liable to the toxins of bias and nostalgia when this book was published. But as illustrated by the air-out-of-the-tires comment, he lives more outside of his era than within it, keeps an open mind, and finds funniness in the arduous task of clear thinking. He sounds a lot more thoughtful than he did in his first Leacock Medal book, *the Grass is Never Greener.* Fourteen years had passed, and Allen spent that time as a freelance writer, separate from the routine world, and working hard as a professional observer of

125 The image above is modeled on Toronto Star cartoonist Duncan Macpherson's Canadian Everyman who was modeled on Allen.

life. It shows in many of the pages of this book.

Like a sociologist doing field work, he studies everyone, including his daughters, with a scientific and analytical eye. He sits in a classroom for a methodical examination of humour and watches the kids at home. He finds that little children know intuitively that it's funny when someone breaks wind, when adults fall down ("Dear Aunt Florence: Last night Daddy fell over a duck," Allen's daughter writes in her first work of humour), or when friends act silly (one boy induces hysteria whenever he does "a little pivot" and announces "I'm a strawberry pie"). But Allen learns that children have a rougher time with jokes that require the context of prior knowledge, socialization, and cultural associations, and they, unnervingly, have to base their judgments on a parent's reaction.

His daughter reads to her family at dinner from a book of riddles. "When is a door not a door?" she asks. Allen invites her to share the answer, and she says "When it's upstairs." Other family members scratch their heads trying to understand why a door can't be a door when it's upstairs. Then the novice humorist says, "Oh. That was for another joke. It's -When it's ajar." At this point, the adults get it, and the little girl smiles with contentment. A few minutes pass, and then she asks "What does ajar mean?"

Thinking about these exchanges causes Allen to recall his own school days, his own biases, and what he thinks is funny, concluding with his comment about "the humor in a joke" not coming "from the joke itself, but from a lot of mental pictures, ideas, feelings, and associations that the joke suggests." He notes that people have their own peculiar associations aligned to gender, age, culture, and their times.

Robert Thomas Allen thought as much as he wrote and, again, was "sneakily profound." Yet Allen's style fell out of fashion.[126] Too bad the post-Watergate world seemed to think that all writing had to

---

126 *Globe and Mail* Columnist and author Roy MacGregor, email to DBD, February 28, 2014 says "RTA would not even be published today. And that's a damn shame."

be obvious, "tough, deep, and serious" in order to be recognized as thoughtful and aimed at making life better.

If I were propelled back to the 1970s, I would (after advising the twenty-something me to think harder and figure out how to accommodate female forestry technicians) tell Allen's publishers to drop the *"wives and wildlife"* title and use an unbiased, more enduring one: something like *"A Bunch of Thoughtful Stuff by Robert Thomas Allen."*

Writing Exercise

Write the story of your five-year-old daughter (imagine you have one) telling a bartender joke with the wrong punch line, showing unfortunate parental influences in her mistake.

1972

THE NIGHT WE STOLE THE MOUNTIES CAR

BY MAX BRAITHWAITE

Lesson 25

How a persevere in a writing career

"Writhed in discontent" seems like a pretty good way to describe some working lives. Not mine. Other people's work. I thought about those poor souls and what they might do about their situations as I read Max Braithwaite's *The Night We Stole the Mounties Car,* the 1972 Leacock Medal winner.

The "writhed" phrase opens the book. Braithwaite's appointment as a school vice-principal in the prairie town of Wannego causes the writhing.[127] He says the $750 per year position constituted "the pinnacle of (his) career as a school-teacher." But after getting that job, he immediately sets out to leave teaching and "get the hell out of Saskatchewan altogether." He wants to be a writer and with this book, he tells us

---

[127] Don't look for a town named Wannego. Braithwaite was born in Nokomis, Saskatchewan on 7 December 1911; One of 8 children, he was raised in Prince Albert and Saskatoon, and attended the University of Saskatchewan.

what it takes to become one. Persistence.

He writes short stories and sends them off in the mail; he reads *Writer's Digest* and digests its counsel; he ponders over rejection letters. But, most of all, he keeps trying even though "scowls and grunts" tell him that writing fiction is beyond the town's pale and "that there in Wannego they didn't take kindly to people who carried on in such a crazy way." His failures pile up, and even his successes crush him with their pennies and dimes meagerness. But Braithwaite not only has commitment, he has techniques that allow him to persevere. One trick is to have an unflinchingly supportive spouse and another is to focus on any crumb of encouragement. Even just being referred to as "a writer" buoys him.

With this, he finds a way to pursue his dream and, at the same time, endure his day job. He joins community clubs, leads school events, and gives his job his working-hours best, modeling his principal, who didn't like teaching either but believed that "anything worth doing was worth doing well."

Readers who would be writers will recognize his novice experience. He tries out scenarios that seem fresh and new to him, but are tired and worn to most editors. He submits essays that are interesting, but do not amount to stories. As his attempts continue, his skills grow, and he eventually stretches himself with themes like fictional child abuse and manages empathy for vile characters like bankers. He recognizes that as much as writing appeals to him instinctively, he's not skilled and can learn a lot from *Roget's Thesaurus* and *Fowler's Modern English Usage*. He attacks the Saskatoon Public Library and some of what seem like "one million four hundred and eighty-four books ... on … the Art of the Short Story."

The teacher-author's lack of a university degree haunts him, and he toys with the thought of returning to school part-time. But Braithewaite decides to save his 5 a.m. free time for writing, believing that as worthy as courses and books on writing are, "none of them will write a story for you."

And so he persists, studies, and practices on his own, motivated by the feeling that even though he lacks technical skill, he is a writer at heart: "a person who pays attention, who ponders, who considers, who assesses (and) ... wonders why. Why is that woman doing that? How did she get that way anyway? What would happen if she were to do this instead of that?"

Ironically, Braithwaite gets his big break by blending what skill he has with the subject before his eyes, the one he knows best, and the one he had viewed as the barrier to his writing career. He co-writes and successfully submits a job-risking report on the state of the education system in Saskatchewan to *Maclean's* magazine.

The "borrowed" Mountie's car episode celebrated in the book's title fits well with the other stories, the characters, and 1930s small town Saskatchewan, but it does not immediately strike you as being pivotal in a way that would warrant its use as the symbol to represent the whole. In fact, Braithwaite cites another incident, the death of an unknown elderly woman in Victoria, as the event that changed his life.[128]

Yet stealing the Mountie's car, even for a ride of a few blocks, is another risky move that parallels his dive into writing and results in a night in jail which jeopardizes his teaching career.

It may have been exemplary of this "taking-a-chance to get out of teaching" story after all.

"Good humorous writing requires detachment," Braithwaite says reflecting on all these stories near the end of the book. "The

---

[128] He taught in rural schools from 1933 to 1940 when he joined the military and moved to Toronto. Discharged in 1945, he remained in Ontario and worked as a freelance writer. He died in Brighton, Ontario on 19 March 1995.

writer must be far enough removed from the situation so that he can view it calmly in retrospect and not use words like bastard and sonofabitch in describing it."

Even though Max Braithwaite fought hard to leave teaching, he remained a teacher.[129] In writing the stories of *The Mountie's Car*[130] with that bemused detachment, he instructed thousands on the craft of writing and described the commitment required of those would-be writers still writhing in discontent.

Writing Exercise

In five hundred words or less, explain how your worst job has helped you as a writer.

---

129 Braithwaite also pioneered educational broadcasting with a radio series called "Voices of the Wild".

130 He wrote plays for radio and TV, scripts for theatre and film, and produced over twenty-five books. He wrote the first radio adaptation of Leacock's *Sunshine Sketches of a Little Town*. For a collection of his work see *Max: The Best of Braithwaite* (1983). He is best known for *Why Shoot the Teacher?* (1965), later a successful movie (by Canadian standards). The book was part of a trilogy that included *Never Sleep Three in a Bed* (1969) and *The Night We Stole the Mountie's Car* (1971). Depression-era themes were also the basis of another Braithwaite book, *All the Way Home* (1986).

1973

SATURDAY NIGHT AT THE BAGEL FACTORY

BY DONALD BELL

Lesson 26

How to write profiles of ordinary people

Bobbing derricks, truck traffic, and puffs of dust surround me on my drive through northern Alberta. But the images that fill my mind are of tall buildings and human traffic in a city back east. Montreal. I've been reading the 1973 Leacock Medal book *Saturday Night at the Bagel Factory* by Donald Bell.

My son, Jonathon, lives in Lloydminster and works on a rig in the heavy oil fields. For six years, his greatest ambition has been to move back to the familiarity and friends of Ottawa.

Donald Bell[131] would have struggled too if he had had to move to Alberta for a job. He loved his home town too much. More precisely, he loved the people of Montreal. The "painters, idlers, hermits, and various city freaks" who populate the pages of *Bagel*

---

131 Donald Herbert Bell was born November 17, 1936, in Brooklyn, New York. In 1941 his family moved to Montreal. His family name at the time was Belitzky. He died in Montreal on March 6, 2003, at the age of sixty-six.

Factory.[132] The all-night diner and bagel bakery on Saint Viateur gives Bell a great venue for the study of urban humanity in action. But he also finds material at rock concerts, wrestling matches, and other gatherings of "Hieronymus Bosch figures in modern dress."

Bell seems, however, most engaged when telling me about individuals like Jacob Kaminsky, "the Balloon Man," who inflates and sells the little balls of latex on the street until weather drives him into Place Bonaventure where guards arrest him for selling without a mall permit. When Bell covers the court case, he tells it as the story of a man who brought colour to the city streets and to the air floating above them.

I think of my time as a public relations guy and my days as a balloon man, stretching, inflating, tying, and tearing my fingers to decorate Legion Halls, backyards, and community centres. My kinship with the Balloon Man causes me to think that Donald Bell's *Bagel Factory* characters likely exist everywhere, and I wonder whether oil patch Alberta has any Balloon Men. Standing in the senior-filled Tim Horton's in Red Deer, I think about Jockey Fleming and Kid Oblay, two Montreal street characters that some label beggars. Bell deems them "old-time moochers" who "work" the intersection of Peel and St. Catherine. He draws their jagged biographies by transcribing what they say about each other and Montreal. The drama in the stories comes in images teased out of their words. Jockey pleads for burial in "the Irishman's cemetery" because "That's the last place the devil will look for a Jew."

---

132 In the 1960s, Bell worked for CBC International Services, the Montreal Herald, the Calgary Herald, and the Montreal Gazette. From 1967 on, he was a freelance writer. For years, he researched the life and death of magician Harry Houdini. Bell's manuscript was published posthumously in 2004 as *The Man Who Killed Houdini.*

Bell's book goes beyond this Jewish sub-culture. The lacrosse game tells the story of urban aboriginals, and the booking agent Don D'Amico, the bohemian artist Luigi Scarpini, and the Carmen Espresso Restaurant touch on the city's Italian community. The story of the flea market in Le Vieux Montreal revolves around Polish entrepreneur Stash Pruszynski. And the Delphi Pool Room with its annual Fluke tournament gives Bell an excuse to explore the mind of Nick, the proprietor, and the city's Greek neighbourhood.

They must have a pool room or two in Lloydminster. Although I email and phone my son fairly often, we have things to discuss, and I'm thinking that sitting confrontation style in a restaurant booth might not be the best way to break the ice. That night, he meets me at the Holiday Inn, and we walk a block to shoot pool at The Sticks on 44th Street and talk for two hours. A Montreal hockey game is playing on big screen TVs, there's a fight, the camera pans the crowd, and I think of wrestling at the Paul Sauvé arena and Hieronymus Bosch. I go back to the hotel room and read more *Bagel Factory*.

Without rolling hills, transport trucks, and jittery odometers, I think less about Bell's stories and more about his technique. He seems to be stepping back from the journalist's role by telling the story of the stories - and describing how he does his work, which involves studying and writing about other people's lives.[133] Bell tells how he meets and engages with his subjects. He obviously didn't bother writing about people he didn't like. He gets involved. He lends them money, he helps when they're in trouble, and he partners with them in business. He gets sued by the Balloon Man, and he gets another "friend" out of jail. He gets more deeply involved. Donald Bell sees the people in the bars and on the streets of Montreal, not as characters or caricatures, but as humans because he cares about them.

Caring makes me think about the people I meet around the oil

---

133 In the 1980s, Bell travelled extensively looking for books for his second-hand bookstore in Sutton, Quebec: La Librairie Founde Bookes. He wrote a column in *Books in Canada* magazine and a book, *Bookspeak*, on these experiences. For more, see the Don Bell Fonds, Concordia University Archives, http://archives.concordia.ca/P235 (accessed November 5, 2013).

rigs. As in multicultural Montreal, they come from many regions and countries, but all are Canadians and interesting to me as those that surround my son. I start to think that someone might be able to write *Bagel Factory*-style essays about the people in this part of Canada too. Maybe this is why a Leacock medal winning book seemingly about a particular city, particular people, and a particular point in time was really about people everywhere.

A month later, my work takes me to Montreal. I go to a Montreal Canadiens game and make a side trip to the bagel factory on Rue Saint Viateur. In front of the bagels and ovens, I think of the people in the heavy oil fields of northwestern Alberta.

Writing Exercise

Write an entertaining profile of the most boring person you know without mocking that person or stressing dullness.

1974

THAT'S ME IN THE MIDDLE

BY DONALD JACK

Lesson 27

What makes good dialogue

That's Me in the Middle, the second Bandy memoir to win the Leacock Medal, wormed its way into my head as a home-made, audio e-book.

It was painful.

The British born author Donald Jack used the English approach to quotation marks, and my digital recorder reads these single apostrophes as something sounding like "Backload."

Listening to this book, [134] I heard an

134 Aside from being borderline copyright-law illegal, the procedure is tedious and not recommended over the simple purchase of an audio book. But I am sharing it with you as a fan of old books that are not available in audio format. I scanned *Me in the Middle* at the rate of two pages at a time into a series of electronic files that I in turn e-mailed to myself. You have to scan to a TIFF file (Tagged Image File Format). Next, you open the files in a standard OCR (optical character recognition) system like Microsoft's and then the files are converted into an older version of Word. You can now open the Word file in a Digital Voice Editor program, which asks you, in turn, to pick a male or female voice, the right speed, and adequate volume and to click through the stages of saving and transferring, eventually

electronic voice say "backload" thousands of times. This technology may have its origins in CIA interrogations. But when you're driving across the Prairies alone, you soon accept the situation, get used to hearing that word, and really, really appreciate how much Donald Jack relied on dialogue to tell his stories. And this is the point.

Donald Jack may be the Leacock Medal winner that I admire most. He won the medal three times by following the same mishap-prone character. Yet it never became tiresome, and from what I have read, Jack passed away after forty years of Bandy stories with people across Canada and abroad longing for more.

World War I pilot Bartholomew Bandy gave Donald Jack a great vehicle for humorous storytelling, but the only sufficient explanation for his long-term success has to be Jack's ability to entertain with words, and it seems he had particular fondness for the words people speak.

As with the previous Bandy book,[135] *That's Me in the Middle* puts our hero through a mix of personal and military adventures.[136] All feature long strings of dialogue and, for me, lots of "backload, backload, backload" listening. The greatest flurry flies around Bandy's relationship with the English girl Katherine Lewis, who is now his fiancé. The two eventually marry despite an episode in Bandy's hotel

---

putting it all into a folder on the digital recorder if the computer successfully recognized the USB input and picked a folder in the recorder with enough e-room. Whew – e-uhh.

135 In the first Leacock Medal winner *Three Cheers for Me*, Bandy serves in the WWI Royal Flying Corps and meets Katherine Lewis, when he crash lands on her family's estate.

136 A government minister elevates Bandy to the rank of lieutenant-colonel, prods him into making a speech that insults the upper ranks, and then leaves Bandy to face the repercussions without political protection. Demoted, Bandy is sent to the 13th Bicycle Battalion back on the front lines. Although he rejoins the Flying Corps, he gets lost landing his plane in militant Ireland. Along the way, Bandy bumps, Forrest Gump-style, up against famous personages including Lester Pearson and Winston Churchill.

room involving Katherine, an amorous older woman, a former Russian prince who is now a hotel waiter, the prince-waiter's lover, her husband, and Bandy.

Donald Jack manages the farce and multi-participant quotes, rarely naming the speaker. Yet somehow he makes it easy to follow.

An award-winning playwright, Jack wrote the first Canadian play to be performed on the main stage at the Stratford Festival, and it's tempting to think that a study of his plays might be a good way to develop a transferable skill in dialogue. But plays are works written for visual performance with obvious speakers.

In a book, you need other tools unless you attribute everything. Sometimes a speaker can address another person by name. In *That's Me in the Middle*, another dialogue technique draws on the military and government context, which associates a junior character with deference and salutations like "Sir." But it's easy to abuse such tools, and it doesn't erase the need for vocal consistency in the mouths of the characters.

Perhaps, the best way to study unadulterated dialogue is to listen closely to radio plays and, if possible, review the scripts without sound. In radio, the speaker is rarely identified by anything more than a voice. The words in a radio play fly back and forth rapidly and yet the listener, even when driving a car, follows along.

The Bandy books, not surprisingly, made for good radio. CBC turned the first book, *Three Cheers for Me*, into a five-episode radio play in 1972 with Don Harron as Bandy. The series was so popular that Radio Canada International sold it as three (3) LP's. This success set the stage for the publication of *That's Me in the Middle* and more Bandy memoirs. In this way, unattributed dialogue and Jack's strength in it really led to Bandy moving from a single book into a series.

Those old CBC records are hard to find now. But it might be worth the effort to track them down. It has to be easier than cobbling an audio book together and listening to hours of "backloads."[137]

Writing Exercise

Using dialogue alone without attribution or explanatory prose, write a short scene of a thousand words to describe a person entering a CBC radio studio to find his or her spouse partially clad and in the arms of another. Use the voice of each of the three characters at least three times. Leave the studio microphone on.

---

137 You might also want to check out the radio play "The Resident Member," based on the story written by Paul Marlowe (currently available online at http://paulmarlowe.com/pm/rm.htm). This is a Victorian-era story set in a gentleman's club and involving the supernatural — it makes a good listening exercise for dialogue students. Marlowe wrote the introduction to the e-book edition of Donald Jack's *Three Cheers for Me: The Journals of Bartholomew Bandy, R.F.C.*, which was the original stand-alone version that won the Leacock Medal in 1963 (subsequently revised in the 1970s to make it the start of the Bandy series). The original version had more "editorial" content than any of the other books, with Donald Jack explaining how he'd acquired the Bandy papers to set up the series. Paul Marlowe (e-mail message to DBD, March 22, 2013).

1975

A GOOD PLACE TO COME FROM

BY MORLEY TORGOV

Lesson 28

How much description is enough

For a long time, I reconciled my meager book sales with typical writer's rationalizations: "Well, it made me feel good, I got something out of my system, and my colleagues laughed." Then, a friend pointed out that I could achieve the same effect with a lot less effort by breaking wind during a staff meeting.[138] So, I admit it. I would like to reach beyond my little circle and touch a larger audience with my writing.

As to how to do that, the answer may lie in the descriptive narration of Morley Torgov's *A Good Place to Come From,* the 1975 Leacock Medal winner.

Torgov's book tells the story of his adolescence as a member of the tiny Jewish community in Sault Ste. Marie, Ontario in the 1930s and early 1940s. He and I would be vying for the same spot on the

138 Federal policy analyst Marc Perreault, communication to DBD February 27, 2012, Ottawa, Ontario.

worstsellers list if he had written his book with only his friends and neighbours in mind. But Torgov invites the rest of the world into his experience by focusing on concerns common to many of us like the centerpiece father-son relationship and by describing the Jewish context in just enough detail for the purpose of the book.

His father, an immigrant who fled the Russian army in 1917, set ups his clothing store in northern Ontario hoping to supply steel workers and become a pillar of that small community. "Not ghetto Jews," Torgov says, adding however that the Soo Jews like his father were always "scratching, scraping, building up, tearing down, conniving and surviving."

In descriptive narration, it's not enough to be skilled in finding words. Writers need to sense when to avoid them as well. It's a talent that likely requires hard work to sustain though Morley Torgov seems to have a natural sense of what we need to know and when to stop.

Yet, sometimes, the situation warrants a lot of description. Torgov, for example, carefully describes the venerated role that two New York Yiddish-language newspapers, *Forward* and *The Day,* played in his home in order to set up the battles with his father over possible careers. His father reads and rereads articles from the papers out loud to make his point: stories on "filial disloyalty," parental suffering, and finally pride when a son graduates in "medicine!"[139] Detail also plays a big role in the chapter "The Making of a President 1944," which describes a failed attempt to recruit a leader for a Jewish community

139 Although Torgov had entered journalism as a *Sault Daily Star* cub reporter at the age of sixteen and would be a writer for the rest of his life, he had also established himself firmly as a Toronto corporate lawyer by the time *A Good Place to Come From,* his first book, was written. As I type this in 2013, he was still writing and lawyering at eighty-five years of age.

group. Not much of an event in itself, but funny because Torgov devotes many pages to the challenge of filling the thankless role.

"A leader could rarely delegate authority simply because his peers were seldom—if ever—in a mood to take orders... The budget made generous allowances for nothing," he explains.

Torgov's father has two wives, endures two flawed relationships, and becomes a widower twice. The book only mentions the death of Torgov's mother briefly but it gives a lot of space to his stepmother possibly because she best illustrates his father's struggles, or maybe because the author felt less pain exploring that relationship. Generally, description should be proportionate to importance, but sometimes omitted words speak more loudly.

On the other hand, in the story of the town's first purpose-built synagogue, Torgov gives a blow-by-blow account of the building design, funding, and construction as a build up to literal blows and a great embarrassment for his father. This story merits the descriptive detail because it comes to define the relationship between father and son.

A Good Place to Come From really describes one great effort to understand and share that relationship. Yet with the death of Torgov senior in the final pages, the author admits that he still cannot understand everything about his father. He settles for just celebrating his father's memory.

In doing this, Morley Torgov tells us a bit more about the Depression, World War II, and Jewish life in Canada. He also helps me understand a little more about how to use words in a way that might make it easier for others to buy my books - or at least understand better why I should settle for meager book sales

---

Writing Exercise

Describe in three paragraphs why your parents regarded the National Inquirer *as the authoritative source of all information when you were young.*

1976

THE LUCK OF THE IRISH

BY HARRY J. BOYLE

Lesson 29

How a tall tale tells a truth.

Harry J. Boyle's 1976 Leacock Medal book *The Luck of the Irish* will make you believe in miracles.

Even though one of his characters says they "were invented by the Irish as a last hope," the events labelled "miracles" in this book are easy to accept as true, and the story could be told as nonfiction. Yet Boyle opts for the style of the tall tale and never acknowledges that his story might be anything other than miraculous. As a product of the culture celebrated in this book, I think I know why.

The saga begins at the funeral of Thomas Patrick "Wee Tom" Macrae where reminiscing swirls around the miracle that defined his life.

When Tom is twelve, he and his older sister Carrie lose their parents in a car-train accident and inherit a rundown farm. Carrie keeps Tom isolated and under foot as the two work to maintain the place. But when the barn explodes in flames, their situation becomes desperate. The local Catholic church, St. Patrick's, with its own troubles, can't help, leading the priest to suggest that only a pilgrimage to the Martyr's Shrine in Midland can save the farm. The Macrae kids head off for a two-day drive and their brush with miracles.

En route, their car has a flat in front of the Feeney family farm, where Tom encounters the kindness, sweet smell, and softness of the daughter, Grace. Later, on the return trip from Midland, Tom drives, with his overbearing sister asleep, around rural roads until the gas tank hits empty – miraculously – back in front of the Feeney farm.

By now, Tom Macrae wears the mantle of glowing miracles, having used $10 of scarce funds to buy hairs said to be from the heads of the 17th century Jesuit martyrs. The thin threads have a phenomenal effect on one woman who had been crippled by the shock of her daughter's poor choice of a husband. Carrie and others in the know don't share the details of Tom's naive purchase thereby encouraging speculation about miracles that would surround the Macraes to the end of Tom's life.

Wee Tom's personal fortunes also change miraculously after his return and his wedding to Grace. His marriage gives him self-confidence and brings in-laws with knowledge of barn building and farming to the McCrae place which prospers thereafter. The story closes with a return to the funeral and a loose-ends tying conversation between widowed Grace and the ninety-or-so-year-old "shanachie" Francis Dee Costello that explains the miracles and makes you believe it all could have happened. This mix of reality and imagination is probably the best way to tell the story of the fading Irish Canadian experience.

My grandmother was part of this world. She and her Ottawa Valley kin had a lot in common with the characters in Harry J. Boyle's fable with one exception. She was a Protestant, who would have no contact with her husband's clan - the Irish Roman Catholic Doyles. Crawling through my family tree a few years ago, I found that the Protestant stream that would lead to my grandmother had once mounted a 19th century temperance campaign against a tavern owned by a forerunner strand of my Catholic grandfather's family. Given this, it's a miracle that couple, my grandparents, got together a century ago. So, it's a miracle that I exist.

I'm not sure how you could do justice to stories like that without making them sound like a tall tale.

Writing Exercise

Write a short story set in 19th century Renfrew, Ontario, that could be read either as a miraculous fable or a true story.

1977

THAT FAR GREATER BAY

BY RAY GUY

Lesson 30

Political Satire and the real "Newfy" jokes

The tail end of a hurricane blew open the door of my motel room, my rental car broke down on a remote country road, and mud and slime ran over my hands every day. It was late August 2010. One of the best weeks of my life.

I spent it with my daughter Becky, then a Memorial University grad student studying slime-covered clams at the Bonne Bay Marine Station in Gros Morne National Park. This was her last summer as a single woman and resident Newfoundlander and a last opportunity to spend Prospero-and-Miranda time together on the rocky island. It was great, but it could have been better. I could have read Ray Guy's book *That Far Greater Bay* beforehand.

The 1977 Leacock Medal winner makes you smile when you think of Newfoundland and helps you value places like Gros Morne even more. It also helps you appreciate Newfoundland humour, the power of satire, and the forms it can take.

Guy, who died at seventy-four just as I was reading his book last year,[140] was best known as a political commentator and a sometimes solitary voice criticizing Premier Joey Smallwood. But by the time Guy and his editors were assembling *That Far Greater Bay,* many of his old political pieces had become dated and would have required too much humour-crushing preambling. Guy said he wanted this book to amuse. For this reason, the book features "flights of fancy,""vicious humor," and writing that has laughter as its exclusive goal.

Guy devotes a chapter to the subject of smells and smelling: "When you think you smell nothing here what you are smelling is the salt water. It's in all the air - so much that it goes unnoticed." Another column describes a failed attempt to fire a gun and smack a tree with a stick (the gestures needed to ring in the Newfoundland New Year); another laments the evolution of picnics into backyard barbeques; and another celebrates "The Art of Doing Nothing."

In everything, the humour flows from unique-to-Newfoundland images and word combinations. Guy recalls the childhood thrill of catching tiny fish with string and worm saying that for thrills "Nothing but an eight-hundred-pound tuna" could take its place: one as "big as the church with two heads and two tails and King Neptune sitting on his back ...all done out with lumps of gold as big as hens eggs and eyes as big as bowls of lime jelly, playing Patience with a

140 Ray Guy (1939–2013), an actor, radio commentator, newspaper columnist, and playwright who collaborated with Mary Walsh, Gordon Pinsent, and other well-known performers, died Tuesday, May 14, 2013, the very day that I finished reading his Leacock Medal book. This was the second time one of the medal-winning authors had passed away during my project. Max Ferguson died a couple of weeks after my reading his 1968 Leacock Medal winner, "*And Now ... Here's Max.*"

large deck of marked cards."

Unlike the pejorative "Newfy" jokes, real Newfoundland humour as in this book bursts with pride. Pride in the face of putdowns, pride in the harrowing history, and pride in the hardiness of the people.

I learned this at Pitt's garage in Rocky Harbour watching my flat tire being repaired and listening to the guys tell stories. The Newfoundlander was always the hero, the toughest guy in town, the one who outsmarts the banker or the boss, and the one who takes the wind and the cold when others run for cover.

In his book, Ray Guy points out that if the Vikings were really all that tough, they would have stuck it out in Newfoundland and there would be Viking "youngsters playing in the yard here today."

"Newfoundland is said to be a have-not province ... but there is one field in which we lead the western world and that is in the field of coarse language," Guy proclaims after the Pierre Trudeau fuddle-duddle episode. "The facts back it up. We have the best coarse language in North America, perhaps the world."

Though seemingly silly and officially just for laughs, Guy could never really escape his political opinions. They lurk below the surface of every piece. His smelling, doing nothing, cursing, and stick-and-worm fishing stories are really about the despised resettling from the remote outports on "far greater bays" into consolidated communities and about anxiety over Newfoundland's natural environment and way of life. Not surprisingly, Guy was a major force in the fight to preserve what is now Gros Morne National Park.

He would have been a powerful voice if his comments on this issue were anything like the pointed parts of *That Far Greater Bay*. In slamming the 1970 War Measures Act, he puts together words that would be helpful in the post-9/11 world, ridiculing the notion that we should just trust our leaders in the mode of an "absolute monarchy." He warns against the absurdity that "desperate times call for desperate measures."

"The stamp on the back of the mind says 'Beware' when the shouts from all throats sound as one or when a leader is set up as something larger than life," Guy says.

When it comes to larger-than-life leaders, Smallwood always gets special attention. Despite the decision to avoid columns on dated issues and events, Guy can't resist including some of his general efforts to humble the Premier.

In one story, two women, "card-carrying Liberals" with heavy accents are upset that anyone would dare to challenge the revered Smallwood for the party leadership.

"It makes me sick, some people. It makes me bile, das da troot... h'ignernt .. nothing but h'ignernt," one says of convention delegates who don't recognize how great Joey is. "Yes, he done a LOT'a good for Newfounlan."

The parody would not be well received if written by an outsider, but Guy's speaking as a Newfoundlander with an outport background.[141] By putting exaltation of Smallwood in backward mouths, he encourages readers to distance themselves from those thoughts in a satire worthy of study. The book closes with a column of optimism: "the sun will shine and it will be fresh and warm and clear. And we will have our soul back." This 1971 column marked Joey Smallwood's election defeat. Guy had an opinion and an ability to mock, and he affected the flow of events in Newfoundland.

But his greatest impact may have come from just being an embodiment of something worth preserving - that Newfoundland pride and ability to keep up the fight with a sense of humour.

---

141 Guy was raised in Arnold's Cove in Newfoundland's Placentia Bay.

Writing Exercise

Write an exchange between two people using misstatements and prejudice to defend a point of view that you do not share. Then do it with a point of view that you support.

1978

WHIRLIGIG

BY ERNEST BUCKLER

Lesson 31

The appeal of silly

Last spring, an Ottawa Valley "Bad Poetry Contest" drew hundreds of entries and overwhelmed the organizers, who were challenged in evaluating all the good bad poetry. It seems more people like the art form than regularly admit it. We stay in the shadows until something like this contest allows us to indulge in the fancy without critique.

I suspect Ernest Buckler[142] might have been pursuing this same awkward pastime when he wrote the essays, poems, and stories bound into

142 Ernest Redmond Buckler was born in 1908 in Nova Scotia. Considered "a brilliant student," he earned a degree at Dalhousie University followed by an M.A. at the University of Toronto in 1931. After university, he worked as an actuary in the "penitentiary" of the Toronto offices of Manufacturer's Life. In 1936, he returned to his family farm in Nova Scotia's Annapolis Valley. In 1938, at the age of thirty, Buckler won a modest magazine article contest, which was enough to encourage him into a writing career. But he stayed on the farm and only maintained contact with the world through his post office. He passed away in 1984.

Whirligig, the 1978 Leacock Medal winner. At the time, Canadians knew Buckler best as the novelist whose first work *The Mountain and the Valley,*[143] sat in the highest rankings of serious Canadian fiction.

Some of the essays in *Whirligig* are clever and generally consistent with his thoughtful persona. They include an account of early social networking (the Rural Party Line) and an examination of the Christmas Card tradition that demands a process for ensuring cards are never sent to the undeserving and never too fulsome in their messages. These essays could, and often did, stand on their own as witty magazine or journal articles.

But I find the book more interesting when Buckler plays with different formats and takes shots at his own profession.

Unlike Farley Mowat, Pierre Berton, and other writers who adapted well to the rise of television and mass media in the 1970s, Buckler was uncomfortable with self-promotion and book-selling based on the personality of the writer. A recluse, who stuck close to his rural Nova Scotia home, he had a hard time with the pressure to produce a "roguish thumbnail sketch" and photo of "excruciating cuteness" for a writer "otherwise as sober as oatmeal."

In "Bestsellers Make Strange Bedfellows," Buckler deconstructs the process of book sales, marketing, and promotion with the insight of someone who worked as a book reviewer as well as an author.[144]

---

143 *The Mountain and the Valley,* published in 1952, is consistently ranked among the best novels in Canadian literature. A follow-up, *The Cruelest Month,* fell short of the commercial and critical achievement of his first. In addition to these and *Whirligig,* his other books include his 1968 memoir *Oxbells and Fireflies.* He wrote text for *Nova Scotia: Window on the Sea,* published in 1973.

144 As a reviewer, he wrote for *Esquire, Saturday Night, the New York Times,* and the *Los Angeles Times.*

Aspiring writers with full-time employment, families, and other demands might be heartened by Buckler's piece on being a writer while also farming with its inescapable demands tied to the seasons and living creatures. These bits of prose are fun.

Yet *Whirligig* is memorable because of the parts when the serious Buckler lets loose in quirky, sometimes bad, poetry. Bawdy limericks, works of many stanzas, and poems of two lines. Poems about animals, religion, culture, relationships, marriage, and often - sex.

It's hard to believe that the bookish Buckler, a life-long bachelor, was not releasing more than a pent up imagination in "Withdrawal Symptoms or Slam, Bam, Thank You Ma'am/I Trust You Wore Your Diaphragm" or the "Matinee Idle" which muses about live sex on stage and the strain of eight shows per week: "But where is the actor - With enough vital factor."

His poems like "Never Laugh at a Giraffe" with its ode to "the elephant who wears no trunks," "the porcupine (that) sports crochet hooks," and other beasts could evoke the animal-based poetry of *Sarah Binks*. But it's not exactly the same.

I have difficulty defining good or bad poetry. But I know Sarah's poems were amusing because they were framed by an admiring biography. Buckler's poems and essays don't have this feature. They can be rhythmic, emotive, and scholarly, but also irregular and disconnected.

The one-time University of Toronto president Claude Bissell said, in the book's intro, that the pieces in *Whirligig* were "written at various times" and this makes the sum "an occasional book," which is another way of saying "a bathroom reader" - a format that might not have propelled Buckler into the upper strata of Canadian literati, but is still, like good-bad poetry, something many of us enjoy when behind closed doors.

Writing Exercise

Write your own author profile for a publisher's website in a way that shows you did it begrudgingly and with contempt.

1979

TRUE CONFECTIONS

BY SONDRA GOTLIEB

Lesson 32

Assuming another persona

A writing course I took years ago still causes me unease when I think about assignments like "tastefully describe the torture to the death of a small child," "detail the sights, sounds, and smells of your last trip to the bathroom," and the daunting one that I could never bring myself to do: "assume the persona of a teenage girl."

I probably dreaded the latter exercise so much because I feared resorting to clothes-food-and-boys clichés that would expose prejudice as well as limited writing competence.

But if I had to confront it today and if the assignment involved the personality of a slightly spoiled, somewhat innocent teenage Jewish girl inching toward adulthood in the North End of 1950s Winnipeg, I would have one model to clutch, *True Confections,* the 1979 Leacock Medal winning memoir-like novel by columnist and diplomat-spouse Sondra Gotlieb.

The autobiographical novel *True Confections,* subtitled *Or How My Family Arranged My Marriage,* traces the life of a girl from her "sweet sixteen party" to her marriage a couple of years later. It talks a lot about clothes, boys, and food.

Teenage girls evidently think a lot about confections. Their preparation, consumption, and impact on bodies. For the party that opens the book, the birthday girl insists on a long menu: a "layered sandwich loaf, iced with cream cheese and olives ... sugared almond shortbreads ... Russian Butter Cake."

Verna, the first-person narrator of the sort-of-autobiographical novel, learns her mother's recipes, takes a job in her cousin's restaurant, and fusses as much about the caterers as the choice of a groom and the linking of families at her wedding.

Always, food and clothing issues swirl around the story, which also never strays far from the subject of boys. Boys like the awkward Harvey Stone, who "is so smart that he thinks in parallelograms" and is from a well-placed family. Harvey would have Verna for sure, but she sees him as only slightly better than Saturday nights with her parents. Another was Kenny "the milkman's son."

"Kenny's brown eyes had a dreamy look ... His shoulders were broad and he was stronger than the boys whose fathers were doctors (and ... and) ... Kenny was interested in the mind." I gathered this was all good stuff for a teenage girl as the first half of the book devotes a lot of space to Verna's imaginations around Kenny. This stops when the sensitive Kenny is spotted with an older man and no female companions at the opera.

Vera eventually falls into her "arranged" engagement to the South End Winnipeg, highly educated, and well-travelled Martin Manheim - M.M. The arranging doesn't mean dowries and match-makers, merely encouragement toward marriage as an alternative to the secular nunnery of graduate studies.

Attracted to marriage as an excuse to drop out, Verna does most of the arranging by allowing M.M.'s offhanded comment that his mother "thinks you might become her daughter-in-law" to evolve into a presumed proposal. It seems to have worked out. Verna's story ends with reference to imperfect marriages but kind words about her own, which was then marking twenty-two years of "getting acquainted."

I like the book, in part, because it celebrates Winnipeg, and the Leacock Medal experience would not seem complete if the only portrayal of the Prairies took the form of the small towns, wheat fields and big sky of W.O. Mitchell, Max Braithwaite, and their kind. *True Confections* convinces you that some people living there – in wintery Winnipeg - might not want to ever leave and could even imagine it as the best place on earth.

This might be my greatest resulting insight about the minds of teenage girls. They live in places like Winnipeg, have families, and have lives, and my sources within the gender tell me that though food, clothes, and boys are not to be ignored, these are just the ornaments on a personality.

The personality in this book is that of Sondra Gotlieb for sure,[145] but not the caricature of a privileged social climber that haunts the real life Sondra. In *True Confections*, Gotlieb assumes the persona of her teenage girl self and, through this, can be candid, self-deprecating, and self-aware.

---

145 Sondra married Harvard–Berkley–Oxford schooled lawyer Allen Gotlieb, eventually the Canadian ambassador to the United States. She was also a published cookbook writer by the time she wrote *True Confections*, her first novel. Later she contributed to *Maclean's* and *Chatelaine* magazines before starting her well-known columns in the *Washington Post.* Over her career, she produced articles for *Saturday Night*, the *New York Times*, and the *National Post.* The Gotliebs now live in Toronto.

So, one other thing I learned about young women is that they access the same tools as the other gender in order to be clever and funny. Maybe, I should give that assignment another shot.[146]

Maybe, I just did.

Writing Exercise

In the first person and in five hundred words of less, describe your sixteenth birthday as if you were a member of the other sex.

146 Like the fictional Verna, Gotlieb was born in 1936 and married her older, scholarly husband in 1955. They had three children, Marc, Rachel, and first of all Rebecca, who was born just a few years after the marriage, which was commemorated in the closing pages of the Leacock Medal book. When *True Confections* was written, Sondra Gotlieb's first child was just entering university and starting studies that would lead to several degrees and a career as a lawyer. Sadly, Rebecca, who also wrote columns on occasion, passed away with cancer at forty-four years of age in 2003.

PART VI

THE 1980'S

HUMOUR AND GENDER

In October 2013, I spent a few days surrounded by thousands of interesting and excited women in Baltimore. It seemed like an okay way to pass the time. My expenses were paid by my hosts, I had extra holidays to burn, and my wife kept her comments to a minimum as I left for the airport.

The National Conference of the U.S. Society of Women Engineers invited me to speak on the history of gender equality because of a book I had written and because of experiences related to two sad events that bookended the 1980s, a decade when, for the second time, no women appeared on the list of Leacock Medal recipients. My brush with engineering issues frames my perspective on the meager female representation on the humour-medal winners list.

One of those sad events left Canada traumatized. On the evening of December 6 1989, a gunman went through classrooms at l'École Polytechnique in Montreal shooting female engineering students. Two of the fourteen murder victims and several of those wounded worked during the day for my employer, which, like other organizations, responded to the tragedy with programs and a commitment to increase the representation of women in engineering.

The other sad event, the November 1980 death of Elsie Gregory MacGill, relates to my book. The book tells Elsie's life story recounting her experiences as the world's first female aeronautical engineer and aircraft designer, and the driving force on the Royal Commission on the Status of Women in Canada.

Polio hit Elsie on the eve of her graduation in 1929, put her in bed and a wheelchair for years, and forced her to pursue a career in a male-dominated profession with a disability. She provided great material for a book.

In researching the biography and promoting the programs at work, I read enough to know that the issues around gender equality are complex and that the merits of specific responses are debatable. Some women see remedial actions as patronizing and other measures can back-fire by implying that women can't compete and need help.

After thinking about this stuff for a quarter of a century and in a big way for the last decade, I find myself certain of only one thing - the positive impact of role models like Elsie. Seeing or learning about someone whom you admire and whom you resemble doing well in a field motivates you with the image of possibility.

Perversely, female enrollment in engineering schools doubled in the 1990s partly because of the profile women in engineering received after the Montreal tragedy. It caused young women to think about such a career.

I'm not sure why the Leacock Medal has not been awarded to more women over the years. Some people have ideas. You don't have to Google too long or scratch too deep to find musings about how tough women in comedy have it or to find flat statements, such as in a 2007 *Vanity Fair* piece by Christopher Hitchens,[147] to the effect that women are just "not funny."

But the Leacock award has a particular context and feels forces beyond what might be explained by broader gender issues or by the brutality of comedy performed on stage. Female writers, excellent ones, abound in Canada, and you could even suggest that women have interests that align well with Leacockian humour.

You might also feel awkward arguing an inherent bias in the

---

[147] Christopher Hitchens, "Why Women Aren't Funny," *Vanity Fair*, January 2007, http://www.vanityfair.com/culture/features/2007/01/hitchens200701 (accessed January 2, 2014).

Leacock Medal given the number of family-oriented themes and the three women among the early winners of the award. But something happened after this initial spurt. A quarter century passed before Sondra Gotlieb expanded the list of women by one, and only two other women have won the medal since: Marsha Boulton in 1996 and Cassie Stocks in 2013. Six out of (the now) sixty-seven in total, something less than a tenth, is certainly statistically significant of something. What exactly though - I'm not sure.[148]

But I am certain that there have been other funny female writers and if more women emulated people like Boulton and Stocks, Canada would benefit. I think that the Leacock Medal program would risk little and gain a lot by making a special effort to promote its female winners, maybe by naming one of its awards for student writers in their honour. The competition would be open to both genders, but the message in the award name would be that women should compete and can be funny too.

I know that women can be funny - because of the look on my wife's face when I first told her about the invitation to Baltimore.[149]

---

148 Even now, a significant majority of entrants in the annual Leacock Medal competition are male (Leacock Associates President Michael Hill email to DBD March 14, 2014)

149 "So, you're the only Dick at this event" was her first response.

1980

ME BANDY, YOU CISSIE

BY DONALD JACK

Lesson 33

How to sustain a book series

As I read *Me Bandy, You Cissie*, the fourth volume of the Bandy journals and the third to win the Leacock Medal for Humour, two questions jumped out of the text.

One, "What happened to his wife?," comes to mind because the last Bandy book on my list ended with the hero marrying Katherine Lewis, the girl with the alluring squint. Now she's dead,[150] and Bandy's thoughts turn to two other women: the sweet Cissie Chaffington and the "hot-blooded" Darya Fillipovna Fokov - Dasha.

Bandy prolonged his World War I experience with Russian

150 Halfway through the book, Bandy finally answers the question of how she died saying "My wife died of Spanish influenza."

imprisonment after his capture at the Battle of Touglas. [151] On the way home to Canada in 1920, he meets Cissie aboard ship, but thinks of Dasha, a woman whom he describes as a sexy pragmatist: "in order to save herself, (she) was forced to lead the (ruthless Red) cavalry to my hiding place ... This action of hers was entirely understandable, of course ... All the same, if I'd seen her again, I'd have cheerfully garroted her."

For much of the book, Bandy dangles on a pendulum swinging back and forth between Dasha and Cissie. Cissie is tall; Dasha is short. Cissie is dependable; Dasha not so much. Awkward and kind. Sexy and shrewd. Neat and prim. Hairy and tousled. Two women or two sides of one or all women. Separately they are comical, but the mixing of the two evokes a real person. That delicate mix of comic and authentic may be the core of the Bandy books and one answer to my second question: "Why is it that I want to write like Donald Jack?"

Knowing that this would be my last occasion to study Jack's work this year, I started making a list of things I noticed and liked about the Bandy books.

> **A Canadian Perspective.** The British Katherine, the Russian Dasha, and the American Cissie. The first Bandy books unfolded in England and Europe. This one is set in the U.S., at times literally revolving around the Statue of Liberty and the Brooklyn Bridge. Part of the appeal surely comes from a Canadian perspective on the U.S. and Europe that appreciates both but is separate from them.

[151] Toulgas was a real combat event, notorious for two reasons. One is its date, November 11, 1918, officially the last day of WWI. Second, it was part of an awkward Allied effort to secure bases within Russia after the new Bolshevik revolutionary government had reached a peace agreement with Germany.

Atmosphere Incongruities: Instead of always matching circumstance with mood, Jack plays with the two. As Bandy leans on the rail of the ship next to Cissie, he gazes out on the "decorative feathery designs on the Prussian-blue surface ... (where) ... the sun was sewing a million sequins, while along the ship's side the rushing waters formed delicate spume patterns." The next sentence shifts to a splash and the sight of "three moldy loaves (washing) ... past, followed by pieces of orange peel, cabbage leaves, and some intestines."

Novel Images: Examples include applying anthropomorphism to the concept of time ("Several obsequious minutes bowed and scraped past before I dared to look up ...") and apt but atypical images around common acts ("She was sandpapering the goose bumps on her skinny arms with her hands").

Character Revealing Descriptions of People: When Bandy meets Cissie's father Cyrus Chaffington, he inventories the great man's features: "At the top end of a pair of heavy, sloping shoulders stood a boulder of a head, on which a thrusting face had been carved ... with its expanse of pallid brow below a mat of uncombed graying hair, its domineering nose and wide, stubborn mouth." As for Chaffington's eyes, Jack, through Bandy, tells us "they were positively alarming ... when they were fixed on you, you could actually feel your own personality draining away into your sweaty socks." When Bandy meets W.C. Fields, he thinks the comedian's head was "formed by an apprentice baker, with two rather mean-looking eyes embedded in the misshapen dough."

Water-Cooler Stories: His side stories are easy to envision and repeat. In *Cissie,* Bandy's family ignores grandma as a cheery, but unintelligible mumbler. When Bandy finds her diary, he learns what she thinks of those around her, and he recognizes what she is really saying to them through her toothless smile.

Research: Jack draws plausible adventures both in war and peacetime for Bandy with well-researched facts not only on the military but also, in this book, Russian history, the barnstorming business, and even silent films. The title *Me Bandy, You Cissie* plays on a comic "Me Tarzan, You Jane" movie that stars Bandy.

Funny Philosophy of Life: Bandy is not a cliché. He's unlucky, but he's also smart and aware of the absurdity around him and the absurdity of his own decisions. He doesn't buy the "master of my fate … captain of my soul" stuff because too many random things can pummel a life and too often our souls betray us, directing our bodies to the Dashas over the Cissies. In everything Jack writes, he tells us just to laugh at it all and press on.

Exemplary of Leacock Medalists: Donald Jack uses the recipe of Gregory Clark's *War Stories*, poignant with a twist, but is also rapid-fire, Richard J. Needham-like at times with splashes of Morley Torgov grace and Robertson Davies urbanity.

That's it. I now know how to write like Donald Jack. All I have to do is go over my stories against this checklist, and I'll be as skilled a humorist as him.

See - I'm already being funnier.

Writing Exercise

Describe your first encounter with your spouse, partner, or closest friend using only the person's physical traits - but hinting at the personality you now know. (Delete after completion and burn all paper copies.)

1981

TAKE MY FAMILY PLEASE

BY GARY LAUTENS

Lesson 34

Domestic humour and keeping it simple

I felt a sensation in my chest and a tightening in my throat after reading the 1981 Leacock Medal winner *Take My Family ... Please!* by Gary Lautens.

Because the author was a newspaper columnist, I assumed the book would be a collection of well written essays, and it is. But more than that, the stories work together as a chest-warming, throat-grabbing record of a man's love for his children.

Lautens never uses the word "love" in this way, and more often he gripes about the diaper-pail misery that small children rain down upon their parents. [152]

---

152 Lautens and his wife Jackie had three kids. They arrived in 1960, 1962, and 1964 as Stephen, Jane, and Richard. In the book, they are the little boy, the little girl, and the baby known as "Rotten Kid." The material was pulled from the thousands of columns that Lautens wrote for the *Toronto Star* and its affiliates over the 1950s, 60s, and 70s.

His affection glows out of his description of the frustrations, anxieties, and befuddlements that are a function of just caring so much for his kids. Lautens was a master of domestic humour, a field that Will Ferguson said in *The Penguin Anthology of Canadian Humour*, seems easy, but is painfully difficult.

Maybe we presume it's easy because it's drawn from the daily events with which we are all familiar. We all think our family and friends are funny and that it is only a matter of recording the things they do to create humour. But a slip on ice or a dinner disaster strikes us as funny only because we know the personalities and thousands of back stories. So, we find it hard to convey the humour of the event to those who do not know Uncle Fred as well as we do.

Life also doesn't actually take place in tightly choreographed, newspaper-column-long episodes that sing with wit and wisdom.

Meanwhile, the opposite edge of the domestic humor sword tolerates little deviation from the authentic because those everyday events are so universally known and understood - any flaws, slips, or exaggerations that cross the line will fall flat.

Yet Gary Lautens excelled at the balancing act for decades. He connected with millions across Canada and was, for a stretch, the most read newspaper columnist in the country. He connected, in part, by keeping it simple and avoiding flowery adjectives and descriptions that might feed other literature but would rasp on the commonplace events of family life.

Lautens also, in tune with his seven-hundred-word columns, kept his stories to one-idea-at-a-time simple. Typically, they begin with a kid or multiple kids driving the parents crazy, then making them smile forgiveness followed by a hint that it's about to start all over again.

Often, he delivers the majority of the text as conversations. Experts suggest that powerful dialogue swims around the word "no," an utterance that is common in exchanges with young children. Even when he deviates from the dialogue format, Lautens still uses straightforward techniques like lists. In one column, he runs through twenty-nine qualities of "a twelve-year-old boy," starting each sentence with that phrase. In another, he gives similar treatment to the "father-of-the-date."

The book naturally made me think of my own kids, their early years, and how fast that time flew by.

Lautens' Christmas stories reminded me of how fleeting Santa Claus was. Before the age of two, the burping, bobbing heads only knew that something was up, but none of the myth around Santa. For a couple of years, they were excited about Santa and Christmas. Then, Becky and Jonathon grew into kindergarten, and exposure to older kids brought the "real story about Santa." Childhood began to drain away from their faces.

This is why my chest and throat reacted as they did to this book and its stories which Gary Lautens kept touchingly simple.

Writing Exercise

Using your own age and gender, write a list of twenty-five common traits in the style of – "A forty-year-old woman or man does not …"

1982

GOPHERS DON'T PAY TAXES

BY MERVYN J. HUSTON

Lesson 35

Telling the story of a whole community.

Digging through personal effects after the deaths of my parents in 2005, I discovered an envelope filled with letters, legal documents, report cards, and a photo-copied excerpt from a book. The words on those tattered pages came from the 1982 Leacock Medal winner *Gophers Don't Pay Taxes* by Mervyn J. Huston.[153] My father, who spent his harvest excursion youth on the Prairies, clearly liked to read and re-read the *Gophers* stories which celebrated Blossum, an imaginary town on the Alberta-Saskatchewan border.

---

153 My dad's excerpt came from *The Leacock Medal Treasury*, the 1984 version of the anthology edited by Leacock biographer Ralph L. Curry. The *Gophers* piece lifted from this book was a chapter entitled "Bootleg Justice." Reading the photocopied story, I learned the source of terms like "The Vested Virgins," "Panther Piss," and having "conniptions" that frequented my father's tongue. At this writing, a comprehensive update of the *Treasury* as an e-book is in the works under the editorship of Dr. George Vanderburgh.

The *Gophers* narrator, a travelling salesman with an outside perspective, passes through Blossum regularly to see how George Ingraham, a lawyer, is getting on. George set up practice in the town during the Depression and is doing his best to fit in as a member of the community. The piece that Dad liked marked a milestone in the lawyer's effort to be accepted. In it, the Mounties arrest the town bootlegger, Jeb Wilson, under pressure from local biddies. But George gets Jeb off after the alcoholic evidence disappears, and the jury becomes inebriated. Even before the bootlegging trial, George had earned points by helping craft the town's claim to independent state status which induced the relocation of the post office and railway station to keep Blossum in the Dominion.[154] The proposed new nation had a population of "About a million and a half." It included gophers, admirable citizens who don't pay taxes but also eschew relief and other social services. In another story, "The Venetian Affair," Blossum survives a scrape when George debates the definitions of oil versus gas versus petroleum before the courts.

Gophers Don't Pay Taxes draws upon the same scenarios and sense of humour that fuelled many other Leacock Medal books - with one difference. The protagonist is the whole town. Huston creates a character out of Blossum through the drama of external threats, common attitudes,[155] and the synthesizing interplay of multiple

---

154 In the book, the independence document was based on evidence that the aboriginal people of the area had never signed a peace treaty with the Canadian government and thus still held title to the land. The Independent Blossum committee intended to negotiate terms with the local native band that would recognize aboriginal language and cultural rights.

155 Those common attitudes include a streak of intolerance, as in 'Poisoned Relations,' a closing chapter that tells of a young man of mixed-race who is wrongly accused of poisoning his bigoted father-in-law.

personalities in venues like the courtroom.

It also helped that Huston's [156] narrator talked about Blossum as a person: "even though plans did not always work out the way they were supposed to. When disaster ensued ... (a) sense of humour came through, she had a good laugh at her own expense and carried right on."

Some writers can find a community no matter where they live: among the street people of a big city, on Facebook, or like the real-life Huston, a scientist and university administrator, within a profession. Others have a harder time. My father loved stories of simple folk out foxing big business and government. But most of all, he liked to recall the time when he felt part of a community, and everyone knew everyone. The kind of community he found in those tattered, photo-copied pages.

Writing Exercise

Describe the personality of your home town as if it were a man or a woman and then say why it is attracted to a nearby town of the opposite sex.

[156] Mervyn J. Huston spent most of his professional life focused on his day job as dean and professor of pharmaceutical sciences at the University of Alberta. Although Huston had published several humour books over the years, he did not complete *Gophers* until his retirement from the university.

1983

THE OUTSIDE CHANCE OF MAXIMILIAN GLICK

BY MORLEY TORGOV

Lesson 36

Metaphors and similes

As a baby, I breathed in ordinary air, made all the usual baby sounds, and sat in my own baby poo while my mother worked in her hair dressing salon next door, and my father held down two jobs. Or so I was told.

Not Maximilian Glick. He inhaled clouds "saturated with love, ***like*** the air of a forest in spring, of a seaside in summer." And Max's parents, grandparents, and friends did not just stand next to his bassinette; they "hovered ... ***like*** overgrown doves, cooing adjectives of praise."

With high expectations swirling around his every step, Maximilian grew up with his "defaults and delinquencies" swelling in guilt to lie "on his slim shoulders ***like*** the national debt."

Everything in *The Outside Chance of Maximillian Glick*, the 1982 Leacock Medal winner and the second book to grab the award for

Morley Torgov, seems ***like*** something else, ***like*** something special.

I know the reader is not supposed to notice well-crafted similes, and writers are to use even the graceful ones with restraint. But checking them off makes me smile and helps me learn from Torgov's stories, and his similes always pass the bar of usefulness. They immediately strike you as apt and reveal a truth, and yet they're unexpected, musical, and literate. The similes in this book are also fun.

The imaginary Maximillian Glick was ***like*** Sault Ste. Marie native Torgov. Max's story unfolds in Steelton, a place ***like*** the Soo where the steel plant "sprawled ***like*** a gathering of dragons, belching smoke and fire." Max is also ***like*** Torgov in his youth committed to music, to his Jewish-Canadian community, and to the opposite sex elements of the other religions (like Catholic piano student Celia Brzjinski). In all this, Torgov, as narrator, says that "on-again—off-again manhood … constantly trailed Max ***like*** an uninvited pet, usually a few paces behind, sometimes drawing alongside, sometimes even a pace or two ahead."

Torgov's metaphorical images are creative and amusing but are not "national debt" heavy and they need only a word or two, like "gathering" or "a few paces," for explanation even when he links machinery to monsters and abstract ideas to puppies.

Max is ***like*** Torgov for sure, but he had something the author did not: a childhood role model for bucking expectations and having fun. If Max is an imagined Torgov, the stand-in for an idealized mentor would be Rabbi Teitelman, the eccentric Lubovitch rabbi who comes to town in time for Max's bar mitzvah training.

"The Lubovitcher," the new rabbi, has a challenge with Max, but he engages the boy by making a confession. The rabbi wants to be a stand-up comedian and, at first, works on jokes at night on the outside chance God is looking the other way. But eventually, Teiteleman comes out by telling a multi-denominational assembly: "what all of us here have most in common is that good old-fashioned sense of guilt ... The difference is that when a Protestant feels guilty about his sins, he climbs on a soap-box at a street corner and shouts his confession; a Catholic climbs into a box and whispers his; a Jew, on the other hand, locks himself in the basement and writes his autobiography."

The rabbi makes an impression in a place where, according to Torgov, "Fun was strictly rationed, ***like*** bread in a time of famine, ***like*** water in the desert."

Lots of "***like*s**" to ***like*** in this novel that's a bit ***like*** an autobiography. But the best simile is, perhaps, the one unspoken and unexpected; Rabbi Teitelman, the would-be comedian, was not only a role model for boys like Torgov, but also a lot ***like*** the author himself. Torgov, a corporate lawyer and a writer, split his life between learned study and humour ***like*** Teitelman.

The book closes with another "***like***" suggesting that Max and the Rabbi might join together someday : "perhaps ... in some spiritual territory where the line between what people are and what people dream of being is invisible, ***like*** a spider's first spinning."

I think they did join - in the lawyer who ***liked*** to laugh: the author of *Maximillian Glick*.

Writing Exercise

Complete the following phrase in the most outrageous way you can "Canadian humour is like ..." Then, in one hundred words or less explain why.

1984

NO SEX PLEASE … WE'RE MARRIED

BY GARY LAUTENS

Lesson 37

How to tell a love story without making love

The night I finished reading *No Sex Please ... We're Married,* I woke twice from the same nightmare. In it, my wife, trapped in our house, watched in distress as an attacker approached through the fog. Standing at a distance, I couldn't reach her and couldn't help. That's all I remember. Not much, but enough for self-psychoanalysis.

Gary Lautens, a kind and funny writer who comforted millions of readers, gave me those nightmares through the story of his own wife's encounter with an intruder. When I put the 1984 Leacock Medal winner down that night, I drifted off thinking "Geez, this is really sad – Lautens cared for his wife so much."

My reading was encumbered by knowing that he had died suddenly of a heart attack at the age of sixty-three, less than a decade after the book had been published.

Lautens' two Leacock Medal books were drawn from columns wrapped around domestic life. The first, published in 1981 - *Take My Family ...Please !* focused on his kids, but the second, *No Sex Please*, concentrated on his love for Jackie, his wife and a woman who lost a 1950s Miss Hamilton Ti-Cat contest judged by Lautens.

I know his skill in family humour cannot be entirely explained by a dissection of techniques, but Lautens did have a bag full of them. At times, he managed to blend laughs and domestic authenticity by merging detailed descriptions of garage sales, laundry, and anniversaries with a slight twist or a focus on the one funny element. When his basement floods, he describes the damage and the consequences of a cleanup, but focuses the story on his wife's greatest concern, the loss of the sugary "rosebuds" saved from their wedding cake.

Lautens also had the ability to dramatize events like a birthday party, switching sides in the bed, his colds and flus, or his wife's change in hair styles by putting the thoughts most of us suppress into spoken words.

"What happened?? ... after only nineteen years of wearing your hair the same way you decided to change it !!"

In this way, the story rings true while still making us laugh with him and at ourselves. Yet, as I said, these techniques do not fully explain Lautens' success. My best guess rests on the thought that his caring for family and his basic nice-guy-ness sprinkled stardust on his words. Even when he is calling people "snobs" or threatening them, he always makes fun of himself and his assumptions. When he talks about his wife Jackie, he mocks her husband and his limited support in her limitless work. A bit like Leacock, Lautens always finds a way to mollify even nasty satire with a few kindly comments at the end.

Consistent with the title and the writer's gentlemanly style, there's no sex in this book but Lautens reflects his passion in euphemisms like flared nostrils.

His son Stephen, a lawyer and newspaper humor columnist today,[157] says his dad was in person just as he seemed in his columns. If so, I would liked to have known Gary Lautens, not because he was funny and famous, but because he lived life as a nice person.

Lots of people felt the same. Still producing columns at the time of his death,[158] Lautens left his fans in shock; many thousands lined up to sign condolences at the *Toronto Star* building in the days that followed. It must have been devastating for his kids and particularly for his wife. I can imagine how they felt because, to use Lautens' words, "You are looking at a person with the above blessings."

That's why this funny, caring book gave me a bad night's sleep.

Writing Exercise

Write a sex scene that could also be read as describing something else and commonplace – vacuuming the rug, fixing a toilet, putting up pictures.

---

157 The one named for Stephen Leacock.

158 Lautens, born November 3, 1928, died February 1, 1992.

1985

LOVE IS A LONG SHOT

BY TED ALLAN

Lesson 38

The novella format and humour

Love is a Long Shot, the 1985 Leacock Medal winner by Ted Allan,[159] made me smile more than many of the books I read last year. I liked it because it was short. Just over 170 pages, some blank space, lots of chapters, and rapid-fire dialogue.

Facing a pile of sixty-six books, I couldn't help but feel a little relieved anytime I knocked one off in a single sitting. This admission reminds me of the crazy concerns that can affect a reader's relationship with a book.

It also causes me to think about the format of the novella.

More than a short story, less complex than a novel, a novella usually focuses on a limited period or a transitional phase in a life; it

159 Ted Allan was born Alan Herman in 1916 Montreal. He died in 1995 at 79, five years after the production of the film *Bethune* based on his book, script, and experiences.

can reference the past and hint at the future, but does not document all of it. The format might be agreeable in humour writing because a few funny incidents loom large in the story and can be enough to colour the whole.

Love is a Long Shot demonstrates the form well. It follows Davie, a teenager in 1930s Montreal, as he passes into adulthood, beginning with the assumption that he got his job in a Cigar Store because he was "absent-minded" and "lazy." The store turns out to be a front for a bookmaker, Eddie Keller. Davie's uncle assured Keller that his nephew, a useless poet and dreamer, didn't have the ambition to interfere in the gambling operations.

The mean street characters pass through the cigar store or the upstairs apartment, which houses two prostitutes: one, Yvonne, is involved professionally and emotionally with Keller, and another, Marie, plays a role in Davie's evolution. But love between humans is not the source of the book's title.

A horse named "Love," the long shot, wins a race and pays big. The success creates an anything-is-possible launching pad for the adventure that would be the rest of Davie's life. His passion for Trotsky, concern about Spain, and involvement in an anti-fascist student group hint at what is ahead, but the novella format obliges an ending before the real world overshadows the humorous interlude.

A writer might find novella material in a first love, a first funeral, a first haircut, or a first taste of beer, but a first job probably works well as a touchstone experience because it colours all job experiences to follow and can affect our lives in many ways.

"The chicken killing plant" in my village hired me, at twelve years of age, into my first paying job. For $5.00 per day, I filled baskets with bird body parts and loaded them onto a truck driven by bulging and glum "Harrison," my boss. A half century later, the bloody feathers, severed heads, and squawking have faded in my mind, but the image of Harrison's belly pressed against the steering wheel haunts me still. It's helped me appreciate my career and my gym membership.

Ted Allan could probably have found a humorous novella in stuff like that and knocked it off in one night.[160]

Writing Exercise

Write a short story about your first job suggesting, but not saying, how it affected the rest of your life.

[160] Ted Allan blurted out his earlier and more famous book *Lies My Father Told Me* in a single writing session. That book was terse enough to be captured in the script for an Academy Award nominated film. Novellas make good raw material for films.

1986

NO AXE TOO SMALL TO GRIND

BY JOEY SLINGER

Lesson 39

A humour-column checklist

When I noticed Joey Slinger's[161] 1986 Leacock Medal book *No Axe Too Small to Grind* approaching on my reading list, I wasn't excited. I knew Slinger had been a *Toronto Star* columnist;[162] I had read his stuff periodically, and presumed, with cause, that his book would be another collection of essays.

This kind of writing might be the most appropriate for my tiny attention span. But last year, I had already read books like this by Eric Nicol, Pierre Berton, Gary Lautens, Gregory Clark, Robert Thomas Allen, Ray Guy, Richard J. Needham, and Norman Ward. I wasn't sure what Joey's book could offer other than more of the same.

---

161 He was born John Edward Slinger Jr. April 14, 1943 in Guelph, Ontario.

162 Slinger retired from *The Toronto Star* on April 15, 2008.

Slinger's one-man audience also had a headache and the flu when it picked up the book around the end of June. But as I put it back on the shelf a week later, I thought this collection would be the one that I would reference again and again in the future.

Slinger disrupted my prejudice right away by saying that his book was originally "commissioned as a Guide to Moral Fitness and was to be illustrated with actual photographs of the author in a leotard." The book's intro then shifted into the description of a novel "about a young boy growing up in a fine old Ontario Family and his quest to become an ethnic," and then it becomes ultimately into something else.

I like being thrown off from low expectations and perhaps being thrown off in general.

Joey Slinger can be unpredictable. His piece linking a rescue from the subway tracks and the process of aging struck me as insightful. When he asks, "Is Mick Jagger smart?," he accesses his silly side, and when he writes about his father's pajamas, he blends the two.

But I may go back again and again to *No Axe Too Small to Grind* to find models for satire. His essay on the city bus that serves the wealthy Rosedale neighbourhood is one such model: "The driver of the Rosedale bus wears riding boots that gleam like black suns and ... A coiffeur fusses over his hair so it will be perfect when he departs ... When the bus slips out of the station a loud cheer goes up from the crowd of well-wishers gathered on the platform." The bus has "Persian carpets ... a dance floor ... shimmering chandelier of Waterford crystal ... twenty-five-piece orchestra ... sauna (and) ... Olympic-sized pool."

I will keep the book as a reference for columns like that, but more for Singer's writing technique checklist. In the piece entitled "How to Write," his first tip is "Learn to read all over again." Learn, for example, how "When Mark Twain describes thunder ... does he make it sound like thunder? ... What sort of detail does Jane Austen give us to make Emma sound too precious by half?" and, of course, why and how do people like Woody Allen "make us laugh."

Learning to read and then reading while simultaneously asking the questions "why" and "how' is his top recommendation. Other tips on his list tell us how to "Practice," "Rewrite," and benefit from reading "your stuff out loud to yourself." His final two recommendations struck me most. One will be fun and natural. It encourages writers to daydream and goof off trusting that a fragment of inspiration will come.

The other one is tough. Slinger says, above all else, "Keep it short." So, I will stop here.

Writing Exercise

Write a five minute speech that you would give to a first-year college or university class on Canadian humour writing.

1987

THE FENCEPOST CHRONICLES

BY W.P. KINSELLA

Lesson 40

How writers find courage

Gang violence terrorizes the town, drugs and alcohol crush lives, and fires kill small children. How dare someone use a place like this to teach us about community, laughter, and sports?

I'm serious.

I'd like to learn how someone dares to do that, and when I had a chance to vicariously ask W.P. Kinsella[163] a question last year that's the one I posed.[164]

163 William Patrick Kinsella, born May 25, 1935, in Alberta, earned a B.A. in creative writing at the University of Victoria before taking the M.A. program at the Iowa Writer's Workshop at the University of Iowa. Kinsella said that he considered himself to be primarily a humour writer in all his work, even his baseball fantasies.

164 In November 2013, at his home in Yale, B.C., Kinsella met with a group of other Leacock Medal winners (four living, Terry Fallis, Joe Kertes, Dan Needles, and Trevor Cole, and one as cremated ashes, Paul Quarrington) along with the Leacock Museum curator Fred Addis. The group was there to spread a portion of Quarrington's ashes, participate in an event at the local auditorium, and ask the *Fencepost* author a few questions, including a couple supplied by me.

My question assumed that the writer had to summon more than a little daring to tell the stories of the Hobbema Indian Reserve as he did in his 1987 Leacock Medal winner, *The Fencepost Chronicles.* Canadians know the reserve as a place of trouble and despair, and Kinsella risked being branded as insensitive by making his stories funny. But I think he brought us closer to the humanity of the place by doing so.

"If they give all us Indians enough hockey sticks, basketballs and volleyballs, we forget our land claims, quit drinking too much, get good jobs so we can have the weekends off to play games," his narrator, the young Cree Silas Ermineskin, says in the hockey-riot story that opens the book.

Silas wants to be a writer, find his voice, and tell his stories.[165] The novice scribe says his friend Frank Fencepost helps him collect writing material because he has a "way of getting (us) into trouble, no matter how hard we try to stay out of it."

After a couple of pages, I asked myself "Is Kinsella really doing what I think he is? Telling stories as an invented Indian, drawing on stereotypes, and in a semi-literate style?" Then after reading some more and looking at the chapters that follow, I realized, "Yes, that's exactly what he's doing !"

But by that point, the story has you hooked, and it's too late to put the book aside. You want to know the truth about the St. Edouard Hockey Riot, what a dog named "Guy Lafleur" had to do with it, and what happens to Ferd Tailfeathers, the Hobbema goalie lying face down on the ice "as if he'd been dead for a week."

My presumptions about courage come from the easy-to-find references to "cultural appropriation," "racialism," and other

---

165 The other stories include those on the Pope's visit to the non-native side of the Northwest Territories, a Canada Council-sponsored road trip to Vancouver, and the land claims settlement with thousands of cattle.

innovative attacks that critics laid on the non-native Kinsella for assuming a Cree voice and "playing the Indian for the White Man."[166]

If you reviewed *the Fencepost Chronicles* from this angle of political correctness alone, you could find many violations in the references to alcohol: "most of the team is serious drinkers" ... "the magic words - Let's go up to your room and have a drink" ..."I'll teach them how to drink ...That's part of our culture, ain't it?"

Yet, with the alcohol served up in context, the Hobbema stories read like a celebration of a community trying to do its best. The characters care for each other, laugh at their struggles, and often outwit their adversaries. Kinsella's aboriginal voice is a respectful one that eschews misspellings and forced slang, leaning instead on verb tenses, syntax, and Indian Reserve metaphors for effect: "Just as the white man is a pale ghost of the Indian, so cattle are weak ghosts of buffalo."

Kinsella had what was needed for this dicey work; he was talented and confident.

"I knew I was good before I was good," Kinsella told a group of fellow Leacock medalists last fall when contributing indirectly to my book.

He had reason for confidence in the late 1980s as movie makers were prepping his novel *Shoeless Joe* for the film *Field of Dreams.* Kinsella may have been at the unique life point to risk the brand of exploiter when he launched the Hobbema series. About a decade after the book's publication, he was hit by a car and suffered disabling head injuries. I wonder whether he would, thereafter, have

---

166 Gerald Vizner, "Playing Indian for the White Man: *The Fencepost Chronicles* by W.P. Kinsella," *Los Angeles Times*, December 20, 1987, http://articles.latimes.com/1987-12-20/books/bk-29947_1_frank-fencepost (accessed February 20, 2014).

had the strength for the challenge imbedded in the Leacock Medal book and for battling critics who made issues personal.

But when asked my question last fall, Kinsella dismissed the idea that writing a story might be a courageous act and laughed at the suggestion that he gave much thought to the potential backlash when assembling the *Fencepost* collection. He also shrugged off the subsequent criticism, labelling "cultural appropriation" as the nonsense of eastern academics and implying that he felt free to explore any subject he liked without considering it a risky act.

Maybe he's right. If you want to look for genuine bravery, you could visit the Reserve and meet people who get up each day to face the gangs, drugs, and poverty with their humanity and sense of humour unbroken. I also laugh thinking that I considered Kinsella courageous for writing a book that portrayed young aboriginals as caring, funny, and creative when an earlier medal winner who had deemed them "dirty ... smelly ... and naturally cruel" drew no negative commentary that I could find.[167] Still, I'm not sure I believe W.P. Kinsella.

In his 1983 novel *Shoeless Joe,* his fictional version of novelist J.D. Salinger says "If I had my life to live over again I'd take more chances. Even if you fail, you've still taken a risk." Kinsella had definitely given some thought to courage and risk taking.

Generally speaking, confidence in your abilities underpins courage; passion about what you are trying to do drives daring. Writers often find that passion in the love of good stories and the compulsion to tell them. W.P. Kinsella, while living in Alberta and

167 Joan Walker, *Pardon my Parka*, p. 181 (see n. 52).

later working as a cab driver in B.C., recognized that young aboriginals had funny stories worth sharing. Like Stephen Leacock and Frank Fencepost, Kinsella had a flair for seeing the fun in a situation. I think this was the force that drove him, and once he wrote those stories, they became his own children. He defended them like a mother cat defends her kittens when attacked.

He could use his claws on admirers as well. As a teacher at the University of Calgary, he was often harsh in what he called the "bonehead" writing courses. Newspaper reports said that he not only burned bridges at the university, he "nuked" them. [168]

So, if I get another chance to quiz W.P. Kinsella and to do it face-to-face, I might ask if he was being honest when he answered my other question and, after that, I could ask him to critique my writing.

Then, I will know for sure that I have found courage and am ready to take a risk.

Writing Exercise

Appropriate the voice of someone about to commit suicide and write a note that is sensitive and humorous.

168 Leslie Scrivener, "Life's more than comfy for Kinsella," *Toronto Star*, November 2, 1986.

1988

KING LEARY

BY PAUL QUARRINGTON

Lesson 41

Flashbacks and fictional time

When you have a central character like toothless Percival Leary, who feels his body withering away, has outlived all of his friends, and spends his nursing home days watching a roommate gurgle and belch, the options for a dramatic story might seem limited.

But it helps if you can draw in dreams, delusions, ghosts, and, most of all, flashback reminiscing, and if you're a Canadian writer, you can also pump up the material by making your protagonist a one-time hockey star with reason to get up out of bed and hit the road for one last adventure.

Without *King Leary,* the catalogue of Leacock Medal winners would not have a single book with hockey as its main theme. Many might think this alone establishes the book's importance. But Paul Quarrington's story stands out for me, instead, as a book that gives voice to the elderly and that induced me to do a little reminiscing of my own.

The character Percival "King" Leary honours real-life player and coach King Clancy, who died a year before the book's publication. Quarrington tells the story with references to authentic Clancy-era hockey history but includes enough fabrications to make it clearly fiction. In the book, Leary's fame comes, in part, from scoring the winning goal in the 1919 Stanley Cup finals. In reality, the Spanish flu pandemic forced cancellation of the playoffs that year.

Now, well into his eighties, "the King" is jolted out of bed by plans for a King Leary Night at the Toronto Gardens and by a television commercial celebrating the hockey star's renowned love of ginger ale.

"Because it makes me pissed!" Leary tells an anti-drinking advocate in explaining his fondness for the beverage. "This is gospel. I get drunk on ginger ale."

Leary heads off on the road trip, escorted by a nurse and Blue Herman, a former sports writer who reminds Leary of past championships and hockey regrets.[169]

Like King Clancy, the fictional Leary was raised in the Ottawa that thinks of hockey, not politics, as the most exciting game in town, and the characters of his childhood dominate his thoughts. Reading this, I realize that this past year I passed a milestone that changed how I define myself and have a flashback of my own. Something like:

> *"It's 7 p.m., Tuesday, November 16th, 1982. I am still twenty-nine years old by just six days. Here in the Centre Block, alone in the darkness, I wait to meet my new boss, to go for dinner in the Parliamentary Restaurant, and to begin a new life."*

---

169 The real life King Clancy was recognized, like the fictional Leary, as "the only man to ever play every position during a Stanley Cup play-off game!"

The years and my age have intersected to mean that I have now spent most of my life in Ottawa, more time than either Clancy or imaginary Leary. I must like it, but never thought of myself as being of this place in the past and probably should care more about its image in literature. Leary's Ottawa, the one that I like, has no politics and no government: It lives in the restaurants, bars, markets, the old Eddy factory, rivers, kids, friends, parks, skating on the canal, toboggans, and a cross-cultural passion for hockey.

Leary's Ottawa childhood links him to the Harold Ballard-esque businessman, Clay Bors Clinton, described by Leary as a "bastard" and his "dearest friend." Another friend from his youth, Manny Oz, meets Leary playing hockey at reform school. Manny, a player who never reached his potential as a pro, died of "alcoholic insult to the brain." Thoughts of both men remind the elderly star of bad decisions and missed opportunities.

In a city pub, the group catches up with the other side of Leary's life, his surviving, "gormless" son Clifford, who resurrects reflections on Leary's wife and his other son, one whose possible suicide and sexual orientation embarrassed the hockey star father. Leary's career ended when he slipped after stepping on the boy's toy truck. His family had lots of raw material for guilt all around.

> *"November 1992 - I feel bad about having rushed Becky and Jonathon through trick-or-treating. They don't have enough time with me. But we zoomed around the block, the baby-sitter met us, and I headed back to the hospital."*

If you want to alter how your characters feel about the past, it makes sense to have them relive it with humour and mollifying imagination. But this tactic can be confusing in a book if not done well.

Quarrington, the playwright and movie script-writer, draws on a sack full of filmmaker tools and his immense creativity.

He mixes the flashbacks, dreams, and ghosts all together, but he avoids confusion by citing places and names that are distinct from the ginger ale and King Leary Night of present day.

Flashbacks only work if done with elegance. Starting with a date for orientation and playing with fonts feels like cheating. I will work more on this, someday, after I finish reading these Leacock Medal books.

> *"November, 2012. Just finished King Leary and reading about its author Paul Quarrington*[170]*. I pause, look out the window, wonder how I would spend this year if it was the last one of my life, decide that there could be worse things than reading humour at my home in Ottawa, and go to the shelf and pull down another book."*

Writing Exercise

You are a ninety-year-old, hard-core Toronto Maple Leafs fan on your death bed. Describe four flashbacks that pass through your mind.

---

170 In January 2010, Paul Quarrington died of lung cancer at the age of fifty-six. When he received the terminal diagnosis in 2009, he had written, in addition to *King Leary*, fourteen other published books, a half dozen produced plays, and dozens of TV and film scripts. A musician and singer as well, he performed as a solo artist and a high-profile member of the country band Pork Belly Futures. It did not surprise his family and friends that he chose to make the last year of his life one of his most creative and prolific, recording another album with his band, touring with a respirator, and releasing his first solo album. He also completed his memoir, *Cigar Box Banjo: Notes on Music and Life*. Published posthumously, it inspired another film. He downplayed the productivity, saying that he was just going along and trying to do what he "wanted to do" for that last year.

1989

WINTER TULIPS

BY JOE KERTES

Lesson 42

Writing of young love

Approaching Guelph, Ontario, from the south, the road rises a bit and then slopes down just before entering the town. The last time I drove that stretch, in June 2003, my car was hit by a dark wave. It washed over me, seeped into my head, and dampened the corners of my eyes. I drove past the university campus and had to turn back. My son, with ear-buds running into a CD player, noticed nothing, yawned, and kept looking out the window. The gloomy wave carried a memory that I had suppressed for decades: the break-up with my university girlfriend and her death.

My son and I were heading to a science conference in Waterloo. I took the Guelph detour to show Jon the campus where I had studied, partied, and aged a bit, thirty-years earlier. I thought about the University of Guelph and that 2003 road trip a lot this past year as I read *Winter Tulips*, the 1989 Leacock Medal winner by Joe Kertes.

The novel, follows Ben Beck, a viola-playing student who moves from his home in Jewish Montreal to study at the University of Toronto. He lives above a Greek restaurant, the Blue Sky, near Queen and Parliament streets, where he hangs out and makes friends with the owner, Stavro Dioskouri, his wife, his son, and particularly his daughter, Diane. The story of young love amplifies the adventure of being away from home for the first time.

"Nice" and largely uneventful by the standard of most modern fiction, the story finds a bit of drama in Ben's light attraction to another girl, the WASP Carolyn, and in the soft drugs and dropping out problems of Diane's brother. Stavro, the father, also takes on a dubious partner in the restaurant business. The family expectations that Ben will marry a Jewish girl and that Diane will settle down with a good Greek cause some tension; Ben's family includes a delusional second cousin, Sarah; and other edgy personalities add to the mix.

But none of these threats ever manifest in the extreme, and they all find resolution with no emotional blood on the floor.

Winter Tulips[171] draws on the author's own life and his love for his Greek wife, Helen, and in the few light interactions I've had with Joe Kertes,[172] there was nothing that would dispel the notion that he is and has always been that "nice" guy in the story. His Leacock Medal book and other works suggest that he is also an amiable storyteller. Kertes may, however, be a better writer today than he was in the 1980s.

---

171 The title refers to the out-of-place plastic tulips that poke through the snow at Diane's Greek-Canadian home.

172 Kertes is today the dean of Creative and Performing Arts at Humber College in Toronto.

I think that sixty-two-year-old Humber College Dean Kertes might make a few edits if he could reach back over the years to grab the pen from first-time-novelist Kertes for a few minutes.[173]

The book might have fewer "wild, passionate love" clichés and a little less wisecracking dialogue, which seemed just a bit too slick for the mouths of first-year university students and Ben's pre-driver's license brother Sammy. The older version of the author might also want to revisit the misspellings and contractions used to represent Greek accents.

But these things did not cause reviewers much discomfort in the 1980s. For the most part, they focused on the book's strength: the celebration of second-generation Canadians who set aside the demarcations of their cultures to build relationships and find love. For this reason, Kertes' book was popular in Canadian schools as a stimulus to multicultural conversations and constitutes a bit of a Leacock Medal landmark.

The one feature of the book that caused reviewers unease came, amusingly, from that pervasive "I like you very much" niceness of the love story. Some seemed almost apologetic when recommending the book because the people are so nice. Good humour, we are told, most often arises out of the sorrows and disappointments of life.

Joe Kertes proved something by writing a nice book for laughs.

My university *"Winter Tulips"* experience would not make for a nice book. It was complicated and messy. A nineteen-year-old's death from cancer is enormously tragic, of course. But my pain comes from my less-than-noble reaction: not "nice," more like self-absorbed, unaware, and ultimately not there.

By humour-writing dictums, my experience should make good

---

[173] There was some tweaking in the story. Kertes, for example, was not a product of Montreal and a Czechoslovakian ancestry like his protagonist. The author was born in Hungary in 1951 and came as a child to Canada after the uprising of 1956, straight to Toronto. The book reflects this background by being less Montreal and more multicultural Metro.

funniness fodder. Yet I have never been motivated to elaborate my own *Winter Tulips* story in writing. Thousands of impressionable students have thus been spared my tale.

Save one. I shared all the awkward, warty details with my son that day in Guelph, hoping that he would see that people make mistakes, that life has unexpected twists, and that we carry on.

I think he got it. He said, "Yeah, shit happens."

We got back in the car, he plugged in the ear-buds, we drove to Waterloo to hear the astrophysicists, and I went back to forgetting for another decade - until the year I read *Winter Tulips.*

Writing Exercise

Write five hundred words describing a first date that is uneventful, but leave readers smiling because of the thoughts that pass through the protagonist's mind.

PART VII

THE 1990'S

LEACOCK MEDAL LIFE EXPECTANCY

Paul Quarrington's death in 2010 at the age of fifty-six was unfortunate for many, many reasons, the very least of which has to be the impact it has on my ability to suggest that winning the Leacock Medal for Humour extends your life.[174]

Quarrington and Gary Lautens stand out as the only Leacock medalists to have died before their statistically anticipated time, and even Lautens' death, as sudden and shocking as it was, could be said to be borderline in this respect.

In the early decades of the last century, Canadian babies would have been advised to bet against life after sixty. The life expectancy of the newly born male did not pass the seventy mark until the 1980s.[175]

Yet most – seventeen of twenty-six - now deceased Leacock medalists lived well past the age of eighty.[176] Four of the first five (Hiebert, Hango, Birney, and Nicol) died in their nineties, and several others (Earl, Boyle, Huston, and Max Ferguson) ended their runs in their ninetieth year. Jan Hilliard was eighty-five. Berton, Mitchell, Clark, Needham, and Trueman all died at eighty-four. Braithwaite

---

174 In his 1989 Leacock Medal banquet speech (June 3, 1989), Joe Kertes said "I believe humour prolongs life."

175 Statistics Canada, life expectancy tables, http://www.statcan.gc.ca/tables-tableaux/sum-som/l01/cst01/health26-eng.htm (accessed January 3, 2014).

176 Death data as of May 2014. This includes Farley Mowat who passed away just days shy of his ninety-third birthday and just before the publication of this book.

was just a year younger. Davies was eighty-two.

A few passed on in their mid-seventies and a couple in their late sixties. Hard-living Mordecai Richler was seventy on the nose, and although his life seemed cut short, he still beat the odds set at his 1931 birth. Even factoring in Quarrington and Lautens, the data suggest that you could have tacked another decade or so onto your life by winning the Leacock Medal sometime over the past sixty-six years.

This may not qualify as noteworthy to the statisticians who like their samples random and significantly larger than a case of twenty-four. But it's the best I can come up with to quantify the view that a sense of humour underpins a healthy lifestyle and is worth promoting for everyone.

If the Leacock Medal serves some noble purpose beyond boosting the careers of a handful of writers and selling a few books, it should be this: engaging all Canadians in smiling and stimulating everyone's sense of humour.

But the medal has been criticized for celebrating "white bread," mainstream Canada to the exclusion of more than just regions and genders. The debate around *The Fencepost Chronicles* came as much over concern that aboriginal humour would not have a voice as over the fact that some guy in Alberta was using it.

Speaking to Professor Allan J. Ryan at Carleton University about this, I learned of his decade-old book, *Trickster Shift*,[177] on the irony and humour in contemporary aboriginal painting and sculpture. I found the art in that book heartening because it seems to be using humour as an olive branch and to be creating a space for people of different cultures to express truth, share, and reconcile. We need to tap into this kind of thinking more. While I believe that the Leacock Medal has done well overall, it could always benefit from more and

---

177 Allan J. Ryan, *The Trickster Shift: Humour and Irony in Contemporary Native Art* (Vancouver: UBC Press / Seattle, WA: University of Washington Press, 1999).

more sources of humour.

In the 1990s, two Leacock Medal books stood out for me as pointing to possibilities for inclusiveness. Bill Richardson's *Bachelor Brothers' Bed and Breakfast* pushed the envelope and disrupted the notion of male-dominated literature to share the lighter side of a culture that still doesn't get enough good press. My Leacock Medal shelf would have a big gap if this feature of west coast life did not appear on it. That book came out just over twenty years ago; maybe if written today, the story would unite the men not as brothers or bachelors.

I also found heart in seeing Roch Carrier's book on the 1990s list not only because of its own merits as a window on rural Quebec, but also because it shows the importance and potential of translation. Carrier's book came to English Canada over one of the great bridges between the two solitudes, the Governor General's Award and Canada Council Prize winning translator Sheila Fischman.

We know that other cultures in Canada - Asian, African, and many more - have tremendous literary capacities and humour references that could enliven the Leacock list and boost all of Canada if shared with wider audiences.

The English language requirement and traditions don't have to be toxic or fatal for a Canadian literary award, but the Leacock Medal will need the Bill Richardsons and Sheila Fischmans of the future if it wants to exceed its own life expectancy.

1990

ACCORDING TO JAKE AND THE KID

BY W.O. MITCHELL

Lesson 43

Telling a story from two different perspectives

"I saw him crying often - he'd get so homesick," my mother once said recalling her family's 1930s hired man. "A boy forced out of his own home - he came to our farm from England."

My father, who worked as a teenage hired man on the Prairies, also lived the experience more as a "boy" than a man. But he had a different perspective. He saw the job as an adventure and loved it. My parents' hired-man stories framed my own thoughts of leaving home with the balance that comes from two points of view.

They also gave me an image that conflicted with the steady older man in W.O. Mitchell's first Leacock Medal book, *Jake and the Kid.* Their recollections align better with Mitchell's 1990 medal winner, which had a slightly different take on Jake.

Like the first book, *According to Jake and the Kid* explores the hired man's bond with a boy on a prairie farm. Jake's worldliness comforts the Kid, and his skill with animals and machinery helps the boy's mother manage the farm after her husband joins the fighting in World War II.

In the first book, CBC radio hooks the boy up with his father for a conversation that the Kid calls "the best Christmas present Ma and me ever got." The second book opens with "my dad got killed just a week after we talked to him ... Maybe I haven't got a father any more, but I got Jake."

Jake now seems, despite his years, less like a father though and more like an older brother, playing games and getting into trouble. As Mitchell explains, "most hired men seemed to have one foot in the adult world and the other in the boy's world."

This book makes the boy within the hired man clearer because it features a few stories told by Jake himself. The Kid was the sole narrator in *Jake and The Kid*, and because Mitchell drew Jake from his own recollections, the picture of a big older man reflected "the low vantage point of a boy."

Mitchell, the teacher and university lecturer, surely told countless students,"that's a good story, now rewrite it from the perspective of another character," and he may have been using the exercise to breathe fresh air into his own work.

But this takes skill if you want to maintain a tone while viewing events from different angles.

When the Kid talks, Jake becomes a wise counsellor and the stories are told with young boy references: the colour of the little colt is like "pull taffy" and two fighting roosters remind the Kid of "those toys you wind." When Jake tells a story, he's a guy who goofs around with friends and compares things to barn doors, trucks, and combines. Jake takes the Kid goose hunting against Ma's orders, and he and his rummy-playing friend Gate sound like bickering children when a storm forces them to spend days together.

Yet the chapters, whether from the perspective of the Kid or that of Jake, all share the same feel and readers recognized them simply as "Jake and the Kid" stories. The consistency comes in part from the farm, the town of Crocus, and the locals[178] common to all stories. But another reason they all have the same feel comes from the core personality. Whether the stories are told by the boy or the man, the central character really rests in the transition between the two. The Kid inches toward it, and Jake reaches back.

That was the space and perspective occupied by others, like *Huckleberry Finn*, *Oliver Twist*, and the hired men of my parents' memories, who helped me make sense of the world when I was the Kid.

From time to time, I can still use a little support and inspiration to figure things out and to transition to something new.

Maybe I haven't got a Jake, my parents, or the others that surrounded me as a Kid - but I got this book.

Writing Exercise

Describe a 1990 writing class taught by W.O. Mitchell from the perspective of a student. Then describe it from the perspective of W.O. Mitchell.

---

178 Characters in the Jake stories include the town barber Repeat Golightly, Old Man Sherry, and the teacher Miss Henchbaw, as well as visitors like the poetess Belva Taskey, the hypnotist The Great Doctor Suhzee, and a medicine man, Professor Noble Winesinger. One story recounts the drive by female curlers for equality. A story cited often by reviewers, "The Face is Familiar," features a slander suit against the editor of the newspaper, who compared a local with a goat. The goat is brought to court as evidence.

1991

WRITING IN THE RAIN

BY HOWARD WHITE

Lesson 44

Regional histories with national appeal

For a year and a half in the mid-1970s, I'd leave work every day, walk to a warehouse near Granville Island, enter a closet, close the door, and talk to myself for a couple of hours. There in the darkness, I read and recorded stories about steamships and B.C. history for the blind.[179] The hypnotic experience changed my life,[180] stamped me forever with stories of the west coast, and haunted my thoughts last year as I read about a truck load of fish guts.

When *Writing in the Rain* by Howard White floated to the top of my Leacock Medal reading list, I assumed its stories of salmon, steamboats, and rainforests would remind me of how much I miss British Columbia.

---

179 I recorded *Whistle Up the Inlet: The Union Steamship Story* by Gerald Rushton (1974) for Vancouver Talking Books for the Blind over 1975 and 1976.

180 The experience recording books led me into a job in Vancouver radio.

When it comes to passion for the west coast, it's hard to match Howard White. He has pretty much dedicated his life to a celebration of the province and its people. After school and a few years of bouncing around on bulldozers and backhoes, White[181] settled on the coast near Pender Harbour, where he not only started a family but also gave birth to Harbour Publishing, the enterprise that, in turn, brought hundreds of B.C. authors and thousands of B.C. stories into the world. The Order of Canada, the Order of B.C., and many industry awards have recognized White, the publisher, as the champion of B.C. regional histories.

Writing in the Rain exemplifies the subject matter, but it differs because publisher White wrote this book himself. It's an anthology of essays that do exactly what I assumed they would. They serve up starfish, hermit crabs, and otters and use terms like "throw it out in the chuck," "gyppo loggers," "haywire," and the "big cumpney's running the show," which I don't hear elsewhere and always associate with B.C.

But instead of making me wistful, the stories usually prompted thoughts of places and people that I encountered after moving away. Now being more elsewhere than of B.C., I see White's coastal characters as just a particular flavour of personalities found in many parts of Canada.

White's comical story of trucking fish guts around the coast, which recalled my B.C. experience, could be easily recreated with the entrails of other animals in other locales; his essay on astronomy and tides, while important to the B.C. coast, touches a global curiosity; and his encounters with aboriginal youth in the B.C. Interior could be

181 He was born in Abbotsford in 1945.

restaged easily in northern Ontario or Quebec. The loggers and fishermen who wrote poetry, sang songs, and told stories reminded me of "versifying" Ottawa Valley farmers, and White's story of the Easthope marine engine sounds a lot like Farley Mowat's adventures off the east coast.

Yet Howard White would have a hard time accepting the suggestion that B.C. is anything but unique. He finds little parallel, for example, in Newfoundland: "one of the bleaker places human beings have chosen to stand" with towns "like lichen clinging to the crevices of a huge windswept boulder." In the rocks, trees, and ocean of the B.C. coast, on the other hand, he sees beauty that gives him a "shivery old feeling" of "mystery and wonder." White has probably eaten more than his share of lotus fruit.

Of course, many writers aspire to tell stories about a specific locale that speak to universals, and this commitment-to-B.C. feature of *Writing in the Rain* probably points to White's strengths rather than a parochialism or fault. I don't think you can find a technique or trick to achieve this effect. It probably flows, when it flows, naturally from a writer's fascination with regional history and caring about the people. This leads into a humanity that can touch everyone everywhere and, in this case, a national audience.

Another challenge I had in studying *Writing in the Rain* was the question of how it rated a humour award. White was not particularly funny in this book.

The chapters that brought me closest to laughing were those that relied, not on White's words, but oral histories told by old timers. I'd never think of terms like "booze kitten" or "Holy Mexican Jesus" unless I'd first read them here. These stories reminded me to quote other authors when I can - and that "none of us is as funny as all of us."[182]

But, as with several other books, the humour of this one may rest in something unspoken. It's the presumption that B.C. does not have a culture and history worth documenting: a hypothesis that does

182 Reference Pending. I'm sure I read that phrase somewhere else before.

not do well in the face of this book and that constitutes a pervasive incongruity. If such a view ever held sway among eastern elites, it's been disrupted over the decades in large part by the work of Howard White and Harbour Publishing, which, in turn, makes the book even less humorous today and its Leacock award more ironic.

Those thoughts give me a headache, yet they're all I have. Perhaps I should go back into the closet, talk to myself, and think of the B.C. coast some more.

Writing Exercise

Record interviews with three people over the age of eighty-five about life in the late 1940s. Transcribe them and use the words as dialogue in a story about an unemployed writer set in 2014.

1992

PRAYERS OF A VERY WISE CHILD

BY ROCH CARRIER

Lesson 45

The humour in unfettered truth

"Well - Kawlin-da-bin - that's just weird, and that's just a weird kid."

My francophone father-in-law's reaction was funny, but honest. He struggled with the suggestion that a French Canadian kid might not want to play for the Montreal Canadiens and could find writing "a lot more fun than winning a hockey game." Weird - particularly since this kid came from the imagination of Roch Carrier, the author of *Le chandail de hockey (The Hockey Sweater).*

"Funny, but honest" pretty well sums up Carrier's 1992 Leacock Medal winner, *Prayers of a Very Wise Child*, a collection of questioning messages to God delivered in the words of a boy in 1940s rural Quebec.[183]

Prayers like these have a lot of potential. A conversation with

183 *Prières d'un enfant très sage*, rendered into Leacock Medal-eligible English by award-winning translator Sheila Fischman.

Someone who knows all of your thoughts and deeds invites candor and the discussion of difficult issues - a combination that often feeds humour. With World War II, poverty, and religious constraints, the times did not lack difficulties, and the boy's prayers tap many.

Some humour comes from the interplay between the church and the child. When a local man hangs himself in the wake of his wife's infidelity and a fire that killed his children, the priest determines that the body should be buried outside the graveyard with the dogs, explaining that the man didn't die like a Catholic, "he died like a dog."

"God, I've never heard of a dog that hanged itself ... Is our religion the best, God, because it's the one where you suffer the most?" the boy asks.

Carrier's boy doesn't sound authentic all the time. He uses too many adult expressions, comparing a saint to "a raving lunatic," fearing that his "grandfather got screwed," and quoting the newspaper *Action Catholique.*

But Carrier did this intentionally and had an impact mixing those references with thoughts like "Sometimes I wish I knew less about grammar and more about (bare) bums" and even sillier stuff from adults: "Our grandmother's greatest hope for the War in Europe is that our French Canadians (fighting there) don't swear too much. Their bad words would scandalize the French, who only know fancy words".

In the end, the little boy sounds like both adult and child, and his prayers mix self-interest with genuine concern for others. In his outpouring over the plight of children in concentration camps ("They look like skeletons, with only enough skin to hide their bones. They have hollow eyes; they're scared. They look like little dead children, but they're alive"), the boy pleads with God to "make a miracle to stop all that suffering."

Then, in the next breath, he announces plans to head to the rink - asking "Please, God, don't forget me. I'd be really glad if Your holy finger could push the puck into the net."

Maybe he's not that weird after all, just honest and more like the rest of us and the hockey sweater kid than we might think.

Writing Exercise

Write a prayer about the Montreal Canadiens, your favorite food, and Peace on Earth.

1993

WAITING FOR AQUARIUS

BY JOHN LEVESQUE

Lesson 46

The mystery of why I like John Levesque

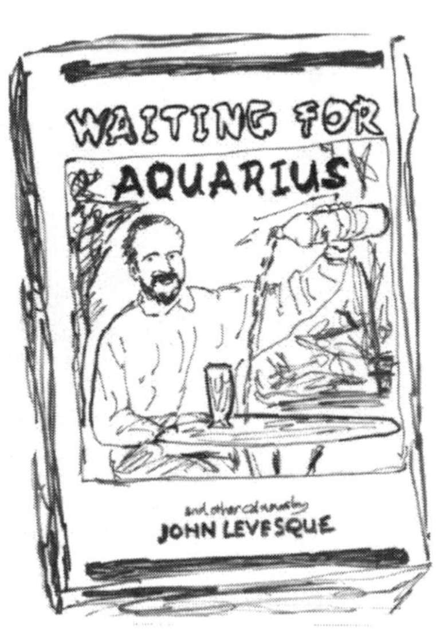

Over the fall of 1970, still living at home, in un-cool small town Ontario, I climbed out of my too-small bed each morning, dressed up in a blazer, and drove my embarrassing beige 1964 Chev station wagon to catch the GO Train. During the commute into college, I stayed alert to read my textbook, prepare for classes, and look at the cute girl who got on the train in Scarborough every day. I knew who she was. She was cool. We were never formally introduced, and we never ever spoke to each other. But she made an impression on seventeen-year-old me because, at our first encounter, she was naked.

She was a performer in *Hair,* the Broadway musical that came to the Royal Alexandra Theatre for a long run that year. Seeing *Hair* combined rock music, rebellion, and, oh yeah, female nakedness with my ambition to grow up and get away. Inexplicably, forty-three-years later, I still think of commuter trains, repeatedly, when I see the word "Aquarius." I can't help it. I don't think I want to help it.

My story hasn't got much to do with *Waiting for Aquarius*, the 1993 Leacock Medal winner by John Levesque, but I don't think I could give an honest account of my experience reading the book without getting that GO Train admission out of the way first.

Waiting for Aquarius pulls material from Levesque's column in the *Hamilton Spectator.*[184] My catalogue of confessions now includes not knowing of John Levesque, another southern Ontario hoser kind of guy around my age, before reading this book. But I really liked his stuff, got his jokes, and found it all consistently smart.

I am not sure why.

Levesque echoes a number of the Leacock medalists I admire. He sounds like a gentle humorist in the Eric Nicol fashion, but like Pierre Berton, he takes on politics, bureaucrats, the media, war, and finance. He also talks of his family in the style of Gary Lautens. If I had to file his columns, I would put them under "Leacock Medal miscellaneous."

His book is a pretty loose collection for sure, matching the physical character of my copy of *Aquarius.* I have lots of Leacock Medal books that are older, but this one shows the most wear. The glue on the binding has given out, and I've stuck in packing tape that bunches up and pushes the pages out in a jagged pile that begs to be wrapped in an elastic band. I'm not sure why I've been so hard on it.

For some people, the book's cover adds to the disheveled look. It features a cheesy photo of the twinkle-eyed, grinning, bearded author. In it, he pours water Aquarius-style, but the liquid hits the table and misses the glass - just as we humans and the other residents of the universe keep missing the mark in the quest for the perfect, harmonic galactic convergence and planetary alignment needed to

---

184 A daily paper with a history of great writers and of punching above its weight class, likely because its competition was the *Toronto Star*, the *Telegram*, the *Globe and Mail*, and other heavies down the road in T.O.

end the age of chaos and usher in the Age of Aquarius. But I like it, and when I call the photo cheesy, I mean it as a compliment. I'm cheesy. I have been the subject of several twinkle-eyed, grinning, bearded author photos as well. I'm not sure why I like Levesque's style.

As I said, there's not much holding the book together. Levesque jumps around a lot, regularly starting off his columns with reminiscences drawn from his childhood and teen years. When he reports on changing demographics, he leads into it with the story of a six-year-old friend who had to keep a back-pocket list to remember the names of his sixteen siblings; he talks about office politics by recalling a grade school exchange of valentines; and he ties Descartes to his dog, physics to sentient trees, and diapers to inventions.

For me, the personal stories give the pieces a genuineness that makes the facts that follow more human and effective. His humour and humanity reach a peak in the closing entry which lists all the things that give him "Happiness." Like me, Levesque avoids resolutions on New Year's Day and, instead, pauses in the gratitude month of October to reflect. I'm not sure why I like his thinking.

All those personal recollections somehow work, and Levesque knows that he has no control over them anyway. When he reflects on the sacredness of Good Friday, he says playing football with his high school friend and "the arc of a football against a ceiling of deep blue" come to mind more than religion, adding, "I can't help it. I don't think I want to help it."

Hmm. That's funny.

Writing Exercise

In a paragraph or two, describe an appropriate but non-traditional way of marking November 11, Remembrance Day, that does not acknowledge war, the military, or veterans.

1994

BACHELOR BROTHERS' BED AND BREAKFAST

BY BILL RICHARDSON

Lesson 47

Finding time and space to read and write

For many years, my one persistent, non-monetary, fully clothed fantasy has been to invent a gigantic "Pause" button to put the universe on hold. With no one growing older, no problems worsening, and no swelling of my in-box, I could dream up new ideas, catch up on emails, take more time to read books, and write.

We will not likely see such a time-and-space Pause button in the near future, but I'm able to imagine it more easily after reading *Bachelor Brothers' Bed and Breakfast*, the 1995 Leacock Medal winner by CBC announcer Bill Richardson. [185] An idyllic, Pause-

[185] Richardson earned a master's degree in library science at UBC and worked as a librarian for a while, but he had his greatest impact as a promoter of books and literacy through CBC radio: Bachelor Brothers' B&B segments aired on the Vicki Gabereau show in the early 1990s. Later, CBC gave Richardson his own arts and letters program to replace hers. A nice bio from his publisher can be found at http://www.annickpress.com/author/Bill_Richardson.

button place "located on one of the islands that populate the Strait of Georgia, between Vancouver Island and the mainland,"[186] the B&B gives guests space to disengage from pressures, relax utterly, and read. Hector and Virgil, the bachelor proprietors, take turns documenting stories about their guests and celebrating written words in their journal-like book.

Helen, one guest who returns to the B&B every year, rereads *Treasure Island* because her first husband carried the name of the central character, Jim Hawkins. He went off to war and his death immediately after their wedding. Other notes, lists of books, mini-reviews, and the brothers' random thoughts make up the rest of the book.

Many of the Leacock medalists muse about writing and make allusions to great literature. But *Brothers* come closest to the format I want for my account of this year of reading humour. It blends the readers, their anxieties, and their experiences with the literature in a way that makes you want to read more books.

It also shows you how to write them.

In imagining the B&B for himself, Richardson creates not only a place where people can enjoy books, but also a space where two men can live together as life partners,[187] dress up as roosters, collect

[186] The fictional B&B sits in a green valley near the Well of Loneliness coffee bar, the Rubyfruit Jungle service station run by New Age lesbians, and other Gulf Island-style amenities.

[187] Richardson left this issue to the imagination, as well as the possibility that the fictional fraternal twins, with "few superficial resemblances" and a paternity that is difficult to corroborate, may have invented their own narrative to live their lives in peace. The closing chapters explore male bonding, the cultural and culinary intricacies of baking a fruitcake, and the inspiration of Liberace, who took "his mellifluous and unabashedly fruitcake voice" on a prideful visit to the rougher side of Vancouver.

flowers, play musical egg cups, use moisturizers, cook, keep cats, and feed birds without their other orientations defining them.

Part of being themselves involves finding time to write their book. They, like many other writers, real or imagined, have busy lives. The B&B can be a dawn to dusk drone of domestic duties: "cooking, cleaning, mending, marketing." But the brothers compartmentalize the day and get it all done.

"The satisfying and consuming rigours of housekeepery rarely allow us time for reflection or inward looking," Hector says. "So, of necessity, these little accounts of our goings-on are set down late at night when the dust of the day has settled; or first thing in the morning, before it has been stirred up."

Last year, I experienced a bit of a breakthrough when, like Bill Richardson's Bachelor Brothers, I decided to commit to writing every day in a different way. Instead of setting dispiriting goals of quantity or quality, I resolved to sit at the keyboard for at least sixty minutes, trusting that I could always squeeze out an hour from my day even if it meant getting up early or staying up late and that this would translate into progress. It was hard at first, but eventually it became much easier to find the time, sit down, and put the universe on pause.

Writing Exercise

Two sisters work as long haul truckers driving eighteen-wheelers. Describe their lives and how they each manage to find time to write while on the road.

1995

FEAR OF FRYING

BY JOSH FREED

Lesson 48

How to laugh at the fear of failure

In my darker moments, I fear that there are only two options for a later-life writer.

I could assemble a mountain of text books and study all the rules so thoroughly that I become not only elderly in body and mind, but in spirit too. In this approach, expanding knowledge would reveal the hopelessness of the enterprise and keep me from ever writing anything other than anonymous, encrypted, untraceable emails to illiterate strangers on other planets. The other frightening option exploits the world of blogging: posting anything and everything that comes into my mind without the filter of editing or education. My unfettered blog would, like many others, attract just a few hits, possibly from illiterate strangers on other planets.

Josh Freed explores such irrational thinking in *Fear of Frying and*

Other Fax of Life, the 1995 Leacock Medal winner. [188] A number of Leacock Medal books mock things that scare us: war, poverty, disease. But this book ridicules the act of being scared.

The book can be therapeutic for anyone who is anxious.

Fear of Frying attacks unfounded anxiety from many directions. Allowing for the reality of the Gulf War and economic recessions, the book shows how silly some of our 1990s "crises" were - constitutional reform, the Goods and Services Tax, and the lingering impact of metric measurement, and it reminds us that we can always find something to worry about and that many issues melt away with time. Frustrations with fax machines, programming VCRs, and setting up answering machines are a few. Freed also points out that seemingly bad events, like minor hotel fires, baldness, and bagel wars, can turn out for the best and often create a feeling of community that did not exist before.

The "Frying" in the book's title refers to food fears that have a flavour of the month quality today, but when Freed wrote this book, the phenomenon was new.

Freed undercuts fear most by making fun of himself.

"I hate takeoff, I hate landing and I hate what comes in between ... And I listen. I listen to the drone of the engine, the creak of the

---

188 A collection drawn from *Montreal Gazette* newspaper columns written by Freed in the first half of the 1990s.

wing flaps and the clunk of the landing gear alert for sounds the captain may have missed," he says of a common anxiety.

A less common one rises from his desk.

"Imagine a ceiling-high pyramid of paper: a leaning tower of yellow newspapers, leaky pens, unpaid parking tickets, bailiff notices, old pizza boxes and petrified coffee cups. All that's missing is a sign that says: DANGER: LIFE-THREATENING MESS," he says.

Although Freed wrote part of the book while living in L.A., takes shots at Americans and mocks the U.S.'s biggest-and-best culture, he targets Canadian cautiousness most, which even extends to learning a language: "ANGLO 1: This person knows all 276 French tenses, and is determined to get them perfectly ... determined not to speak another word until he has finished five more years of intensive French." Freed prefers "ANGLO 2 (who) has a vocabulary of 15 words and one tense, usually the present, and talks like a cave man ... (and goes around speaking) French with the confidence of Moliere."

He encourages us "to plunge ahead and fill the air with words ... (for) ... If you speak French badly for long enough, you may eventually learn to speak it correctly." We should not, however, speak in a vacuum, and we need to interact with those who know what they are doing.

Sounds like a plan for writers too. We should plunge ahead knowing we might be doing it badly as long as we listen to others who do know what they're doing and as long as we can park those irrational fears.

Writing Exercise

Write five hundred words on why writers should consider the fear of failure as absurd.

1996

LETTERS FROM THE COUNTRY

BY MARSHA BOULTON

Lesson 49

The caring yet practical perspective of farmers

Our family christened my sister as "the caring one." When her lamb died, we dug a grave by the barn, held a funeral, and tried to comfort her. When my pig, Herkimer, left the mortal world, we put him in the freezer and then ate him. That was fine with five-year-old me, "the practical one."

From that time, my sister was not tagged to be a farmer because she was seen as too sensitive and squishy for the necessary dispatching of livestock. I too was not farmer material because I, on the other hand, did not seem to care enough for animals. We learned at an early age that farmers need a perfect blend of caring and practicality. Farmers should also have a sense of humour, and great farmers know how to share these characteristics with others.

By all these measures, Marsha Boulton makes a great farmer even though farming was not her first career choice. Sometimes caring, sometimes practical, and always seeing the humour in our presumptions about farm life, the 1996 Leacock Medal winner could also communicate it all well.

Letters from the Country, the medal-winning work, describes the routine events of rural life in central Ontario with the amusement and awe of someone who came from the city. Boulton moves to the farm after years of glamour as editor of the People section of *Maclean's* magazine, where she had spent her days interviewing "celebrities, actors, writers, musicians, poets and politicians." Her farm stories read like a series of reports to former colleagues and friends in a magazine article/ CBC feature kind of way.

Her transition to the farm was not direct or obviously preordained. Although her book mentions a brush with cancer, it doesn't link this to the change in lifestyle.

The practicality and caring combo comes through clearly in reports on her sheep. She shears the wool, cleans hooves, and measures scrotums. She oversees hundreds of births, cradles young lambs in her arms until they fall asleep, clears their noses, and helps them wean. Then, she takes pride in seeing her babies listed as "Lamb from Marsha Boulton's farm" on the menu of Toronto restaurant Bistro 990.[189]

Although she identifies herself as a shepherd and her sheep are the most common subject of her stories, Boulton's collection covers a range of rural experience from snakes to porcupines and cats to cucumbers. Non-farmers learn that geese have bad breath, turkeys are so dumb they drown while drinking rain, hermaphrodite sheep are money makers, and chickens caught in fly paper are hard to

[189] A once trendy place, but now closed.

manage. Anyone from a rural area will nod at her stories about skunk encounters and deals at local auctions.

She says rural experience has a dark side too. It includes vandalism and theft beyond worm rustling, mailbox smashing, and Christmas tree thieving. But Boulton mitigates these stories with an ambiance of caring for two-legged animals, her neighbours and friends. She can even see humour in that practical, caring construct.

"City people often live under the fantastical notion that the kindly farmer always has room for another dog," Marsha Boulton says with charity toward the practice of dog dumping; "When they have an unwanted puppy, they drive out into the country and drop the animal off near the end of a laneway for the kindly, anonymous farmer to find."

Of course, before someone finds the puppy, it has to dodge traffic, hawks, and other hazards. If the dumped puppies and kittens live long enough, they join other wild animals that harass the livestock. This usually means that "the kindly farmer ends up having to get out the varmint gun" and do the practical thing.

Boulton wrote this book about a decade after her move to the country, and while her writing, radio work, and editing of a local history suggest she could not leave her first self behind entirely, you get the feeling that she has settled on the farm for good.

I am glad that no one told Marsha Boulton that she was not suited to farming, or if they did, she ignored them. She certainly seems better suited to living and celebrating the two-pronged requirements of rural life than either my sister or me.

Writing Exercise

Write a story about farmers who leave their unwanted livestock in the city assuming that urban dwellers will figure out a way to deal with it.

1997

BLACK IN THE SADDLE AGAIN

BY ARTHUR BLACK

Lesson 50

Why Google-era writers still collect trivia

Forty years ago, the radio station in Oshawa, Ontario had a teletype machine that rattled out something like three lines per hour, typewriters that jammed continuously, and a subscription to one newspaper. Interesting printed words were scarce, and my colleague disc jockeys and I gnawed on every scrap of trivia like starving rats.[190]

Someone with an iPhone and a head of coloured hair may think of trivia as an overflowing stream to be scooped up with a flick of the finger. But 1997 Leacock medalist Arthur Black,[191] who began his radio

---

[190] I worked at what was then CKLB and its sister station CKQS-FM in Oshawa from 1973 to 1975 as my first job after university.

[191] Arthur Raymond Black was born in Toronto on August 30, 1943. After dropping out of Radio and TV Arts at Ryerson, he travelled and worked in different jobs overseas.

career in 1970s Thunder Bay, [192] would know what I am talking about, and I'm sure that this explains why he became a trivia stalker and compulsive "Idea Thief."

In the opening of his medal-winning book *Black in the Saddle Again*,[193] Black admits to stealing from "books, magazines, TV programs, things I see on the street, conversations I deliberately overhear in the supermarket." He sounds just like another guy formed in the atmosphere that attached great value to information tidbits, factoids, and odd expressions, and all of the essays in this book profit from his obsession.

The Table of Contents might be one of the funniest sections because it earnestly tries to categorize a grab bag running from dumb criminals, snoring, weird music, and worm eating to pirates, hot dogs, Shakespeare, and hockey sticks.

Mostly repackaged rants from Black's CBC show,[194] *Black in the Saddle* does not have the aura of great literature. Black, for example, doesn't sweat over transitions, usually resorting to some form of "which reminds me of the story ..." or even "which for some reason reminds me." Often, the essays read like one-sided arguments after the third or fourth round at a bar.

But they make you laugh because Black finds reason for outrage in the trivial, loves words, and always makes bizarre connections. Sometimes he uses tidbits to lead into a personal story, sometimes he tells a personal story to introduce a news item, sometimes he pulls up trivia from history, and other times he describes something that happened that day. Sometimes, he does none of the above.

---

192 Black hosted the CBC Radio *Noon* show in Thunder Bay, Ontario, from 1976 to 1985.

193 Today, Black can look at three Leacock Medals on his mantelpiece - for this one in 1997, for *Black Tie and Tales* in 2000 and for *Pitch Black* in 2006.

194 By the late 1990s, his show *Basic Black* had been on the national airwaves for over a decade. It ran until 2002. Black received a number of awards for his radio work as well as his writing.

He can act the straight man simply rattling off absurd facts for our consideration or he can question a world of diets, tummy tucks, and corsets paralleled by the kind of starving that takes place in Somalia, Ethiopia, and Bangladesh.

With blogs that feature bullet lists, 140-character messages on Twitter, and email jokes, we now swim in a tsunami of information that has no context or purpose beyond momentary amusement. Arthur Black recognized trivia as having this power as well and sometimes seemed satisfied with that.

Today, there might be little market for an Arthur Black who merely hits us with more odd facts and trivia even if skillfully knitted together.

But Black, when he produced award-worthy material, made trivia the starting point not the goal and packaged it within a ball of original thinking – "ideas." This might be the reason he called himself an "Idea Thief" and not a collector of trivia.

Whether plucked from newspapers, TV, or eavesdropping at the coffee shop, odd information has more worth when wrapped in personal reactions, feelings, thoughts, and associations – our own "ideas," the things we can't find with Google.

We should probably collect and save those ideas, whether on our iPhones or in our heads, not just the trivia that spawns them, and that's the idea I will steal from Arthur Black.

Writing Exercise

Find out the average body weight of a housefly and use this information as a spring board for a discussion of ethics and morality.

1998

BARNEY'S VERSION

BY MORDECAI RICHLER

Lesson 51

The role of an unreliable narrator

A cancerous kidney and a surgery in a Montreal hospital forced Mordecai Richler to cancel his trip to Orillia for the Leacock Medal banquet in June 1998.[195] He died three years and one month later,[196] cementing the similarities between his medal-winning book, *Barney's Version*, and the classic that inspired it. Richler wrote *Barney's Version* as his final novel and as his own version of *Don Quixote*, a book ranked as the most influential in history by Nobel Laureates, literary scholars, and me.[197]

The motivation for using the *Quixote* structure might have come from the intellectual test or the seduction of a great story idea. But I

---

195 Charles Foran, *Mordecai: The Life and Times* (Toronto: Knopf Canada, 2010), pp. 646–47.

196 Richler died at the age of seventy in 2001.

197 *Guardian*, "Don Quixote is the world's best book say the world's top authors," May 8, 2002.

would guess, given Richler's personality, that he liked the format's capacity to tease and challenge.

Richler has fun with his readers in many ways. He twists the characters and the plot, and he tries to hide his model. For example, the narrator, Barney Parnofsky, cites dozens of novelists and thinkers - Faulkner, Twain, Joyce, James, Shakespeare, and many others - but he purposely leaves out Cervantes, an author who also fell ill and died shortly after finishing the final version of his book.

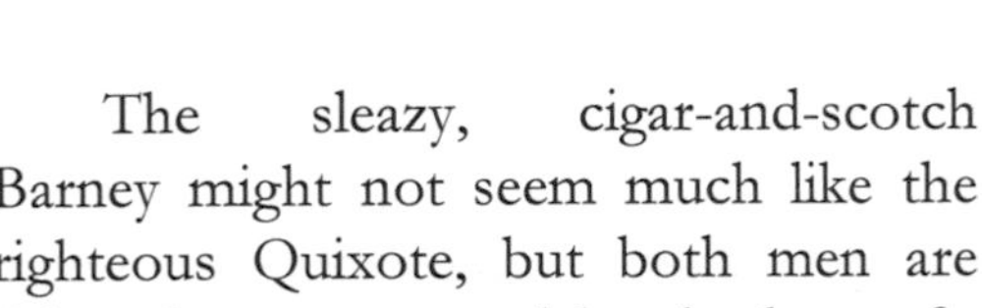

The sleazy, cigar-and-scotch Barney might not seem much like the righteous Quixote, but both men are driven by a quest and by the love of a woman. Quixote dedicated himself to the ethereal Dulcinea. Barney engages in the impossible dream of winning back Miriam, his third wife. Just as Quixote saw the world as rose-tinted, Barney has his own take on people. His first wife Clara, dismissed as a flake by others, enchants Barney, who sees her and his drinking buddies, just as virtuous as Quixote perceived ladies of the evening and inn keepers.

Barney's best friend, the addict Boogie Moscovitch, does not map perfectly onto Sancho Panza. Yet both sidekicks have a dependent relationship with their protagonist, act as foils, and fluctuate between common sense and the silly.

Barney, like the Cervantes classic, uses a huge cast. Quixote and Sancho encounter and spoof all elements of religious, cultural, and economic life in 16th century Spain. *Barney's Version* pokes at 1990s separatists, Jewish Montreal, and hockey while passing through a crowd that includes wives, children, foreign friends, conniving businessmen, Barney's policeman father, and Duddy Kravitz. *Don Quixote* often followed other characters without the hero, thus being split into different stories. *Barney* also pursues separate narratives, a murder mystery and a love story; it loops back and forth from flashbacks to leaps into the future and the recitation of letters written as vengeful pranks.[198] Even the love story is divided into distinct parts around Barney's marriages: first to the bohemian Clara, then to a Jewish princess, and finally to Miriam[199] whom he meets on the night of his wedding to Wife No. 2.

Aging writers might find cheer in a story populated with forgetfulness and misstatement that still engages. *Barney* also helps those racking up the years with a reminder of the impact that bitterness can have when not mollified with imagination. *Don Quixote* carried this message as well. Other parallels reside between the lines and in the details of the two books, but none of this fully describes the inspiration Richler pulled from the pages of *Don Quixote*.

The CanLit icon wanted most of all to exploit the interplay between the real and the imagined through the mind and voice of an ultra-unreliable narrator. Barney, whose unreliability flows from creeping Alzheimer's, alcohol, age, and a weakness for irony, put his story in writing as a reaction to the memoirs of his former friend McIvor. Miguel de Cervantes narrated Quixote in the guise of a translator of Arab text based on second-hand accounts and, in the second volume, in reaction to a fake Quixote sequel. Not surprisingly, both stories jump around and digress.

More than other formats, the unreliable narrator forces readers to think for themselves, to do their own research, and to read more. This makes *Barney's Version* and *Don Quixote* worthy of repeated reading and study. It's also a good idea to check them again after reading this because I see Don Quixote in every novel, and I made up some of this stuff about Mordecai Richler.[200]

---

198 Barney's fantasies include painful ways for his nemesis McIvor to die: nibble by nibble consumption by sharks or suffering paralysis within a burning building.
199 Richler also met his third wife at an earlier marriage.
200 The parallels in the two books are real, but I found no references to Richler and *Don Quixote* to support the notion that he did this by design.

Writing Exercise

In one to two thousand words, tell the story of your life as if you were in the advanced stages of Alzheimer's and had just finished a bottle of scotch.

1999

HOME FROM THE VINYL CAFE

BY STUART MCLEAN

Lesson 52

Why we sometimes like "boring" stories

The protagonist of the 1998 Leacock Medal book[201] marries three times. His first wife commits suicide after providing ideas for bizarre porn. The second drains his bank account and has sex with his best friend, and the third leaves for a younger man. Alcoholic hallucinations and a murder investigation envelop the mess. Stuart McLean's *Home from the Vinyl Cafe,* the next medal winner, tells a slightly different story.[202]

McLean's book features Dave and Morley, a devoted couple who suffer mild misunderstandings and commonplace experience. They meet at

---

201 That would be Mordecai Richler's *Barney's Version.*

202 Andrew Stuart McLean was born in Montreal on 19 April 1946. He began his career with CBC radio in the 1970s as a freelancer, moving on to become a regular contributor to programs like *Sunday Morning* and Peter Gzowski's *Morningside,* leading into the launch of *Vinyl Cafe* in 1987.

a skating rink, correspond, get married, settle down, have kids, go on road trips, rent a cottage, send the kids to school, organize birthday parties, worry about teenage dating, and, at the beginning and the end, celebrate Christmas.[203]

By the murder and porn standard, the stories can seem bland and even boring. Yet humdrum Dave and Morley have comforted listeners to McLean's radio program for over twenty-five years and have made the *Vinyl Cafe* books, like the 1999 Leacock Medal winner, bestsellers.

McLean's radio delivery adds a lot, and although his voice floats faintly in the back of your head, a book will disappoint CBC fans who like McLean in audio form. But for the humour student in me, the text in isolation made it easier to consider the patterns and analyze the appeal.

After putting the book down, I realized that many Canadian readers could probably recite the story line, characters, and incidents of each episode in greater detail than they might recall burn-into-your-brain dramas designed to titillate and traumatize. One reason for this lies in the Canadian flavour of what writing scholars call "profluence,"[204] the cause and effect sequence of events that readers willingly buy into. For many, the simple *Vinyl Cafe* tales have a familiarity that gives the flow a logical feel and that slips easily into the average Canadian mind.

Because Dave, the husband and father, usually screws up in the

---

203 For many, the opening story, "Dave Cooks the Turkey," and the closing chapter on Polly Anderson's party epitomize the *Vinyl Cafe* brand.

204 As described by John Gardner in *The Art of Fiction.*

Vinyl Cafe, I tremble thinking that McLean's stories could be popular because there are so many men out there like Dave with partners who see themselves as Morley. But maybe.

In each story, McLean describes intentions and decisions that make it easy to cast thoughts ahead in anticipation while, at the same time, turning the pages in anxiety. Canadians feel anxious because they care about what is going to happen next. They care because Dave and Morley are so darn nice.

Dave wants to keep his daughter safe and to save time, so he locks his keys and kid in the car. He sticks his tongue to the frosty TV antenna when boyhood curiosities blend with adult defiance. Dave feigns illness to spend an amorous day with Morley after fifteen years of marriage, and this decision leads to a visit from his concerned mother-in-law. Perhaps people laugh because they can laugh at themselves, and if this quality defines Canadians, it's not such a bad thing.

Still, even with this cause-and-effect flow and ability to pull readers along, more drama and action would enliven these stories, and maybe McLean should conjure up at least a few that mix Dave and Morley with alcoholic hallucinations, murder, and bizarre porn.

While I reviewed these questions and wondered how far to pursue the issue, an admitted *Vinyl Cafe* listener, who identifies with one of the characters and who happens to share my bed and bookcase, provided me with guidance. I asked whether one could explain the phenomenon by describing *Vinyl Cafe* fans like her as typical, "boring" Canadians.

"Well, I suppose," she said, adding "so, what then do you call someone who spends his time analyzing and deconstructing the *Vinyl Cafe*?"

Writing Exercise

Tell a story about doing your laundry in a way that makes readers tense.

PART VIII

2000-2009

MULTI-MEDIA MILLENNIUM

In the first decade of the new century, it looked like the CBC headquarters in Toronto might need a new wing to house Leacock Medals.

In just over a decade (1997-2007), CBC radio personalities Arthur Black and Stuart McLean won the award a combined six times, raising the question, " What purpose does a book award serve when it celebrates material that originated in another medium and sometimes seems best suited to that other format?" After all, the Leacock Medal doesn't purport to celebrate humour from all media. Yet the Black-McLean cluster merely highlighted a phenomenon that has characterized the writing and writers honoured by the Leacock Medal from its beginning. Many medal winners have flowed from or into other media ranging from radio and TV to scripts for the stage.

Eric Nicol, Robertson Davies, W.O. Mitchell, Ian Ferguson, Donald Jack, Dan Needles, and others wrote humour for in-person, human performance. Gary Lautens, Pierre Berton, and others indulged professionally in T.V. writing, and Paul Quarrington, Max Braithwaite, Ted Allen, W.P. Kinsella, and Morley Torgov arguably experienced their greatest success directly and indirectly through movies. *Turvey*, the *Bandy* series, *Jake and the Kid*, and, of course, Max Ferguson and Bill Richardson provided CBC radio with piles of material well before Arthur Black and Stuart McLean came onto the combined book-broadcasting scene, and the CBC, in turn, has provided writers with profile in its programming and in the CBC Literary Prizes and *Canada Reads* competition for years. Even the second medal winner Paul Hiebert, the author of *Sarah Binks*, had a regular gig on the CBC. Leacock himself enjoyed success in lectures and stage presentations as well as in writing books and articles. If you regard daily newspapers and magazines as distinct from written words in bound books, the cross pollination between Leacock Medal winners and other media feels furious and incessant.

This activity may swirl around other types of writing as well, but it could be drawn to humour in particular because of its inherent goal of amusement, which can transcend the mode of communication or obstinate allegiance to one platform.

In the 21st century, those platforms are proliferating. I started this book by noting that a single word tossed onto the Internet had more impact than most humour writing this past year. If someone could take all the resulting comments on Twitter and put them into a coherent novel or essay collection, they would have a very funny work inspired, in part, by new technologies.

These new trends really surfaced in the Leacock Medal world in 2008 when Terry Fallis won the award for something that began as a podcast, a website posting, and a self-published book that exploited the new paradigm of online tools for layout, editing, and simple submission.

You can bet more of this stuff and flavours of communication we can't even imagine lie ahead, and this probably bodes well for the propagation of Canadian humour. I know I will have to adapt, get more engaged with e-communication, and join the 21st century.

Still, I found it comforting to know, as I typed these words, that *The Best Laid Plans* has been transformed once again, this time into a television series, and might end up having its greatest reach through the Leacock Medal's old baby boomer buddy, the CBC.

2000

BLACK TIE AND TALES

BY ARTHUR BLACK

Lesson 53

Why humorists mix facts and fancy

My mind will forever associate orgasms with humour thanks to *Black Tie and Tales*, the 2000 Leacock Medal book by Arthur Black. In this, his second medal winner, Black quotes a number of authors and recites many observations on humour.

But the remark that "laughter is an orgasm triggered by the intercourse of reason and unreason"[205] lingers. It haunts me, not only because of the image, but because Black's entire book, directly or indirectly, argues for this concept.

In his earlier medal-winning book, Black, a confessed "Idea Thief," showed how odd information can stimulate thinking and ranting. *Black Tie* collects and presents more of the same, but it takes

---

205 Attributed by Black to American writer and critic Jack Kroll (1926-2000).

readers a step further with musings on how interactions between the unreasonable and the rational can make us laugh.

These interactions also, according to Black and those he quotes, bring us closer to the truth.

In the 1990s, when Black generated many of the essays in this book, literary critics were still picking at the merits of creative nonfiction, a mix of facts and fancy, and a lot of the debris fell on Leacock medalist Farley Mowat. Arthur Black, a fan of the format, defends Mowat with the environmentalist and author's own words: "Truth I have no trouble with. It's the facts I get mixed up."[206] Black amplifies the point with Saskatchewan writer Sharon Butala's explanation of how all good "nonfiction is fiction" anyway. Butala suggests that in "The backward search through happenstance, trivia, the flotsam and jetsam of life, to search out a pattern, themes, a meaning ... is by its nature an imposition of order onto what was chaotic ... what is (really) true are thoughts, dreams, visions."[207]

The idea of mapping thought onto the flotsam of life appeals to Arthur Black. Even though he recognizes the power that trivia tidbits have to engage ("Any storyteller knows that the first thing you've got to get from an audience is attention"), his best rants merge trivia with thoughts to grasp at a truth.

So, if "truth lies at the root of much humor"[208] and humour arises from the incongruities of life, truths that make us laugh may be those revealed by thoughts in conflict with fact. It seems to me that such incongruity can only be achieved in one of two ways: (1) with humorous thought spread upon dull facts or (2) with sound thinking in the face of unreasonable fact. Black's curmudgeon persona prefers

---

[206] Mowat, as quoted by Black, was responding to a critical 1996 cover story in *Saturday Night Magazine.*

[207] Taken by Black from Batula's bestseller *The Perfection of the Morning.*

[208] Fully "The love of truth lies at the root of much humor" as attributed to Robertson Davies.

the latter - the one that rails at reality.

To this end, he seeks stimulus from everywhere he can, using a brain that operates on "the same principle as the lint mitt. It picks up fluff, dust, stray hairs like a magnet ... and lets the big stuff slide right on by."

Arthur Black uses the fluff for orientation and a hint at what is coming. He links his own experience to broad issues and ties trivia to his feelings. The death of his aunt leads into an essay on gift-giving. The story of a biologist in the Brazilian rain forest revives memories of Black's father. His experience wrestling with a tangle of battery cables sends him into a study of neuro-functioning.

Arthur Black would chuckle at all this seriousness around the subject of humour. It is in this book that he cautions, "Trying to define exactly what is funny is like trying to braid a rope out of smoke." Still, I am convinced by the suggestion that the intercourse between the odd and the thoughtful can reveal a truth and make us laugh.

Not all truths fit this frame though. Too bad. It would be a different world if truth telling always induced an orgasm.

Writing Exercise

Identify a belief that you hold dearly and write a convincing essay to argue for your position, but fill the essay with many obvious factual errors.

2001

VINYL CAFE UNPLUGGED

BY STUART MCLEAN

Lesson 54

Why any Canadian would try to make a living from creative writing

My den looks like a furnished dumpster. I love books, real books, not pixels on a screen, and I have too many. Pages bound together, inside a cover, and in my hand make me feel things inside, and they pile up around my home. I have too many.

Yet when I decided to read the Leacock Medal winners, I resolved to buy more and add to the pile. Although e-books and scans are better instruments for searching and referencing, I wanted bound-paper books for souvenirs as well as study. This irrationality led me into a treasure hunt that not only brought treasures into my hands, but brought me into bookstores and homes where I met other enthusiasts.

It also made me a better audience for *Vinyl Cafe Unplugged*, the second book to win the Leacock Medal for Stuart McLean. The first winner, *Home from the Vinyl Cafe*, did not really talk much about the

Vinyl Cafe, Dave's record store. It focused on domestic life - being "home from" the store.

Unplugged, on the other hand, devotes a lot of attention to Dave's store, his career choice, and his back story as a rock group manager. The 2001 medal winner reflects an evolution of the Stuart McLean series with a move into general themes, such as the wistfulness we feel over life choices – the practical, career and money-oriented type or the dreamy, used-record-store kind. This question can trouble anyone who has deigned to pursue a career in creative writing or, alternatively, has rejected the idea as absurd.

The issue surfaces in many of the *Unplugged* stories: those about Morley's university friend Susan, Dave's exchanges with neighbour Mary Turlington, and the visit from "Overweight and overbearing" Cousin Dorothy from the village of Hawkhurst, South Kent, England. Comparisons make Dave and Morley twist over their priorities and their commitment to the Vinyl Cafe.

Dave has the hardest time. He strains "to open his record store ... more or less on schedule every morning" and bristles at official processes. The story of his late Uncle Jimmy, an electric razor held together by twisted wires and duct tape, and airport security illustrates his tension with the rigid world.

Despite their Vinyl Cafe tendencies, Dave and Morley try to maintain a rational side. They save $200 per month without precise plans for its use. Morley has practical ideas. but Dave dreams of buying an Austin-Healy. He tries to do some electrical work to preserve the nest egg and in the process induces renovations that consume the money for responsible purpose.

Together the stories suggest that life will always be a struggle to find balance. I saw this tug of war in the musings and decisions in almost every book I read this year. We all have to find our own balance between the rational and irrational, the dreaming and the practicality. Dave and Morley's success rests on a Canadian compromise.

My pile of old books now makes me think of my Leacock Medal

whimsy, of how hard it would be to sell old records or write for a living, and of the possibility that the time has come to give in a little, tidy up the den, and do some chores. Someday.

Writing Exercise

Think of the most absurd business you can and then explain why running it would make for a great way of life.

2002

GENERICA

BY WILL FERGUSON

Lesson 55

How to laugh in the book publishing business

"This is brilliant - too bad it's written by a Canadian."

When I first heard about Will Ferguson's novel *Generica*, I liked the idea but thought the book would fail. It describes the devastation caused by a self-help manual that really works. The concept appealed to me because it took advantage of the self-help craze without buying into it. But I thought that sales would plod along under the yoke of the Canadian literature brand.

In 2001, people like me could still assume that a first novel by a Canadian, no matter how clever, would flounder, and the *Ottawa Citizen* could still regard Will Ferguson as neither an "A-list" nor a "B-list" writer and presume that any book he wrote would be "uninspiring."[209] None of these presumptions would endure beyond 2002 and the success of *Generica.* The book ultimately made it onto store shelves in thirty-three countries.[210]

I can pinpoint when I first learned about the book because I remember being confused when another based on the same concept came out. That second novel, entitled *Happiness*™, appeared in late 2002, had the same author, and had almost exactly the same content. Eventually, I figured out it was the same book with a different title.[211]

In time, *Happiness*™ took over the book's cover throughout the world, but *Generica* persisted in Canada long enough to make this the name of the 2002 Leacock Medal winner. The award celebrates that original title, the one that was about to disappear. The Leacock Medal can be proud of its prophetic association with the book's *Generica* phase.

But Ferguson must have suffered in the irony. The award for a disappearing title could have been a scene from the novel, [212] which mocked book writing, publishing, editing, marketing, and consumption even more than the subset "self-help" industry.

Funnier than many others on the Leacock Medal list, this book has an edge that probably flows from Ferguson's years of stewing over his subject: how to sell books in quantity into the baby boom bubble and the U.S. market.

---

209 Paul Gessell, "Turning the page on 2001: This year's non-fiction lineup has a disappointingly familiar ring to it, while this spring's new fiction lacks big names," *Ottawa Citizen*, sec. F6, January 3, 2001.

210 And in twenty-six different languages, according to the publisher's note in the 2003 edition of *Happiness*™ by Will Ferguson (Toronto: Penguin, 2003).

211 The title change was in response to marketing feedback, particularly from Britain, where people mistook *Generica* to be science fiction or fantasy.

212 In the book, characters debate the importance of title selection at length, citing statistics that showed the optimum number of words for a title as 4.6 and debating how to generate 0.6 words for this purpose.

The book business can dispirit anyone who has made it their life's purpose. Even with the liberation of e-books and print-on-demand, works that are innovative, thoroughly researched, and well written by respected standards (like this one) never find a publisher let alone a market, whereas formulaic novels, the autobiographies of professional wrestlers, books written within days to exploit hot news, and 21st century snake oil sell in the millions.

Generica/ Happiness™ not only puts these trends on steroids but also satirizes the society that feeds their success and feeds off them. For this reason, Ferguson sets his story in a large U.S. city, unnamed but New York-like, of "scurrying office workers ... on a merry-go-round where the horses have emphysema." Those scurrying through the streets to their giant "filing cabinets" include Edwin Vincent de Valu, slush-pile editor at Panderic Inc., a publishing house that relies on an author known as "Mr. Ethics." When Ethics[213] flees from charges of tax fraud, Edwin's boss, a boomer with a Chihuahua's penis pony tail, puts pressure on Edwin to find a replacement book of the self-help ilk.

Edwin had just skimmed *What I learned on the Mountain,* a manuscript submitted by the unknown Rajee Tupak Soiree. Soiree's book presents the world with a manual for losing weight, quitting smoking, getting rich, enjoying great sex, and achieving eternal, blissful happiness. After episodes that put Edwin in a trash compactor and seagull feces, the self-help work finds its way into publication, triggers the collapse of world economies, causes a cultural upheaval, and reduces almost all of humanity to a generic, vacuous personality. Soiree becomes a cult leader whose worshipers include Edwin's wife Jenni and his true love Bea.

Edwin, his boss, and Ethics, unaffected by the plague of happiness, see the darker side. They set out to kill Soiree, learning in the quest that the true author, a trailer park hermit in Paradise Flats, Texas, invented Soiree and hired an actor to play him.

---

213 Mr. Ethics is author of the popular *Seven Habits of Highly Ethical People.*

Through these characters, Ferguson laughs at authors, editors, publishers, and promoters while, sometimes, weeping inside.

Today, the reprinted *Happiness*™ opens with dozens of rave reviews from around the world. But when it first came out as *Generica*, Canadian critics were the only ones paying attention and were not so kind. Several complained that Ferguson took too much time to move the story along, went overboard in pounding his pet peeves, and was at his weakest in putting long philosophical speeches in the mouths of his characters. Yet even those most critical admitted to finding the book, at least in sections, very funny.[214]

The humour pokes out of the unCanadian, unkind, unsophisticated bits: the breaking of Edwin's finger, on principle; the severing of Soiree's nose-picking digit while it was at work; Edwin musing a miserable death for his co-worker Nigel; the guru's devotion to lots of sex and the recruitment of fawning underlings; and the parody of the *Seven Habits of Highly Ethical People, In the Name of the Tulip,* and *Chicken Broth for Your Aching, Needy Heart* style.

Ferguson does, however, beat the novelty out of the happiness-linked-to-sadness idea. He starts on page 11 of my copy of *Generica* with *mono-no-aware*, the Japanese term for "the sadness of things" - the ever present pathos that lurks below the surface of life. He repeats it periodically throughout and then again in the closing confrontation.[215] The repetition of this idea made me laugh at my evolving "insights" on humour and their link to "the pathos lurking below the surface" of my own life. It reminded me too of something Ferguson said at an Ottawa book event this past year: "Everybody thinks they're deep – everybody - we all think we have profound

---

214 I must have liked it a lot. In spite of my determination to move on to the next Leacock Medal book, I read *Generica/Happiness*™ three times and bought five copies (one *Happiness*™ for me, two for gifts, the entertaining audio version read by American actor Jim Frangione, and an old grey copy that I could not pass up: a 2001 Canadian edition of the *Generica* version signed by Will Ferguson).

215 Edwin accuses the hermit and author of murder because bliss is not true happiness and the Soiree books make people disappear into a mass of nothingness bereft of the things that make them sad.

thoughts."[216]

Ferguson's book shows Canadian writers not only how to laugh at the frustrations of their context and at themselves, but also how to do something about the situation.

Will Ferguson succeeded in doing what he ridicules in this book, purposely feeding the U.S. and international markets. But he also induced people to part with their money at the book stores by writing about something that interested and motivated him personally.[217]

Writing satire requires such a balancing act. You want to make a point, but equally you want to be funny. Those early CanLit critics, who wanted Will Ferguson to move the *Generica* story along more quickly and edit out the obvious jokes, were probably ignoring the importance of the second objective: the funniness of the journey.

If Ferguson had taken such advice and listened to the "everybody thinks they are deep" voice in the back of his head, he would not have written *Generica.* But he could have produced another proud, well written work of literature; one that was neither funny nor popular beyond our borders; and one that might have melted into the generic mass of nothingness - too often coupled, in the past, with that phrase "it's written by a Canadian."

Writing Exercise

Write a short story about a book on humour writing that actually helps writers.

---

216 Will Ferguson, Ottawa Writer's Festival, 18 April 2013

217 The now three-time Leacock medalist and Giller Prize winner insists, in response to the routine audience question, that he does not try to chase the market or try to write what people want; rather, he says, "What I write about is for me, how I write is for the reader." Ibid.

2003

WITH AXE AND FLASK: THE HISTORY OF PERSEPHONE TOWNSHIP FROM PRE-CAMBRIAN TIMES TO THE PRESENT

BY DAN NEEDLES

Lesson 56

How to put the humour in our history

My Uncle Ed worked as the fire chief in a Northern Ontario town that burned to the ground four times.[218] His fire crew resigned en masse when Ed took the pool table away, and Ed's wife died in a house fire while he was out promoting fire safety. He and I share ancestors who believed they were descended from a heroic Celtic king.[219]

Lots of writers could tell this story with an ironic twist. But when I wrote about the town and Ed's life a few years ago, I focused solemnly on the angles of

---

[218] It was about Cochrane, Ontario. Fires (mostly forest fires) destroyed the town in 1910, twice in 1911, and in 1916.

[219] Cassivellaunus, a British Chieftain who fought Julius Caesar in 54 B.C.

persistence and dedication to encourage community pride.[220]

I don't think I did justice to Ed's memory, the story, or readers by running away from the perversely funny perspective. Intent on doing better in the future, I hoped to learn how to tease the humour out of history by reading the 2003 Leacock Medal winner, *With Axe and Flask: The History of Persephone Township from Pre-Cambrian Times to the Present* by Dan Needles. Opening up the book, I braced myself because I knew the exercise would make me itch. *With Axe and Flask* parodies local histories like mine on Uncle Ed.

Dan Needles has been working at funny pretty much since Pre-Cambrian times, and he has small-town storytelling credentials as well. After university and other work, Needles took a job as editor of the weekly paper in the fiddle-contest community of Shelburne, Ontario. The barrage of school boards, soccer tournaments, and sewers often leads small town editors to seek diversions and ask questions like "Why does this place exist?" and "Who decided those people deserve respect?"

Such thoughts make us laugh at ourselves, and if we can, we make others laugh too. With this goal and his power at the paper, Needles started a regular feature in the early 1980s: letters to the editor from the fictitious Walt Wingfield. Walt, a stockbroker turned farmer, amused readers with his naiveté and outsider's perspective.

After a few years, the popularity of the invented Walt took him to the stage in plays that continue to run thirty years later. The plays have morphed into television productions and DVDs, making Needles a two-pronged oddity as a Canadian writer who earns money at it and, indirectly, as a farmer who actually makes a living from agriculture-related activity. [221]

---

220 Dick Bourgeois-Doyle, *Stubborn: Big Ed Caswell and the Line from the Valley to the Northland* (Renfrew: General Store Publishing House, 2010).

221 Now best known as a playwright, Needles kept up his small-town editor self over the years with columns in publications like *Harrowsmith Country Life*, before its demise, and other regional and national publications with a rural bent. He also produced a couple of books drawing on Walt's letters.

All this suggests I could learn a bit from Needles about how to mix history and humour even though *With Axe and Flask* stands apart from his portfolio as a story not by and about Walt but about the township around his farm.

In this book, the narrator, another man from the city, finds time on his hands and turns to the study of a 1930s manuscript written by his late grandfather. The old book also carried the title *With Axe and Flask: The History of Persephone Township from Pre-Cambrian Times to the Present.* This means Dan Needles wrote a book about writing a book about another book and coupled it with the narrator's personal interpretations, experiences, and bits of stumbled upon trivia.

It felt kind of familiar.

With two imagined authors and one real one at work, digression threatens, and Needles himself suggests the book falters at times. But it generally holds tight to a retracing of the Township history that, as expected, made me smile and scratch at the same time.

In looking for humour in history, you can usually rely on a politician or two to grab more than their due when things go well, and when things go badly, a scoundrel or two can usually be found hiding in the bushes. The challenge comes when nothing much happens. Needles tackles it with a *Sarah Binks*-style effusiveness.

The technique underpins most of the book, but it's really hard to miss it when the narrator tells us that his grandfather devoted a chapter of the source manuscript to "The Economic Inactivity of Persephone, 1870 to 1900." In another chapter, "The Modern Era," the narrator's grandfather paints a "picture of a community that has dwindled into calm resignation at its fate as a quiet backwater in the Ontario countryside." With this as substance, words like "greatness" have a particularly ironic impact.[222]

History with hyperbole will resonate with anyone who has studied small town Canada. But the sections that might make Canadians twist and smile most deal with more recent developments such as "the invention of the pickup truck ... (which) relieved a great burden on the local ecosystem ... (as it) gave the men much greater range for hunting and a greater carrying capacity for weapons and beer ... (as well as) a measure of independence and privacy to young couples ... (that) ... considerably reduced the need to abduct women by force."

Biting stuff, but I don't know if Needles can help me much until I'm ready to cross the line and satirize rather than celebrate.

I might be looking for too much by thinking I could do both at the same time.

Even in fiction, one-liners and sarcasm can test a community's sense of humour. Stephen Leacock enjoyed a prickly reception in Orillia after *Sunshine Sketches of a Little Town* first appeared, and the imaginary book within a book in *With Axe and Flask* was remembered as an "unfortunate foray ... into the realm of literature" and a deviation from an "otherwise unblemished life."

"It was a different time," the narrator is told. "In those days, people just didn't think it was seemly to discuss in public where a person's family came from, how they made their money, or, worse, how they lost it. It made everybody squirm."

"But how do they feel now?"

"Probably the same."

---

222 Wikipedia proudly describes the Shelbourne economy as follows: "Major local employers have included automotive part manufacturers Johnson Controls (until 2009) ... A recently zoned industrial area has been established in the south end of town ... (Roads) have been constructed to provide access to *potential industries* ... Shelburne is also home to *a small retail sector.*"

Assuming they and their Canadian counterparts still do, the dependable options for humorous history would include the mode of parody chosen by Needles. The satire can still smart when real events and personalities are sprinkled throughout. They destabilize any reader who wants to think of the whole book as a yarn.[223] Still, I might have to keep looking to find a model of "true" history with humour. Perhaps it lies in writing that includes humour but ghettoizes it, keeping it separate from the factual.

Regardless, any foray into humorous history, when personal and local, carries risks beyond how others might react. As the narrator of *With Axe and Flask* notes: "When you examine your own history properly, it does offer a rich source of speculation about why you have turned out so badly." Those remarks have a particular sting for someone like me who is descended from a heroic Celtic king.[224]

Writing Exercise

Write a short account of the first meeting of the Fathers of Confederation, noting that there was an open bar at the event.

223 *With Axe and Flask* brings the real and unreal worlds together with references to the War of 1812, John A. MacDonald, William Lyon Mackenzie, and the 1859 visit of the future King Edward VII, then the Prince of Wales, touted in local headlines as "H.R.H. to make pilgrimage to Persephone."

224 Needles invited me to give him a few shots, but the best I can do is to suggest that he might have done more writing like *With Axe and Flask*. You could accuse him of having found a format in the Wingfield letters that worked and of being just too comfortable to ever abandon it completely. But my spirit wouldn't be in it because I know that it's more challenging to stick with something, sometimes beyond reason, and to follow it through. As consumers of food and drink, Canadians are better off because so many farmers don't consider other options.

2004

VILLAGE OF THE SMALL HOUSES

BY IAN FERGUSON

Lesson 57

How to create an effect by not saying things

My parents stayed in the same home for almost four decades, cradled me in a sense of security, and always furnished the essentials. Their behaviour really limited my opportunity to build character and an interesting life story. They affected my life by not doing things.

Ian Ferguson never had that problem.

His parents dragged him through bone-chilling experiences while he was still in the womb.[225] Lucky Ian had the kind of childhood that forms personality and aligns well with a creative life, and he exploited this advantage to win the 2004 Leacock Medal with *Village of the Small Houses.*

---

225 His book opens with a harrowing story leading up to his own birth, which took place after his parents managed to catch the last ferry of the season over the ice-clogged river, realizing only then that Ian's older brother had been left back in the cabin on the other side.

Ferguson's "memoir of sorts" begins in the late 1950s when his parents flee Edmonton with the unborn Ian. The group settles in the bitter cold and minimal plumbing of Fort Vermillion, and Ian's father works as a teacher on the local Cree reserve until his lack of credentials comes to the attention of the school superintendent. Dismissed from his job, Hank Ferguson takes the expanding family, which eventually numbers seven, eight, or more depending on how and who you count, on another road trip, eventually settling everyone in Regina, where Hank wrestles with the bottle and disconnects.

Ian's parents end their marriage there, giving their children motive to make jokes about Regina decades later. Their mother, a nurse, takes her children back up to the Fort, where they have a house and she finds work. The kids rarely see their father again.

Already, I'm sure you're thinking this is a sad story.

Proximity to the Indian Reserve, Ian's health problems, and the small house-like tombstones in the Fort's graveyard add to the potential for tales of insecurity and woe.

But Ian Ferguson rejects this route, and he never comes close to assuming the guise of victim.

Early in *Small Houses*, for example, Ferguson mentions his mother's exposure to L.S.D. treatments and thalidomide, but he paints her, not the unborn son, as the wounded one. At the end of the book, Ferguson touches on his own battle with alcohol, but distances it from anything that might point to paternal culpability. I admire this, but I was a little surprised, given the Leacock award, that Ferguson also declined the easy option of spinning the recollections as wildly comic, even though he had experience in comedy.

A playwright, actor, director, and producer, Ferguson had a well-honed imagination and a reputation as a joker. He ran a comedy club in Edmonton for a while and made money with *How to be a Canadian,* a book of jokes and rants on history, culture, and Regina, which he co-authored with his Leacock medalist brother, Will.[226] Those who knew older brother Ian's career might have understood had he chosen the mode of blatant comedy for his memoirs.

Instead, Ferguson tells his experience in simple terms and stresses the family and friendships more than the adversity.

You sense that he wrote the book as a tribute to his mother, his siblings, and even his father and that he cared more about this message than book sales or reviews. The disadvantaged native people who walk in and out of Ferguson's sort-of-remembered childhood also appear as uplifting and cheery figures. The Indian community formally adopts Ian to legitimize his treatment through aboriginal medicine, and the personalities of Bud, David, and Lloyd brighten his life despite their issues and their destinies.

But again, in this book the most intriguing parts come between the lines in what Ian Ferguson does not do. We can always find something to mock or complain about - even seeing a downside to a stable and secure "waste of time" childhood like mine. But Ferguson tells of long winters, outdoor bathrooms, illness, his dad's departure, and Christmas with no presents without any hint that he considered his childhood as anything but a joy. In fact, in the last lines of his book, the guy I called "Lucky Ian" with irony says, "I was born lucky."

Against Leacock's formula for humour, you can easily see the influence of a kindly contemplation in Ferguson's account. The

---

226 Fans of Ian's well known sibling might look to *Village of Small Houses* for a window on Will's childhood. But from beginning to end, the book tells Ian's story. Will or "Little Billy" was about five years younger than Ian, and this alone distinguished their experiences. The older Ferguson brother also had unique health problems, friendships, and memories of his parents.

incongruity requires a longer stare. It sits in that simple retelling combined with the absence of the obvious clichés that normally surround rugged childhood stories. It makes you smile, but you aren't completely sure why.

When the book came out, a few critics suggested that Ferguson fell short in the "artistic expression thereof" side of the humour writing equation. But they usually presumed one of those clichés which Ferguson did not use, and they missed the things unsaid.[227]

Writing Exercise

Write a first-person account of your own birth.

[227] For such a review, see Gordon Phinn, "The Various Fictions of Autobiography [Village of the Small Houses: A Memoir of Sorts]," *Books in Canada*, May 2005, pp. 16–17.

2005

BEAUTY TIPS FROM MOOSE JAW

BY WILL FERGUSON

Lesson 58

Humour in travel writing

Looking across the surface of bluish grey and swirling green, I feel the breeze brush my face, listen to the flapping sounds, and watch the tumbling leaves. I'm flipping through a book and wondering if I have it in me to become a travel writer.

The bluish grey-green paperback contains *Beauty Tips from Moose Jaw*, the book that brought Will Ferguson his second Leacock Medal in 2005.[228] It encouraged thousands to learn more about Canada and prodded me to learn more about grammar.

---

228 *Beauty Tips from Moose Jaw: Travels in Search of Canada,* the book draws upon three years of travel across Canada. Ferguson still managed to eat and pay the bills during this period, writing stories for *MacLean's* magazine and other publications that drew on the travels that fed into *Beauty Tips*.

I like to see new places, meet different people, and research both, but travel writing as an enterprise has always intimidated me. I've avoided it like time-share seminars and resorts under quarantine because I have a problem with verbs.[229]

When I read travel articles, I can never figure out how or why the writer has chosen a specific tense. Some stories are told as if events are unfolding as the traveler transcribes them. Other travel articles tell similar stories completely in the past tense, but sometimes with the air of reportage. It seems writers can set their own rules, which I wouldn't mind except that I'm easily confused. The disorder usually reaches cruise-ship proportions when the writer tries to be both funny and factual.

Will Ferguson, however, has it mastered. In *Beauty Tips*, he uses verbs to choreograph his travels, humour, and first-person narratives in a way that cues his readers, avoids the confusion, and makes a better book.

Beauty Tips, subtitled *Travels in Search of Canada*, follows Ferguson through a selection of tourist sites across the country. The adventures fall on the mild side of travel, not too far from hot showers, warm beds, and grilled cheese sandwiches, but Ferguson makes each place interesting with his personal accounts, information on geography, the local lore, and, mostly, the history, which he shares with zeal. He also makes you chuckle.

He travels sometimes alone, sometimes with one of his brothers,

229 To the extent that I have managed the verbs, punctuation, and other grammar issues in this book, I owe a debt to editor Kelly Bogh, recommended to me by my friends at Canadian Science Publishing.

sometimes with his wife, and regularly with his infant son Alex.[230]

Ferguson tries to tie all this together by picturing Canada as an assortment of "outposts," which may seem like weak analysis but serves the purpose here because his style and his skill with those verbs hold the stories together better than any umbrella image.

He starts each chapter with a humorous experience, like the poetry night that starts his overview of Victoria, B.C., using the present tense, then slips into the past tense when sharing the facts of history. A past tense description of the Underground Railroad and the Henson settlement sits within a comic road trip with his brother Ian. In the title chapter set in a Moose Jaw spa, Ferguson tells of his first-ever massage in funny terms and the present tense, [231] but he turns serious and invokes the past tense when railing about distortions of local history. Pooping-and-peeing Alex provides the ambiance for the real time drive to the Republic of Madawaska and the venue of an almost-war in northern New Brunswick. Similar dual-tense stories tell of Ferguson's search for the polar bears near Churchill, his stop in the Saguenay region of Quebec, and his tour of the Viking settlement in L'Anse aux Meadows.

A single -tense exception comes in his visit to St. John's, which is dominated by present day human interaction and less history than usual. And his recollection of his childhood in Fort Vermilion, which seems to be dropped into the book as an afterthought, has its anomalous feeling amplified by the almost exclusive use of the past tense in its telling.

But even these examples do not break with the pattern picked by Ferguson to tell his stories: when he really wants us to laugh, he talks

---

230 He dedicates the book to Alex.

231 The Temple Gardens Spa is a two decade old effort to revitalize a piece of the city's history and recall the Moose Jaw spa, which reached its zenith in the 1930s when people came from afar to bathe in the city's not-too-hot hot springs pool lined with marble and underwater lights.

in the present; when he wants us to learn, he sticks with the past. This may be the lesson for those who aspire to write humorous travel stories. Whatever you decide to do with your verbs, be consistent.

My effort to reduce Ferguson and his book to verb tense technique threatens to bleed all of the beauty and humour out of *Beauty Tips*. But the pencil notes on the flapping leaves of my blue-grey book suggest I'm not imagining it.

If I was, Ferguson might forgive me anyway. He thinks that Canada exists as a function of our imaginings and "is a sum of its stories"- stories that are easier to share when you know what to do with your verbs.

Writing Exercise

Write a travel essay about a visit to Vatican City with your brother-in-law, a professional magician.

2006

PITCH BLACK

BY ARTHUR BLACK

Lesson 59

On the need for continuous curiosity

"I plan to improve with age, like fermenting wine," I said.

My wife asked if this meant she should stuff a cork in my mouth and keep me in the cellar.

"No, no … I have to breathe and swish around in the real world – you know, just like post-retirement Arthur Black."

The fear that age equates to an inability to keep in touch with human events and the issues that interest others can be challenged in lots of ways, but a potent one would be to point to Black's third Leacock Medal book, *Pitch Black*, which won the award in 2006. Four years earlier, Black had taken official leave from his CBC job where he had developed his style and produced material for his earlier medal winners.

Now settled in B.C.'s Gulf Islands, he could have pulled back a bit. But instead, he stayed curious and connected, contributing to newspapers and giving speeches. In many ways, the post-retirement Black reads a lot like the pre-retirement one. His pieces, still around seven-hundred radio-friendly words, cover a wide range of subjects running from animal rights, public nudity, and marijuana to coffee drinking as a profession, talking toilets, and the invention of macaroni and cheese on a stick.

If anything, he may have broadened the scope of his preoccupations and peeves with rain coast references and his stories about Salt Spring Island life.

Black did not mellow either.[232] In this book, comments like "this is nuts" or "Does it get stupider than this?" routinely introduce his rants. Black sounds, in fact, like someone who has decided that the time has come to take a few more risks, go out on a limb, and lob a grenade or two that may not have survived the political correctness of a CBC script.

He likes the terms "nutbar" and "Right-wing nutbars" and uses them on those who see *The Simpsons* as a threat to family values and "the Amurrikan way of life." He calls Howard Hughes the "Famous nutbar" and lists then U.S. President George W. and a string of European royals as inhabitants of the "nutbar department." The federal Cabinet is "a collection of submissive human sock puppets" and "nutbars."

He also throws around the "Nazi" label, identifying his childhood dentist by name and saying he "had the forearms of a longshoreman and the compassion of a Nazi." Diet guru Atkins leads the "Carbo Nazis."

Finally, Black directs a tirade at the missing Al-Qaeda leader

---

[232] *Quill and Quire* described Black as "sort of like your favourite crank uncle," a role that then living "Andy Rooney tries to play ... on *60 Minutes*, but he's not as good at it." Harbour Publishing, "Praise for *Flash Black*," http://www.harbourpublishing.com/excerpt/FlashBlack/reviewquote (accessed December 15, 2013).

saying how much he loathes "Osama bin Hidin' and his venomous pack of psychopathic lunatics." That may not seem harsh, given the subject, unless you know that Black's rant was actually inspired by Bin Laden's chin whiskers which, he says, have "given beards a bad name."

Together, these rants might suggest that Arthur Black had crossed over into the fermented-wine, old-man phase. But read in context, they come across as amplifications of the personality Black always had, maybe with a touch more pluck. One way to write naturally, to be yourself, and to express feelings without concern, of course, lies in basic goodwill and dedication to coherence and quality. Black shows this when he talks about writing style and words.

He mocks those who think of writing as effortless typing by quoting Stephen Leacock: "Writing is simple: you just jot down amusing ideas as they occur to you. The jotting presents no problem; it's the occurring that is difficult."

Black was open to learning from any source and admits to having admiration for tabloid newspaper journalists "because writing even a mediocre tabloid story is fiendishly difficult. You have to deliver a maximum amount of impact with a minimal number of words - and simple words at that." Black definitely doesn't consider writing for publication to be a hobby or something to pass time in retirement.

On the never-ending need for hard work and study, he repeats the Margaret Laurence story of "an eminent Canadian brain surgeon (who) once made the mistake of telling ... Laurence over the hors d'oeuvres that when he retired he planned to become a writer. 'What a coincidence,' she responded sweetly. 'When I retire, I plan to take up brain surgery.' "

Maybe novelists like Laurence and even people like me can pursue neurosurgery in retirement if we live long enough and have Arthur Black's inclination to keep learning, working, and jabbing at people.

Writing Exercise

Write an analysis of the last Federal or Provincial Budget in memo format as a government policy analyst. Then re-write it using the words "Nazi," "idiots," and "nutbars" at least three times each.

2007

SECRETS FROM THE VINYL CAFE

BY STUART MCLEAN

Lesson 60

The secret to storytelling

In mid-December 2012, with the *Vinyl Cafe* Christmas concert coming to the National Arts Centre, CBC radio challenged listeners to write three-hundred words in the style of Stuart McLean's "Dave and Morley stories." My entry drew on an experience chauffeuring a semi-famous person around Ottawa,[233] but in the story, I became Dave and my guest was Morley. The show picked it as a runner-up. Many people heard my name announced, listened to my story read on the air, and assumed I had won something. Several asked how I managed to imitate McLean so closely.

"I know the secret of the Vinyl Cafe," I would say. "Just take real experiences from wherever you can and then squeeze them into

233 A federal cabinet minister.

the ever-so-sweet Dave and Morley format - easy."

Now, all you have to do is repeat the process hundreds and hundreds of times over decades and in a way that resonates whether as text, radio broadcasts, stage performances, or presentations on rolling trains. That's all Stuart McLean did. Easy.

With enough pharmaceutical support, I might have maintained this delusion through the first two *Vinyl Cafe* Leacock Medal books, but not the third.

The first two were pretty well rooted in the Dave-and-Morley soil. The third book, *Secrets from the Vinyl Cafe*, which took the medal in 2007, presents a different collection, which, more often than not, features a protagonist that is neither Dave nor Morley. A few stories follow their children: teenaged Stephanie, who comes of age as a tree planter, and Sam, who navigates schoolyard sports.

But most revolve around previously peripheral characters: Dave's mother Martha, Italian neighbour Eugene, Carl the retiree, Kenny Wong, and Mary Turlington for the requisite Christmas story. The book was promoted under the "Secrets" theme with the pretense that each character had a secret to hide. Most of the secrets are mild embarrassments that beg forgetting, but they can be *Vinyl Cafe* funny and maybe, together, show the progression of McLean's skill as a fiction writer.

Even admitted fans of the radio program find the stories predictable and confess that part of the appeal flows from the comfortable normality of it all. This perception likely caused many of McLean's writing students to assume that he had a predictable, learnable pattern.

He's been pretty open about it all and acknowledges that, particularly as a fiction writer, he spent years trying to fix on an approach to build his Dave and Morley franchise on. As someone who regarded himself as a journalist, McLean started out writing his stories by interviewing people, conducting research, and then pushing his material into a fictional framework: not too much different than my three-hundred-word CBC contest approach.

Yet, by 2007, too many sober people were touting McLean as a great storyteller and creative writer to attribute it to such a technique alone. If he did achieve such greatness, his persistence and the experience of those hundreds of stories in hundreds of venues probably played a role in it. McLean also had a couple of other forces working on his writing hand: his humility, with its associated willingness to learn and his work as a teacher, with its obligation to observe other learning.

The poor student who failed in high school became, during a short sojourn from CBC, an instructor at Ryerson University (then Polytechnical Institute) in 1984 and later the director of the broadcast division of its School of Journalism. Eventually, Ryerson granted him status as a tenured professor. Trent University also picked him as its first Rooke Fellow for Teaching, Writing and Research.

It's pretty hard to evaluate others without evaluating your own writing, and it's pretty hard not to want to walk the talk when you have students watching you, as a high-profile prof, closely. Still, as I read the last-to-that-date McLean Leacock Medal book, I was still searching for a magic-bullet secret to his success.

Finally, the answer jumped out, not from his book, but from his *Secrets* promotional tour.

When being interviewed, McLean always, always tried to divert the questioner from the subject of his new book, his show, and his life. He wanted, more than anything else, to tell another story. It's impossible to watch Stuart McLean on stage or listen to him speak without sensing that this is a person who just really loves stories. Oh yeah - and Christmas.

Writing Exercise

Think of the stupidest thing you ever did. Then, tell the story with generosity and with Dave or Morley as the protagonist.

2008

THE BEST LAID PLANS

BY TERRY FALLIS

Lesson 61

Seeing the humour under your nose

Terry Fallis and I might not get along.

I wish it wasn't so. He seems like an interesting and friendly guy. But if Terry got to know me, he'd probably see me as an irritating evil twin to be avoided. He already has a twin, whom he likes and looks like, and probably doesn't need an older one.

My resumé looks like a cracked reflection of his. As an engineering student at McMaster, Fallis got involved in campus politics and fell in love with words. Just down the road in Guelph, my math studies had been disrupted by politics and campus radio.

In the 1980s, when Fallis haunted Liberal backrooms, I toiled as a Conservative Party drone. He supported Jean Chrétien's first leadership bid in 1984, the year after I devoted hours to the Mulroney leadership campaign. We then worked on opposing sides in testy elections. He once scurried around as an aide to a Liberal cabinet minister; I did the same thing a few years later for the Conservatives.

He founded a public relations company with the accounting firm-style name Thornley Fallis; I had a PR business that specialized in clown-delivered balloon-a-grams and operated under the name Hot Air from Ottawa. He moved away and now mocks the government city, which has been my home for over thirty years. I look forward to our first formal encounter.

Actually, Fallis is probably not inclined to loathe too many people. He sounds, in his public comments, like one of those "progressive and enlightened" Canadians who is all about "tolerance and acceptance" - you know, the way Liberals like to think of themselves.

He might even count me among those whom he hoped to amuse when he podcasted and self-published his first novel, *The Best Laid Plans*, the 2008 Leacock Medal winner. For those of us who've spent time bumping around the buildings between Wellington Street and the Ottawa River, the book was a kind of obvious chronicling of all the facts of political life. It documents the talk that can be overheard any day of the week in bars and boardrooms around Ottawa, but in an engaging story.

Everyone in politics has fantasized that a reluctant maverick might come from behind to take another party's stronghold or that their opponent's star might get caught in an awkward vote-crushing scandal on election eve. These have been the damp dreams of Canadian political hacks since Confederation was consummated.

But the dream is more often nightmarish - the tug of war between what Fallis calls "the cynical political operators" and "the idealist policy wonks" that plague every party from the roots to the crown; the problems with polls; the theatre of Question Period; toeing the party line against all reason; the incest and dirty dancing of politicians, journalists, and pundits; and the partisanship that transcends even the inanity of ideology and policy in its destructiveness.

It can get really, really bad and begs a lampoon. So, if it was right under our noses, why didn't someone write a book like this before?

Well, some tried, but PR-savvy Terry Fallis succeeded in communicating it more effectively than others by stringing all those oddities together in a readable narrative - a real story with a beginning and an end and other parts.

The Best Laid Plans has both a Terry Fallis-like protagonist, Daniel Addison, and a hero, future MP Angus McLintock. Unfortunately, many early reviews and even some publisher promotions presented the book as a simple story about Addison's adventures as the suffering aide of a wild, incompetent goofball. Yet Angus clearly embodies Terry's idea of a great politician and the ideal boss: quirky, but thoughtful, inspiring, and full of integrity.

I'm pretty sure that Fallis did not base his idol on a Conservative cabinet minister. But I'm struck by how many people have suggested that McLintock was inspired by my old boss.[234] An odd coincidence and interesting to me but maybe no one else. Still, I take this to be a reflection of how much *The Best Laid Plans* resonates with Ottawa readers and to be more evidence of material that was always under our own noses.

"Everybody in Ottawa thinks they are in that book," Leacock scholar, author, and fellow Ottawa-resident David Staines said when I told him my story.

---

234 A former Minister of National Defence, Indian Affairs, Fisheries and Oceans and Science and Technology, who, like Terry's hero, (1) was a Ph.D. mechanical engineer and a university professor, (2) was initially uncomfortable in politics, (3) was keen about his field of aerodynamics and liked to tinker in his shop with motors and machines, (4) broke into Parliament when the popular incumbent dropped out unexpectedly, (5) confronted his own party over issues of values and the future of Canada, (6) is an expert in water systems and a passionate advocate for the environment, (7) won his seat only to be thrust immediately into other campaigns (1978, 1979,1980) one when a minority government was brought down by a budget-related vote, and (8) made a memorable entry into the House. I worked for him from 1984–86.

You certainly don't have to be associated with politics to recognize Ottawa in *The Best Laid Plans.* Despite the emphasis on stereotype and political cliché, this book, like *King Leary,* also treats Ottawa like a place in which real people live, and this appeals to people who are not always preoccupied with policies, polls, and media spin and are more focused on groceries, mortgages, weekends in the park, and getting the kids to school.

The book celebrates the rivers, the village of Cumberland, the Ritz restaurant, the Canal, the universities, the bilingual ambiance, the Chateau Laurier, the museums, and the enlightened part of Parliament, the Library. Even the slipping in spring-time dog dung story speaks to quintessential Ottawa. As I mentioned in reference to *Leary*, after thirty-one years, I am starting to see this town as my home and, like Terry's protagonist Daniel Addison, as the place where I fell in love. These other elements of *The Best Laid Plans* were also sitting under my nose.

I am even looking more charitably upon my life in the public service. In fact, when I read political theories that talk of cynical operatives and policy idealists, I always think there is something missing: the people who take those airy policies and make them real - civil servants. Like lots of things, governing flows from a formula of three variables, but usually, politicos and journalists dismiss the latter group as irrelevant or worse.

Terry Fallis was typically "liberal" in portraying government officials in his novel, further ingratiating him to me. Add to this Daniel Addison's recurrent musing about "Canadian comedic novels" and his desire to study writing, and you have the full picture and the reason why I might have been more than mildly intrigued by this book.

So, while Terry Fallis may not want me trailing along behind him as his embarrassing evil humour-writing twin or triplet, I hope he understands why I might do that.

Writing Exercise

Describe your vision of the ideal boss from the perspective of your current job or one from the past. Then write a short story that shows how hard it would be for someone like this to assume a managerial position.

2009

NEVER SHOOT A STAMPEDE QUEEN

BY MARK LEIREN-YOUNG

Lesson 62

How to write the fish-out-of-water story

You breathe heavily all the time, flail around in angst, and hope someone will intervene to put you out of your misery. A fish does that when pulled out of water, Mark Leiren-Young behaved much that way while living in Williams Lake, B.C., and I usually do that when I read a journalist's memoirs.

Leiren-Young's account of his time in the Cariboo in the mid-1980s, as told in the 2009 Leacock Medal winner *Never Shoot a Stampede Queen,* amounts to what reviewers called the standard "fish-out-of-water" story. Playwrights and movie scriptwriters like the form for its comic get-your-hero-in-trouble potential. This means they have pretty well worn it out, and Leiren-Young's book doesn't break from the routine. But I liked his stories despite the formula and their journalist-memoir aura because I believed them, learned a bit, and laughed.

His publisher calls his book the tale of "a city boy" in "a cowboy town," and the title promotes the tenderfoot in the Cariboo image.

But when you read it, the floundering fish you see laying on the page has the body and soul of a playwright trying to survive in a weekly newspaper job. He could have been anywhere, even in the big city. The cowboys and Stampede setting have less to do with his stories than his personality and perspective.

I say this with confidence because I lived in Williams Lake around the same time as Leiren-Young, knew all of the places he cited, and floundered around as a reporter in small towns myself.[235] Please accept my word on that because an elaboration would flip me into old journalist boasting, the kind that makes me wheeze.

Leiren-Young's stories don't do that, and I think this is partly because they mix the fish-out-of-water structure with the newsroom memoirs. Mixing formats always blows air on a story, but first you have to master each one individually.

Stampede Queen has all the fishy elements for anyone wanting to study them. First (1) you have to set up the protagonist and his point of view, and Leiren-Young does that by telling us how he recognized the theatre as his calling at UBC and later at the University of Victoria.[236]

Next, (2) the book pulls the fish out of the water. Leiren-Young's post-graduation appointment as artistic director for a children's theatre falls through and the job offer from the *Williams Lake Tribune* presents itself as the only alternative to $6 per hour on the line in an Ontario cookie factory.

Now with empathy for the fish and its waterless situation

---

235 I lived in bunkhouses as a forestry worker around Williams Lake a few years earlier. I was a reporter in Richmond and Vancouver and also worked for a spell as legislative assistant to Lorne Greenaway, member of parliament for Cariboo–Prince George. I will stop my memoir here to maintain credibility.

236 He worked at the UBC Student Paper, the *Ubyssey*, which also trained other Leacock medalists (Birney, Nicol, and Berton) and for a term at *The Vancouver Province.*

established, the third phase (3) is introduced: the flailing.

Abuse and assaults, car accidents and robberies, bikers and bears, municipal politics and Stampede Queen photo shoots thrash him around for about a year. Leiren-Young's accounts have an authentic ring for anyone who has had a police scanner next to his pillow or covered dog shows in the morning and murders at night, and they might still be a good primer for journalism students. But they make other people laugh too because of Leiren-Young's imagination and outsider's perspective. He looked back on the experience as an anomaly in his career and not a step on the path to glory. As usual, I'm awed by stories that make something out of nothing like the explosion that doesn't happen but had so much drama that Leiren-Young used it to open his book.

In another illustration of how strangely personal humour can be, I also laughed at the problems caused by his hard-to-spell, hyphenated, half-Anglo/half-not name. A Vancouver paper makes his cheque out to "Neil Leisen-Young," and irate Stampede Queen contestants complain about the "Horrible (photographer) Mark Leiner-Young."

His stories feel bright because they were written not like faded and fabricated memoirs, but while still fresh. Mark Leiren-Young fell ill with mono shortly after leaving the Cariboo. Housebound, he put the stories to paper in 1988 and didn't change them much even though they went unpublished for over twenty years. As a result, the stories remained vivid, but with a touch of perspective and bemusement.

The final phase (4) in the standard fish story flows from hoping someone or something will intervene to either pull the fish back into its natural habitat or help it grow legs and live in the new environment. In fact, the typical Hollywood exercise ends with the out-of-water hero learning to adapt to his new surroundings, usually well enough to mate and spawn.

Leiren-Young left the Cariboo and went on to a career as a screenwriter, playwright, performer, and comedian. Yet he still sometimes describes himself as a "freelance journalist" and did manage to mouth "maybe living in a small town's not so bad after all" before swimming away from Williams Lake. The sum makes you want to jump out of the water, take a chance, and maybe even read more journalist memoirs.

Writing Exercise

Describe your personality and passions.

Then think of the worst employment circumstance for a person like you and write a story with you in it, explaining how you got there, what happens while you are on the job, and how you leave.

PART IX

2010-2013

DEFINING A "KIND" OF NICHE

This past year my dad's younger brother Murray died, taking away my last connection to stories from that side of the family. A regular guy and a bit of a hoser, Murray liked to tell jokes. As his last one, he asked to have his ashes put in a whisky bottle and thrown in a river near his home in eastern Ontario. This happened, and I smile thinking of his memory and his sense of humour.

People don't tell jokes to each other anymore. We email gags, upload them on the Net, and pass around links to YouTube clips of cats using toilets and people falling. Murray tried to adapt, but his e-messages contained no comments or personality. They seemed like spam. He should've stuck to what he did best: telling jokes in person.

Humour manifests in many ways, and the vehicles for conveying humour and making others laugh have changed a lot since 1947, when the first Leacock Medal went to a book that reads like a guy telling you funny stories face-to-face.

To serve a purpose in the age of hyper-communication, the Leacock Medal, it would seem, will need to define a niche around what it does best, presumably by focusing more intently on its role as an award that honours humour in literature. The last four Leacock Medal winners on my list, three novels and a work of literary travel writing (2010-2013), would provide a good stage to launch a renewed commitment to such an approach.

To some, this focus might not seem like a major shift. The

mandate to honour books has always meant some exclusivity. Famously funny Canadians like Wayne and Shuster, Rich Little, Charlie Farquharson, Dan Akroyd, Jim Carrey, John Candy, Martin Short, and many others of the *Second City* and *Saturday Night Live* ilk, for example, have never taken a Leacock Medal home. The medal list can never be a comprehensive representation of Canadian humour - not even written humour. The Canadian writers and editors of the *National Lampoon's* "Bad Taste" days represent an overlooked era and attitude, and Ian and Will Ferguson won for memoirs, travel writing, and a novel and not for their very funny book of jokes, *How to be a Canadian.* Still, strict adherence to a literature imperative would likely have eliminated many of the funniest past medal winners and, ironically, even collections of satirical sketches of the type that Leacock himself would have written.

So, I think that the literature thing probably makes sense as a bias, but not a concrete rule, because I wouldn't want CanLit snobbery to ever suppress the humour imperative. I see the Leacock Medal as an award that prods accomplished writers to access their funny side - and that encourages naturally funny, but developing writers toward greater literary skill.

These two features speak to Leacock's notion of humour - "artistic expression thereof" literature and an acute sense of relevant "incongruities of life" humour. As I suggested at the outset, I would like the Leacock Medal to be weighted to prefer works with strengths in both features, but allow for winners that might excel in one while being a little lighter in the other.

This leaves us to factor in the troublesome "kindly contemplation" element of the Leacock triad.[237] On this point, I

[237] Interestingly in this context, triads - groups of three - feature in a lot of humour and appear often in the Leacock Medal winners. Typically, the writer will say - something ordinary, something ordinary, and then something absurd - or something expected, something expected, and then something unexpected. It works as well conversely with - something extreme, something extreme, and something every day. The technique is a function of the incongruity quality of humour and operates by hitting the reader with a twist. Two items provide just enough repetition to establish a pattern without boring the reader. The third provides the surprise.

sought illumination from two Stephen Leacock scholars who happen to live here in Ottawa, Professors David Staines and Gerald Lynch. [238]

Staines, who has published massively on Canadian literature as well as researching Leacock's life and letters, made the suggestion noted in the opening pages of this book, that Canadians merely "like to think they are kind" and that our humorists don't have to be kind, they just have to write within the context of that delusion. He also concluded from his study that Canadians, like the British, might have a more finely tuned sense of irony than Americans.

Professor Lynch, author of *Stephen Leacock: Humour and Humanity*,[239] had a similar view as well as a strong position on the kindly contemplation notion. Lynch believes, based upon a study of other references and Leacock's life, that the humorist had a specific, different 19th century meaning to the word "kindly" in mind - one tied to the word's origins around our "kind," "kin" or "kinship."[240]

Comedy scholars (yes, there are comedy scholars[241]) talk of

---

238 Bios: http://www.english.uottawa.ca/faculty/dstaines.html and http://www.english.uottawa.ca/faculty/glynch.html (accessed January 3, 2013).
239 Gerald Lynch, *Stephen Leacock: Humour and Humanity* (Montreal: McGill-Queen's University Press, 1988).

240 Aaron Paquette, the very 21st century #Ottawapiskat writer, also promotes the idea that "To be kind means to be kin. To be family." http://www.aaronpaquette.net/ (accessed February 3, 2014).

241 Mel Helitzer and Mark Shatz, *Comedy Writing Secrets*, 2nd ed. (Cincinnati: Writers Digest Books, 2005). Also check out the work of Dr. Peter McGraw, a professor at the University of Colorado Boulder who collaborated with journalist Joel Warner on the recently released *The Humor Code: A Global Search for What makes things Funny* (New York: Simon & Shuster, 2014) – definitely something you would find interesting - if you have come this far in my book. They talk, not of "kindly contemplation" and "incongruities" but "benign violation" focusing on comedy. There is no mention of Leacock, but they authors give generous space to Canada with a chapter on the Montreal *Just for Laughs* Festival.

humour as being the interaction between the material, the performer, and the audience – perhaps mirroring the incongruities, artistic skill, and kindly elements of the Leacock concept.

In this context, the "kinship" interpretation of "kindly" provides that needed illumination and might also be a good label for the obvious, but often unmentioned Leacock Medal criterion; a winning book should be Canadian, should contribute to a sense of "kinship" among Canadians, and maybe should, just once in a while, tell the kind of stories and a few jokes that Murray and my own kin would have enjoyed.

2010

BEYOND BELFAST

BY WILL FERGUSON

Lesson 63

Plotting and plodding

Last spring,[242] in an old stone church overlooking the Rideau Canal, I went up to a table by the altar and converted. There, in the sanctuary of Southminster United, I broke my vow to buy only used copies of the Leacock Medal books. I paid full price for *Beyond Belfast: A 560-Mile Walk Across Northern Ireland on Sore Feet,* the 2010 winner by Will Ferguson. Ferguson came to the church for the Ottawa Writers Festival, and I had a chance to get a book signed if I bought it on site.

After a brief exchange, he wrote out his signature, a salutation, and the note "Funny is as Funny

[242] Will Ferguson was interviewed by CBC's Alan Neal, April 18, 2013, Ottawa International Writers Festival.

does." I read a lot into that comment, probably more than warranted, because I associate it with something he had told the audience that night. [243] Earlier in the evening, Ferguson had said he doesn't like stories that feature introspective personalities and that he always tries to reveal character through dialogue and action.

"I believe deeply that our character is decided by the choices we make," he said in reference to his Giller Prize winning novel, *419*. "I think character in fiction and in life is defined by the actions that characters do and not who they think they are or the slights and the grudges and regrets that they dwell on."

The comments echo standard writing text advice to tell stories through vivid experience, action, and deeds. If you wanted to extend that to writing humour, you might express it as "funny is as funny does."

When I got home that night, I looked down at the scribble in the front of my new book and broke another pledge. I started reading this 2010 winner out of chronological Leacock Medal order, keen to find words that would illustrate Ferguson's point and to make that the theme of my review of his book. I saw a few examples, but not enough.

Beyond Belfast follows Ferguson on a solo journey along the Ulster Way, the long, looping footpath around Northern Ireland. The book documents action - the action of walking across streams, up mountains, along cliffs, and over dung-filled pastures - and it presents dialogue - in dank pubs, dank B&Bs, and dank city streets. The book makes the slipping and sipping experiences pretty funny, but *Beyond Belfast* also contains more than just a little dwelling and thinking too.

Fewer people had completed the sore-feet feat than had climbed Everest at the time Ferguson set out on it just over a decade ago, but he was not motivated entirely by the physical challenge. He wanted to understand his ancestry, which he saw not in the Fergusons, but in

---

243 A few months earlier, Ferguson won the Giller for *419,* a novel of murder and internet scams, set in part in Nigeria.

the Ulster line leading to the single mother who raised him in Fort Vermilion. I don't think that Ferguson could suggest that this book kept entirely clear of introspective thoughts and feelings.

He mused not only about his orphaned grandfather but also about the history, politics, and religion of Northern Ireland. In the front end, he frames his journey with the basics of William of Orange, the 1916 Easter Uprising, and the 1969 events that sparked the more recent terror.[244] Although Ulster issues defy understanding, Ferguson wades in, perhaps feeling he had earned a connection with his blisters and his research on family history. As he flops his cowshit covered hiking boots around Northern Ireland, he passes all the points of sadness: Armagh, Derry, Enniskillen, and, of course, the starting and end point, Belfast.

I don't know what kind of person could avoid introspection on that route, and I don't blame Ferguson for failing to provide me with an easy, exemplary book of telling by showing.

Still, I felt a little dejected. As I pondered this hurdle, I thought about my decision to buy a new book just because of the convenience and wondered if I was giving up. Having read the 2010 Leacock Medal winner out of sequence, I knew that when I put *Belfast* down, I would be slipping back to 1992 and would be facing twenty more books.

Maybe in part to put off the backward slide, I started flipping through *Beyond Belfast* again, and I took greater notice this time of the

244 In 2008, when he was wrapping up the traveling part of his project, a decade had passed since the Good Friday agreement.

maps and charts that introduce each section, thought about the plans and preparations and the plodding along in the pastures, and remembered something else Ferguson had said in the Ottawa church.

He told the pews that he puts more time into planning and working on the plot for his books than writing them. He spent over a year and a half on the outline for *419*.

"I should have brought the actual outline - it's about 80 pages," he said. "It's a scene-by-scene breakdown. The trick is to outline and outline and outline ... before you start."

Ferguson said that he thinks that a detailed plot ensures that a writer doesn't follow ideas into a corner or get swept up into the fog of endless possibilities. He told the audience that this applies equally to fiction and travel writing.

"My sister is a sculptor - she prefers to work in marble, but it is quite expensive and so she also works in clay," he said in what seemed like a non-sequitur. "She says with clay you build something up ... with marble you cut something down."

Ferguson said travel writing like *Beyond Belfast* is like sculpting in marble because you typically have this huge block of experience, history, and destination information. You have to make choices and cut away.

"But with fiction it's like writing in clay ... you are building things up from something," [245] Ferguson said, adding that you can be overwhelmed in either of them - in one by information and in the other by ideas. Then he repeated that a detailed plot can be the answer.

---

245 The example Ferguson cited was the story of C.S. Lewis who had an image of a fawn under a snowy street lamp from which he built Narnia. A week later, I would read in *Beyond Belfast* of Ferguson's surprise encounter with a stag on the trail in the midst of the Mourne Mountains, which the author describes as being the place that inspired Lewis's vision of - Narnia.

"With a good plot outline, you can skip ahead and work on a scene out of sequence and then come back to your plan," he said. "Don't worry about themes – themes come out of the story" - if you stick to the outline. Maybe I jumped ahead in reading *Belfast*, but I did it within an outline: my Leacock Medal book reading plan. Now, I just need to do the same kind of planning with my writing.

So, I plodded along thinking back on Ferguson's varied advice, his 560 mile walk, and my book. I visualized his sister's work with chunks of marble, the towers and castles of Ulster, the rock of the Mourne Mountains, the stone walls of the Ottawa church, and then the craft of writing. A unifying theme emerged - "this stuff is hard."

Writing Exercise

In 560 words, plot a travel adventure story based on the circumnavigation of Prince Edward Island in a canoe.

2011

PRACTICAL JEAN

BY TREVOR COLE

Lesson 64

How a creative spark leads to a story

In April 2005, I tried to kill my father.

We declined permanent life support and wanted his pain to end. Teeth out, struggling for every breath, and mouth contorted, he looked like a grey version of Munch's *Scream.* My attempt to bump him off (with lies to get excess morphine) failed, and he came back to life long enough to grab my collar and remind me of what he wanted. I laughed nervously and said "I'll do what I can, Dad."

I told that story after his funeral with the same confliction.

That memory and the nervous laugh visited my head again and again this year as I read the 2011 Leacock Medal book, *Practical Jean* by Trevor Cole. The book tells the story of Jean Horemarsh, a woman who cared for her mother on the way to a nasty death. Jean vows to spare her friends the same fate and sets out to kill them in a prophylactic way while they're still relatively young and healthy.

Sometimes, it seems that everyone, save a few newly born babies, has a story, like me, of a loved one who suffered too long and has likely thought about the issues raised by *Practical Jean*. But Trevor Cole takes those thoughts just one step further into a twisted, but also kind of honest realm that does what all good story ideas do. It touches on a universal in an unusual, creative way.

When you're struck by the creative spark, you feel an energy that flows from other ideas, or, at least that's what I've read. Reflecting on the idea of *Practical Jean* and the book that sparkled out of it, I have a guess as to why this happens.

An unusual thought, contrary to a usual one, raises questions. Who would think that way? Why would they do that? How would they pull it off? And what will happen as a consequence? The questions tickle your mind.

So, after seizing on this concept of proactive euthanasia, you would naturally try to think of a sensitive protagonist who has attended a bad death and doesn't want to endure it again. Jean, a ceramic artist with a bland but comfortable husband and home in small-town Canada, fits the requirements. Then, you would need a back story that makes euthanasia an acceptable approach to such problems, and this produces Jean's childhood at the ringside of her mother's veterinary business and multiple puppy terminations.

Jean, the sister of two police officers and the daughter of another, has lived all her life labeled as the one incapable of doing the "practical" thing when required. Then, the death of her mother pushes her to take action. As a caring person, she sees the plan to end the lives of her closest friends as the means of saving them from the "ruthless" and "pulverizing" experience of age and the bleakness of a "slow and agonizing" death.

Trevor Cole sticks with this portrait by having Jean give each of her victims/friends one last bit of happiness and beauty. One time, this beauty comes as sex in a car with a youth; another time, it's sex with Jean. She hacks with a shovel, strangles with wire, and poisons with drugs.

I can easily imagine how Cole generated each element, from the dead puppies to the murder mystery-style climax, building on his initial idea. But what makes Cole's words better than a pile of clay is his execution, if you can excuse that word here. A one-time journalist with decades of experience in magazines and daily newspapers as well as fiction, Cole enjoyed recognition as a talented and literate writer before receiving the Leacock Medal.

Practical Jean impressed me because it sought to get into the heads of middle-aged women. As a mouth-breathing male, I may be a poor judge of how well Cole does this but I can say for certain that he twists the mind, draws detailed characters, and generates thoughtful dialogue that doesn't go on too long. For this reason, I was surprised by some not-so-great comments in early reviews of *Practical Jean*. Most of the negative stuff struck me as conflicted.[246]

It made me think again of my conflicted feelings about my dad, his suffering, and his sense of humour, and it gave me a twisted but creative idea on how I could spare humorists like Trevor from the "vicious, ruthless ... grinding ... pulverizing ugliness" of confused reviews in the future. I'll work on it after this project is over.

246 Dave Williamson calls the book "morbid and silly" (I think he meant that was a bad thing) and says, "It just ain't funny" (*Winnipeg Free Press*, "A woman running around killing her friends? Funny, right?" October 2, 2010). In his generally positive review, Randy Boyagoda says the book is "faltering" and has "a series of flat chapters" (*Globe and Mail*, "Mordantly murdering the middle class," September 18, 2010).

Writing Exercise

Write a short story about a serial killer who bumps off humour writers before they can experience bad reviews.

2012

THE SISTERS BROTHERS

BY PATRICK DEWITT

Lesson 65

The incongruous setting

At the Leacock Medal award banquet last year (2013), the regular attendees at my table told me that they found Patrick deWitt's 2012 acceptance speech to be the funniest and most memorable one ever. They laughed because the speech was exceptionally short. Some of them recalled his remarks as being limited to a modest and soft "uh... uh ...thank you." But that's an exaggeration – just a modest and soft bit. DeWitt did add a few crumbs on the subject of creativity for those listening closely.[247] But that was about all. My tablemates thought this was funny and kind of cute because of their own

[247] In those brief remarks, he mused a bit about the craft of humour writing, noting some people think "life itself is a joke" and adding, "if that is true, it is a complex one." The author also managed to hint at his inspiration by quoting the British playwright Joe Orton. Orton, who was brutally murdered in his mid-thirties (Patrick deWitt was about the same age when he wrote *The Sisters Brothers*), was a champion of black comedy, calling it "a weapon" and a "dangerous" one.

expectations.

The annual bunfest, always held in or around Orillia, gives locals a night out that includes a cocktail hour, book signings, and a chance to meet current and past medalists. The performances of previous winners have created the anticipation that the medal recipient's speech will be funny and thought-provoking and will help justify the $65 per ticket cost of the evening out. Patrick deWitt is funny and thought-provoking when writing books, but not so much when asked to perform on stage – unless unintentionally, because of the setting.

Patrick probably finds it more comfortable in the spotlight now after over two years of picking up honours for his dark, but comical novel *The Sisters Brothers*, the book that won the 2012 Leacock Medal. Still, I suspect he remains most at ease in the context of written words.

In another way, the issue of context probably constitutes the greatest factor in the humorous effect of his medal-winning book. Please allow me to illustrate with the following lifeless summary of *The Sisters Brothers*, which I prepared as an exercise.

> *The Sisters Brothers*, the second novel by Canadian-born, Oregon-based Patrick deWitt describes a transforming journey made by Eli and Charlie Sisters, two men who are different in many ways but have a fraternal bond that keeps them together as business partners. They do contract work, now exclusively for a powerful entrepreneur identified as "the Commodore," who has asked them to travel to California on his behalf and negotiate with Hermann Kermit Warm, an inventor with a special process for mineral exploration. The brothers are to deal with Warm through Henry Morris, an intermediary in the Commodore's employ.
>
> The Commodore puts hard-nosed Charlie in charge. Eli, the sensitive narrator of the story, thinks about leaving the business because of all the travel and the tense interactions with customers. Eli also worries about his weight, his teeth, the lack of female affection in his life, his widowed mother,

and his brother Charlie's taunts. Charlie drinks heavily and focuses clinically on work.

Whew! That was tough, trying to outline the story of *The Sisters Brothers* without the 19th century context of cowboys, gold rush prospecting, horses, guns, knives, and killing. I pulled those elements out of the description to try to evaluate the impact of the incongruous setting and the writing style.

The book teases us into compassion for the brutal and reminds us of the universality of human concerns in the tradition of recognized literature. It has carried off so many literary prizes[248] that any comment on the quality of the writing seems redundant, and critics in Canada, the U.S., and abroad have detailed the book's literary merits many times.

So, I focused my thoughts on why the book made me laugh, always coming back to the gun-slinging, the dirty work of mid-1800s hit men, and the violence of the Old West in contrast with the clowning and bickering of the brothers.

When Eli confesses a fear of spiders, cares for his one-eyed horse, fusses over toothpaste flavours, or feels hurt over his brother's teasing, we might not find it funny if he wasn't also an assassin ready to blow a stranger's head off or do what was "necessary" to extract information from an old woman. Because Eli, the narrator, relates all this in the formal old-time western ("that's some nice shooting, brother") sort of way, he enforces the incongruity in almost every passage.

248 He won the Governor General's Award for Fiction and the Rogers Writers' Trust Fiction Prize as well as spots on the short lists for the Man Booker Prize, the Scotiabank Giller Prize, and the Walter Scott Prize.

Patrick deWitt definitely knows the importance of setting and context, and he may have been more aware of the expectations at the Leacock Medal banquet than it seemed.

In verifying the facts of the 2012 event, I read that Arthur Black and Dan Needles bookended deWitt's acceptance speech. Both are polished speakers and hard to match. In similar circumstances, I too would have limited myself to "... uh ... uh ... thank you."

Writing Exercise

Write a short story about a pair of humour writers doing contract work in the Old West.

2013

DANCE GLADYS, DANCE

BY CASSIE STOCKS

Lesson 66

Caring about characters

I felt relieved after reading the 2013 Leacock Medal winner *Dance, Gladys, Dance*. Having completed the last book on my list may have had something to do with it. But the feeling flowed mostly from knowing that I could look Cassie Stocks in the glasses, should we meet again, and say, "I liked your book." Cassie has a well-tuned bullshit detector, so I would be bound to the truth.

A down-to-earth Albertan, now Saskatchewan dweller, Cassie makes fun of herself, laughs a lot, and connects with lots of people. She lists one-time biker chick, actress, gardener, waitress, office clerk, aircraft cleaner, fowl farmer, and Eston Co-op employee in her author bios.

When she added award-winning novelist, it gave her more opportunities, but in addressing the June 2013 Leacock Medal banquet, Cassie said that she enjoyed the profile mostly because of the young women who identify with characters in her book. Cassie said many "don't think they're like everyone else, and don't feel normal." She liked the thought that her book may have helped them.

"Women are by and large less likely to believe in themselves as artists," Cassie, the first woman to grab the medal since 1996, said. "And when an artist gives up their dreams and gives up their work then we'll never know what we have lost."

Cassie Stocks cares about people, including fictional dead ones and people who only exist in her imagination. In a banquet speech that went on a lot longer than Patrick deWitt's thank you, she described her characters one by one, saying she not only loved fleshing them out as an ensemble, but loved them individually.

"I like to call them freaks; they are odd and a little bit outlandish … strange … and I think they're beautiful, all of them."

Frieda, the narrator, lacks self-esteem, dwells on imperfect decisions, and shares some of Cassie's curriculum vitae and sense of humour. Frieda decides to give up on art, get a "real job," and become "ordinary." She stops seeing the world as a "series of potential paintings" and starts talking about the weather.

A classified ad for an old phonograph, ending with "Gladys doesn't dance anymore - She needs the room to bake," launches Frieda's adventure and the encounters with her disembodied mentor.

"I made Gladys a ghost because I wanted her to tell her own story rather than, you know, through someone else or someone reading a diary," Cassie said. For many reviewers, the characters make *Dance, Gladys, Dance* work.

Caring about your characters provides a pretty good starting point in writing fiction. With no exception I can recall, characters are the vehicle for moving a story along and exercising all those techniques of action, dialogue, and thinking. To be believable, no matter how nice or disagreeable, they have to tap into something human, usually a bit of the author. In Frieda, the relationship between author and subject was glaring but Cassie tweaked the superficial details to create a character with her own energy. Some of Cassie's characters had little in common with the author, but enough for a connection. All of them had their own interests and motivations.

"Kurt Vonnegut said make your characters want something ... right away … even if it's just a glass of water," Cassie said, explaining that Vonnegut recognized that even characters paralyzed by the meaninglessness of modern life are human and have to drink water.

Her central character wanted something: to be ordinary and get a real job.

I have a real job of sorts, and this made the trip from Ottawa to Orillia and back difficult to justify. But attending the 2013 banquet struck me as something that would be good for me to do given all the time I'd spent studying Leacock Medal books this past year, especially after my wife said, "this would be good for you to do given all the time you've spent on this thing this past year."

It was a five and a half hour drive each way. So I decided to stay overnight at the Geneva Park Conference Centre on Lake Couchiching. It wasn't much of a hardship.

But because most people attending the banquet live in Orillia, only a handful stayed overnight - mostly people from far away. People like Cassie Stocks and me. We had breakfast together. Cassie was dejected because she thought her sometimes rambling speech was a flop. She wanted to "crawl into a hole like a gopher."

Cassie Stocks could not have picked a better bacon and eggs partner. I pumped her back up by telling her how much I enjoyed the talk and connected with it.

"Don't worry only a few hundred heard your speech," I said.

"Millions will read my glowing account of it someday."

She laughed again, and we talked about the craft of humour writing and how funny it is to study funny. In her speech, she cited sources such as the *Humor Reference Guide: The Comprehensive Classification and Analysis*, which identifies some ninety-seven different types of humour or flavours of incongruity. These include the liar paradox, the deviation from the ideal, the unexpected honesty, and anti-humour humour: "the intentional violation of the expectation of the joke: the joke turns out not to be one, and it's funny because ironically it's not funny!"

"Now, I think that definition is totally hilarious!" Cassie said also noting humour-writing advice from the previous female Leacock medalist Marsha Bolton. "Wear tight pantyhose at readings 'cause it makes you stand up straighter."

So, I like Cassie Stocks. You don't need to like every author you study, but I think that, like working on characters for a book, you need a human connection that makes their mistakes yours, their humour something you might appreciate, and their lessons something you might want to write down and remember.

Writing Exercise

Write three paragraphs to introduce a ghost who is doing something not normally associated with the spirit world, like brushing teeth, going to the bathroom, or doing a humour writing assignment.

PART X

2014 - A LIFE LESS SERIOUS

The Leacock Associates have just announced that *The Promised Land: A Novel of Cape Breton* by Bill Conall has won the 2014 Leacock Medal competition. If you have read the rest of my book, you might guess how happy I am to learn that a story about the 1970s can still resonate with 21st Century readers and award givers.

I wish I could say who the next and the next and the next medal winners will be in order that this book would not feel dated for a while. But I can only predict with certainty that whatever books add medal stickers to their covers in the future will have their critics as well as their admirers. I find this oddly uplifting.

Studying the Leacock Medal books, I learned that critics often cut up winning books when they were first released and now scoff when reading them out of context. Too bad for the award winners. Great for me. It reminded me to keep Kipling in mind - not just to treat both "triumph and disaster" as imposters but also to not make serious thought the solitary aim of any exercise. My other aim in studying these books, as you might recall, was to laugh.

For this reason, I have tried to offset cheerless musings with amusing material from the books and to mollify pompous thoughts on writing with funny episodes from my own life.

If studying humour has any value on a personal level, it must come from a prod to laugh more, to take life less seriously, and to maybe share that attitude with others.

This book purports to hold lessons on both laughter and life, but, of course, the best approach treats the subjects as intertwined.

Selected Bibliography

For a complete list of the (now sixty-seven) Leacock Medal books and their original publishers check http://leacock.ca/

For a rich resource on author bios, see - St. Pierre, Paul Matthew, ed. *Dictionary of Literary Biography*. Vol. 362, *Canadian Literary Humorists*. Detroit: Gale, 2008.

Burroway, Janet. *Writing Fiction: A Guide to Narrative Craft*. 8th ed. Boston: Longman, 2011.

Cameron, Elspeth. *Earle Birney: A Life*. Toronto: Viking, 1994.

Carroll, Jock. *The Life & Times of Greg Clark: Canada's Favorite Storyteller*. Toronto: Doubleday Canada, 1981.

Curry, Ralph L., ed. *The Leacock Medal Treasury: Four Decades of the Best of Canadian Humour*. Toronto: Lester & Orpen Dennys, 1984.

Curry, Ralph L. *Stephen Leacock: Humorist and Humanist*. Garden City, NY: Doubleday, 1959.

Davies, Robertson. *The Papers of Samuel Marchbanks*. New York: Viking, 1986.

Ferguson, Will, ed. *The Penguin Anthology of Canadian Humour*. Toronto: Viking Canada, 2006.

Foran, Charles. *Mordecai: The Life and Times*. Toronto: Knopf Canada, 2010.

Gardner, John. *The Art of Fiction: Notes on Craft for Young Writers*. New York: Vintage Books, 1985.

Grant, Kay. *Robert Stevenson, Engineer and Sea-builder.* New York: Meredith Press, 1969.

Gordon, Charles. "Afterword." In *Sarah Binks*, by Paul Hiebert. Toronto: McClelland and Stewart, 1995.

Heintzman, Ralph, ed. *Tom Symons: A Canadian Life.* Ottawa: University of Ottawa Press, 2011.

Helitzer, Mel, and Mark Shatz. *Comedy Writing Secrets.* 2nd ed. Cincinnati: Writers Digest Books, 2005.

Huston, Mervyn J. *Prescriptions for Humour.* Edmonton: Faculty of Pharmacy and Pharmaceutical Sciences, University of Alberta, 1989.

Leacock, Stephen. *Feast of Stephen.* Edited by Robertson Davies. Toronto: McClelland and Stewart, 1970.

Leacock, Stephen. *Humour: Its Theory and Technique, with Examples and Samples.* 1935.

Leacock, Stephen. *The Greatest Pages of American Humour.* London: Methuen & Co, 1937.

Lynch, Gerald. *Stephen Leacock: Humour and Humanity.* Montreal: McGill-Queen's University Press, 1988.

MacMillan, Margaret. *Stephen Leacock.* Toronto: Penguin Canada, 2009.

McKillop, A.B. *Pierre Berton: A Biography.* Toronto: McClelland & Stewart, 2008.

Mindess, Harvey et al. *The Antioch Humor Test.* New York: Avon, 1985.

Mowat, Claire. *Travels with Farley.* Toronto: Key Porter Books, 2005.

Nicol, Eric. *Script Tease: A Wordsmith's Waxings on Life and Writing.* Toronto: Dundrun, 2010. E-book.

Robins, John Daniel and Margaret V. Ray, eds. *A Book of Canadian Humour.* Toronto: Ryerson Press, 1951.

Ross, Val. *Robertson Davies: A Portrait in Mosaic.* Toronto: Douglas Gibson Books, 2009.

Ryan, Allan J. *The Trickster Shift: Humour and Irony in Contemporary Native Art.* Vancouver: UBC Press / Seattle, WA: University of Washington Press, 1999.

Staines, David, ed. *The Letters of Stephen Leacock.* Toronto: Oxford University Press, 2006.

Leacock, Stephen. *My Financial Career and Other Follies.* Edited by David Staines. Toronto: McClelland and Stewart, 1993.

Staines, David, ed. *Stephen Leacock: A Reappraisal.* Ottawa: University of Ottawa Press, 1986.

Walker, Alan, ed. *The Treasury of Great Canadian Humour.* Toronto: McGraw-Hill Ryerson, 1974.

ACKNOWLEDGEMENTS

I am indebted to everyone quoted directly or otherwise referenced in the text and footnotes of this book. This, of course, includes my wonderful wife, kids, and family members both living and departed. Many helped with their enthusiasm as well as advice.

ABOUT THE AUTHOR

Dick Bourgeois-Doyle has contributed to many books, articles, TV features, and radio programs on the history of science and creativity in Canada. His biographies of inventive and heroic Canadians have been dubbed "fascinating and inspiring … thorough and engaging" and been celebrated by reviewers in Canada and abroad. His books include *George J. Klein: The Great Inventor, Her Daughter the Engineer: The Life of Elsie Gregory MacGill* (both Canadian Science Publishing-NRC Research Press publications) and *Stubborn: Big Ed Caswell and the Line from the Valley to the Northland* (General Store Publishing House). Bourgeois-Doyle also edited and co-wrote *Renaissance II: Canadian Creativity and Innovation in the New Millennium.* A former Chief of Staff and Director of Communications to the Minister of Science and Technology, he currently serves as Secretary General of the National Research Council of Canada.

ABOUT CANUS HUMOROUS

The title is meant to evoke "a year of reading Canadian humour" in the style of Annus Mirabilis and Annus Horribilis.

My initial attempt, Anus Humorous, drew odd Twitter followers and too many unfortunate web-references to my blog. Canus Humorous had a nicer ring, and when I learned that "canus" is Latin for "grey-haired and aging," that sealed it.

With my cartoons of book covers and authors, I tried my best to respect the Leacock medalists as well as copyright laws.

For more:

http://canushumorous.blogspot.ca/

@CanusHumorous on Twitter

canushumorous@gmail.com

http://billconall.com/

http://cassiejeanstocks.wordpress.com/

http://patrickdewitt.net/

http://www.trevorcole.com/

http://www.willferguson.ca/

http://leiren-young.com/

http://terryfallis.com/

http://www.wingfieldfarm.ca/

http://www.ianferguson.s5.com/

http://basicblack.homestead.com/

http://www.cbc.ca/vinylcafe/home.php

http://www.joshfreed.ca/

http://www.marshaboulton.com/

http://www.humber.ca/scapa/programs/school-writers

Proof

31633687R00182

Made in the USA
Charleston, SC
21 July 2014